T0302269

"With the increasing relevance of social media in the business world today, understanding 'corporate cancel culture' is extremely important to maintaining relevancy. As social media continues to evolve, considering consumer perceptions of companies through the lens of social media is critical for upholding and protecting reputation, managing public relations and guiding leadership decisions. Companies and social media users who wish to preserve their brands would be wise to read this book."

Wendy York, Dean, Wilbur O. and Ann Powers,
College of Business, Clemson University

"This research-based book examines 'corporate cancel culture' and how it affects brands and business. Chapters on misinformation, cancel culture, the dark side of memes, and issues with livestream social media shopping provide a modern take for marketers and social media users alike."

Jonah Berger, *Wharton School Professor and bestselling author of* The Catalyst and Contagious

CORPORATE CANCEL CULTURE AND BRAND BOYCOTTS

This topical book examines and tests the complexities of unintended consequences of social media that often impact brands and companies from both an economic and a reputational lens. This book introduces the term "corporate cancel culture," highlighting the growing trend among customers to leverage social media to communicate their grievances with companies.

This book reports challenges of social media platforms to brands and companies. The challenges addressed entail including social media trolls, the power of influencers, the dark web, cancel culture in sports due to political constraints, social media influencer livestreams, and misinformation. Written by a team of experts from North America, Europe, South America, and Asia, this book showcases real world expertise in marketing, branding, consumer psychology, economics, and communication. This book also considers solutions for brands and companies who need to address the dark side of social media by offering insights on fostering accountability among brands and business leaders and providing a roadmap to mitigate consumer resistance.

Corporate Cancel Culture and Brand Boycotts: The Dark Side of Social Media for Brands is a must read for students of psychology, marketing, public relations, management, and social media. It will also be of interest to users of social media – both consumers and business/organizations. It is especially valuable for marketing/advertising professionals, social media professionals/influencers, and business executives. It is designed to be read alongside *The Dark Side of Social Media: A Consumer Psychology Perspective*.

Angeline Close Scheinbaum (PhD, University of Georgia) is a scholar of consumer behavior and integrated brand promotion with a focus on contexts of sport and e-commerce/social media. Within branding, she measures event sponsorships and their economic impact, fanbase psychographics and behavior, consumer brand perception, and experiential marketing effects. She has worked with global brand sponsors such as Ford, Dodge, Volkswagen, Suzuki, Mazda, and Lexus. Dr. Scheinbaum is co-author or editor of *Advertising & Integrated Brand Promotion*, *Consumer Behavior Knowledge for Effective Sports and Event Marketing*, *Online Consumer Behavior: Theory and Research in Advertising, Social Media, and E-Tail*, *The Dark Side of Social Media: A Consumer Psychology Perspective*, and *The Darker Side of Social Media: Consumer Psychology and Mental Health*.

CORPORATE CANCEL CULTURE AND BRAND BOYCOTTS

The Dark Side of Social Media for Brands

Edited by
Angeline Close Scheinbaum

NEW YORK AND LONDON

Designed cover image: Image created by Angeline Close Scheinbaum and Benjamin Harvey, Clemson University

First published 2025
by Routledge
605 Third Avenue, New York, NY 10158

and by Routledge
4 Park Square, Milton Park, Abingdon, Oxon, OX14 4RN

Routledge is an imprint of the Taylor & Francis Group, an informa business

Library of Congress Cataloging-in-Publication Data
Names: Scheinbaum, Angeline Close, editor.
Title: Corporate cancel culture and brand boycotts : the dark side of social media for brands / [edited by] Angeline Close Scheinbaum.
Description: New York, NY : Routledge, 2025. | Includes bibliographical references and index.
Identifiers: LCCN 2024027493 (print) | LCCN 2024027494 (ebook) | ISBN 9781032670492 (paperback) | ISBN 9781032670515 (hardback) | ISBN 9781032670546 (ebook)
Subjects: LCSH: Corporate image. | Corporations—Public relations. | Branding (Marketing) | Consumers—Psychology. | Social media—Psychological aspects.
Classification: LCC HD59.2 .C665 2025 (print) | LCC HD59.2 (ebook) | DDC 659.2—dc23/eng/20240711
LC record available at https://lccn.loc.gov/2024027493
LC ebook record available at https://lccn.loc.gov/2024027494

ISBN: 9781032670515 (hbk)
ISBN: 9781032670492 (pbk)
ISBN: 9781032670546 (ebk)

DOI: 10.4324/9781032670546

Typeset in Sabon
by codeMantra

CONTENTS

ABOUT THE EDITOR

Angeline Close Scheinbaum (PhD, the University of Georgia) has a range of experience on social media platforms. The first social media platform she used was MySpace, where a fond memory of that platform was getting to choose a signature song to go along with the MySpace page. Next, she became active on Facebook back when a college email was required to be on the platform. While less active on Facebook (Meta) since this line of research began, she is still a member of the platform, albeit more mindful of the time on it and the nature of the content. The next social media platforms she joined included Twitter, Pinterest, YouTube, LinkedIn, and Instagram, each of which she uses for various purposes. At this time, she has managed to not join TikTok (due to some of the concerns with the platform as expressed in this book) and Snapchat. After almost two decades as a thoughtful social media user and scholar in consumer behavior/consumer psychology in the context of social media, she is an advocate for social media breaks, more mindful social media usage, avoiding toxic content, keeping children off of social media, preventing social media addiction/disconnection anxiety, and for using social media for good.

Dr. Scheinbaum is the Dan Duncan Endowed Professor in Sports Marketing and Associate Professor of Marketing at Clemson University. Professor Scheinbaum is an expert in the dark side of social media, consumer psychology, integrated brand promotion, and sponsorship/experiential marketing in contexts of sports and social media/online consumer behavior. Her research is often based on 15 plus years of industry and research funding experience working in sports marketing with event sponsors such as Dodge, Ford, Volkswagen, Toyota, College of Southern Nevada, Shell, Lexus, Suzuki, Mazda, USA Cycling, and AT&T. Dr. Scheinbaum has published in the *Journal of Academy of Marketing Science,* the *Journal of Business Research,* the *Journal of Advertising,* the *Journal of Advertising Research,* and *European Journal of Marketing.* Professor Scheinbaum is an author or editor of the following books: *Advertising & Integrated Brand Promotion, Consumer Behavior Knowledge for Effective Sports and Event Marketing, Online Consumer Behavior: Theory and Research in Social Media, Advertising & E-Tail,* and *The Dark Side of Social Media: A Consumer Psychology Perspective.* Her research has won awards including the American Marketing Association Sports SIG Paper of the Year and The Academy of Marketing Science's DeLozier Best Conference Paper Award.

Dr. Scheinbaum integrates research and industry experience in the classroom. She has taught many different courses ranging from undergraduate to doctoral and has experience mentoring and publishing with doctoral students. She serves on the Editorial Review Boards for journals such as the *Journal of the Academy of Marketing Science,* the *Journal of Advertising,* the *Journal of Advertising Research,* and the *Journal of Business Research.* She also has a long-standing commitment to service with the American Marketing Association and the Academy of Marketing Science, where she served as VP Membership and Director of Social Media. She is also an active member of the Association for Consumer Research. Prior to Clemson University, she served as the University of Texas at Austin, Associate Professor at The Stan Richards School of Advertising & Public Relations, and Associate Director of Research for the Center for Sports Communication & Media at the Moody College of Communication at Texas.

ABOUT THE CONTRIBUTORS

Hyeong-Gyu Choi (PhD, University of Memphis) is an assistant professor of Marketing at Nebraska Wesleyan University. He received his MBA from the University of Findlay prior to the doctoral program. At Nebraska Wesleyan University, he teaches an MBA course on Marketing Management and lectures in undergraduate programs on the topic of Principles of Marketing and International Marketing.

Medha Reddy Edunuri (MS, Clemson University) is a marketing graduate from Clemson University's Wilbur O. and Ann Powers College of Business. Her research interests are consumer behavior, advertising, brand loyalty, pop culture, social media, and influencer marketing. She is experienced in digital marketing and market research through her work at Just Cause Apparel and Clemson Small Business Development Center.

Kevin Flynn (DBA, Cleveland State University) is a clinical assistant professor of Marketing from Clemson University's Wilbur O. and Ann Powers College of Business. His research interests are AI and marketing, marketing productivity, hybrid and remote work productivity, and marketing graduate technical and professional skill readiness research. He received his MBA from Case Western Reserve University and a BS from the U.S. Naval Academy. He has experience in market research and business intelligence in consulting and private equity.

Sayan Gupta (PhD, University of Pittsburg) is an assistant professor of Marketing at Clemson University, whose research and teaching interests focus on digital and social media marketing, marketing analytics, brand management, and the marketing-finance interface. His dissertation titled "Essays on Brand Actions and Love-Hate Relationships with Consumers" investigated various aspects of consumer polarization in response to brand crises and won awards from the ISMS and the AMA. He received his PhD in Marketing from the University of Pittsburgh in 2023 and has published in the *Journal of the Academy of Marketing Science*.

Jingyun Hu (MA, Northeastern University) is a doctoral student in Economics from Clemson University's Wilbur O. and Ann Powers College of Business. Her research interests are social media and influencer marketing, social network, causal inference, and machine learning. Currently, she is working on research on collaboration between brands and influencers in the livestream market and presented this research in ISMS 2023 and Informs Annual 2023.

Kevin W. James (DBA, Louisiana Tech) is Department Head and Associate Professor at the University of Texas at Tyler. Dr. James has experience in teaching a wide range of marketing classes including principles of marketing, consumer behavior, personal selling, business-to-business marketing, international marketing, public relations, sports marketing, and promotions with a social media focus. Dr. James enjoys conducting research on a variety of marketing topics but specializes in value elements within the marketing mix. Dr. James has published in the *Journal of Business Research* and *European Business Review*. Dr. James is also active in participating in a variety of marketing conferences around the world including The Academy of Marketing Science, American Marketing Association, and Society for Marketing Advances.

Andrew Gavin Leach (PhD, University of New Mexico) is a lecturer in Marketing at Clemson University's Wilbur O. and Ann Powers College of Business. Dr. Leach's diverse academic background includes degrees in business, communication, and instructional design. He has taught courses such as Social Media Theory and Application, International Business, Marketing Principles, Mass Communication, Communication Theory, and Sociocultural Dynamics as well as instructional design. His research interests are social media, influencer marketing, neural networking/data analytics, and artificial intelligence.

Darren Linvill (PhD, Clemson University) is a professor in the Department of Communication at Clemson University and co-director of the Clemson University Watt Family Innovation Center's Media Forensics Hub. His master's and undergraduate degrees are from Wake Forrest University. He is an international expert on online deception, with a particular focus on state-sponsored social media influence operations. His research has appeared in *Political Communication*, *Computers in Human Behavior*, and *Social Media + Society*. He has also written for *The Washington Post*, *Foreign Affairs*, and *Rolling Stone*.

Jonathan R. Oliveira (MA, Federal University of Parana – Brazil) is a doctoral student in the Recreation, Sport & Tourism Department at the University of Illinois Urbana-Champaign (USA). His research interests rely on sport event management, community development, facility management, and sport tourism. His research has appeared in the *Journal of Sport & Tourism*, *Sport in Society*, *The Journal of the Latin American Socio-cultural Studies of Sport* (ALESDE), *Brazilian Journal of Sport Sciences*, and *Tourism in Analysis Journal*.

Janna M. Parker (DBA, Louisiana Tech University) is an associate professor in the Marketing Department at James Madison University. Her research interests include retailing and consumer behavior and social media use and its impact on individuals, brands, and society. Dr. Parker has published on employee termination due to social media use, online predators, and cancel culture. Her research has been published in the *Journal of Business Ethics*, the *Journal of Business Research*, the *Journal of Consumer Marketing*, the *Journal of Marketing Education*, the *Journal of Marketing Theory and Practice*, and *Journal of Retailing and Consumer Services*. She is a co-author of the textbook *Social Media Marketing: A Strategic Approach*. Dr. Parker provides workshops on teaching digital and social media marketing. She has been a board member of the Academy of Marketing Science. Dr. Parker is the social media editor for the *Journal of Business Research*, a role for which she launched and directs the journal's social media accounts.

Renan Petersen-Wagner (PhD, Durham University) is a senior lecturer in Sport Business and Marketing at Leeds Beckett University. His research interests lie at the intersection of media studies, sport, and social theory. His research has appeared in *Global Networks: A Journal of International Affairs*, *Convergence: The International Journal of Research into New Media Technologies*, *Annals of Leisure Research*, *Current Sociology*, *International Review for the Sociology of Sport*, the *Journal of Sport & Social Issues*, *Sport in Society*, and *Leisure Studies*. He is the co-author of *The UEFA European Football Championships: Politics, Media Spectacle and Social Change* (Routledge).

T. Andrew Poehlman (PhD, Yale University) is an associate professor of marketing from Clemson University's Wilbur O. and Ann Powers College of Business. His research interests are all connected to unconscious influences on behavior: the divide between conscious and unconscious control, the unconscious effect of social information on consumption decisions, and the effect of unconscious influences of time-related perceptions on mental states. His work has spanned analyzing the predictive validity of unconscious thoughts on behavior, the influence of historical Puritanism in American culture, and most recently the role of historical narratives in heritage branding.

Adam Stone (MBA, New York University) is a professor of Practice at Clemson University. Mr. Stone has 30+ years of experience including over a decade in CEO roles for omnichannel retail, restaurant, service, and manufacturing businesses ranging from multi-billion-dollar companies to small- and mid-sized, entrepreneurial high-growth companies. In the fall of 2022, he joined Clemson University's faculty as a professor of Practice in the Marketing Department of the Wilbur O. and Ann Powers College of Business. Before Clemson, Mr. Stone was a chief executive officer in the apparel industry for 11 years, most recently as Chief Executive Officer for Palmetto Moon, a Charleston, South Carolina company selling apparel, footwear, home goods, and accessories. Here, he helped the company strengthen its brand development and marketing capabilities as well as implement a robust retail channel expansion strategy. Mr. Stone holds a bachelor's degree in mechanical engineering from Lehigh University and an MBA from New York University's Stern School of Business.

Scott R. Stroud (PhD, Temple University) works on topics at the intersection of philosophy and communication. He is a professor in the Department of Communication Studies at the University of Texas at Austin and the author of *John Dewey and the Artful Life* (Pennsylvania State University Press, 2011), *Kant and the Promise of Rhetoric* (PSUP, 2014), and *The Evolution of Pragmatism in India: Ambedkar, Dewey, and the Rhetoric of Reconstruction* (University of Chicago Press, 2023), which was also published in India as *The Evolution of Pragmatism in India: An Intellectual Biography of B.R. Ambedkar* (HarperCollins India, 2023). He is the founding director of the Media Ethics Initiative and the program director of Media Ethics for the Center for Media Engagement at the University of Texas at Austin.

Felipe Bertazzo Tobar (PhD, Clemson University) is an assistant professor in the Parks, Recreation, and Tourism Management Department at Clemson University (USA). His research interests gravitate around sport in relationship with fandom, management, tourism, heritage, events, and politics. His research has appeared in the *Journal of Sport & Tourism, The International Journal of Sport Policy and Politics, The International Journal of Sport and Society, Sport and Society,* and *Soccer and Society.*

Patrick Warren (PhD, Massachusetts Institute of Technology) is an associate professor in the John E. Walker Department of Economics at Clemson University and the co-director of the Media Forensics Hub. He studies political economy, organizational economics, and the public information environment.

Kat Williams (MA, University of Texas at Austin) is a doctoral student in the Communication Studies Department at the University of Texas at Austin, with an emphasis on rhetoric, language, and political communication. Her research interests lie at the intersection of ethics, pop culture, and social movements. She is a graduate research assistant with the Moody College of Communication's Center for Media Engagement and Center for Advancing Teaching Excellence.

Dr. Debra Zahay (PhD, University of Illinois Urbana-Champaign) is Professor of Marketing in the Department of Marketing, Operations and Analytics at the Bill Munday School of Business at St. Edward's University in Austin Texas. She holds a doctorate from the University of Illinois, Urbana-Champaign, MBA from Northwestern University in Evanston, Illinois, JD from Loyola University in Chicago, Illinois, and AB from Washington University in St. Louis, Missouri. Dr. Zahay has been teaching digital marketing for over 20 years. She researches how firms use customer information for competitive advantage and the impact of social media on the society at large. She has published in journals such as *Decision Sciences* and the *Journal of Interactive Marketing*, *Marketing Letters*, and the *Journal of Business Research*. She has co-authored three textbooks in digital and social media marketing.

FOREWORD: A LEGAL PERSPECTIVE

Tik Tiking Away

This writing takes a recent legal perspective to the dark side of social media, and literally a discussion of "cancel culture" at an entirely new level – that of an entire and exceedingly popular social media platform of risk of change or cancelation. On March 14, 2024, the US House of Representatives passed legislation that gives TikTok a historic ultimatum; find a buyer or face a nationwide ban in the US. This bill achieved significant bipartisan approval despite the upcoming 2024 presidential election. This political season is especially filled with an intense political tension, divineness, and attitude silence. This current issue with social media (particularly TikTok), however, is in the line of debate between free speech and national data security.

President Biden expressed his support for the bill by stating that he would sign the law with approval from the Senate. This momentous decision marks the first time that the US government would remove access to a social media platform for its citizenship. However, the potential impact of this legislation transcends the tension between free speech and data privacy. Issues of mental health, loss of identity, restriction of expression and experience, and viable alternatives are just some of the important topics of research and inquiry.

While some aspects of this bill are yet to be settled, what is known is that Congress has given ByteDance (the Chinese, parent company of TikTok) six months to find an approved buyer for its social media platform. This may prove difficult if not impossible, as some market valuations are estimating TikTok to be worth 84 billion (Thomala, 2024). If the company does not comply, the US government will force telecommunications giants Apple and Google to remove TikTok from their app stores. While those who have downloaded the app previously will still have access, the inability of management to update, upgrade, or support the current TikTok version would render the application essentially useless. This removal of access to a platform created and owned by a "foreign adversary" is not a new phenomenon.

There are, as of this writing, 39 American states that have restrictions on TikTok. States such as Texas, Maryland, Utah, and Alabama have laws in place that prohibit employees and contractors associated with government agencies from using TikTok while communicating on their state-issued devices. The rationale for this prohibition is clear; state-designated confidential or classified information may be inadvertently shared while "engaging" with the application and/or mobile device. The state of Montana goes a step further by banning the downloading of TikTok on any electronic devices regardless of classification. Montana SB 419 states, "TikTok may not operate within the territorial jurisdiction of Montana." This geolocated limitation was the first of its kind and set the stage for future legislation.

The result of this removal of the more active users on TikTok is yet to be seen. While countries like India, Afghanistan, and Taiwan have restricted access to TikTok for similar reasons as the US (data sharing, national security, and misappropriation of information), the sociocultural impacts are yet to be fully understood. Recent studies show that the citizens of these countries felt TikTok was a waste of time, included unrealistic content that ultimately leads to a discussion on digital sovereignty (Chakraborty, Kapoor, & Ilavarasan, 2020; Kumar & Thussu, 2023). What is yet to be investigated is the psychobiological impact this forced removal might have on its more active users. American consumers of this platform tend to skew young, and these consumers may heavily resist having a choice of social media platforms taken away from them by the government, even if it is well intended to protect national security.

Disciplines such as psychological, sociology, communication, and business have explored the impact of various usage levels on key constructs such as mental health, addiction, social involvement, loneliness, depression, self-identity, and consumer behavior. The key difference between then and now is social media agency. These studies investigated the voluntary choices made by individuals to engage with a particular platform. This new legislation opens the door for future exploration into the impact that involuntary removal has on these same constructs.

It is the intention of this book, *Cancel Culture and Brand Boycotts: The Dark Side of Social Media for Brands* (Scheinbaum, 2018, and in this current volume 2024), to shed light on the dark side of social media and cancel culture. As this book highlights a variety of problems related to social media for business and society (e.g., misinformation, the dark side of influencers, brand boycotts, consumer resistance, social media as a tool to harm, cancel culture going from people getting canceled to what Poehlman and Scheinbaum term "corporate cancel culture"), this legal TikTok case is one solution that is currently proposed. It remains to be seen at the time of this writing if and when it goes through, and either way, what the business and consumer reactions to a change will be.

Andrew Gavin Leach, PhD
Clemson University

References

Chakraborty, I., Kapoor, U., & Ilavarasan, P. V. (2020). There is nothing real! a study of nonuse of TikTok in India. In *Re-imagining Diffusion and Adoption of Information Technology and Systems: A Continuing Conversation*. IFIP WG 8.6 International Conference on Transfer and Diffusion of IT, TDIT 2020, Tiruchirappalli, India, December 18–19, 2020, Proceedings, Part II (pp. 287–302). Springer International Publishing, New York.

Kumar, A., & Thussu, D. (2023). Media, digital sovereignty, and geopolitics: the case of the TikTok ban in India. *Media, Culture & Society*, 45(8), 1583–1599.

Scheinbaum, A. C. (2018). *The Dark Side of Social Media: A Consumer Psychology Perspective*. Routledge, New York.

Thomala, L. L. (2024, February 22). *TikTok Brand Value 2023*. Statista. https://www.statista.com/statistics/1324424/tiktok-brand-value/#:~:text=The%20short%20video%20brand%20enjoyed,of%20200%20billion%20U.S.%20dollars

FOREWORD: A CEO'S PERSPECTIVE

Brands Can't Wake Up and "Be Woke"

Companies are increasingly vulnerable to serious damage from mishandling social issues, especially with Gen Z and younger customers that grew up using social media on a daily basis. The combination of heightened awareness of social issues over the last decade, particularly on the important LGBTQ and Black Lives Matter fronts for social justice, and the ability for negative "news" to go viral can put companies in a very precarious position. This generation has very little tolerance for "tone-deaf" companies or "tone-deaf" instances of brand communications that do not understand or react appropriately (such as with authenticity and sincerity) to all of their constituents' concerns.

The challenge for leaders in business is that the "upside" from handling these issues well from a brand communication perspective is nowhere near the downside of mismanagement. Customers can cancel companies overnight via social media and sales, stock prices, and business reputations can plummet. Most companies and consumers are all too familiar with the case of Bud Light's Dylan Mulvaney campaign. For a helpful review of the Bud Light case, please refer to the business teaching case, *This Bud Light's for You-Him/Her/Them* (Wood & Allan, 2024).

This is the most notorious example in 2023 of how mismanagement can alienate customers, causing incredible brand damage and serious financial consequences. The "cancelation" of Bud Light also brought job losses. Imagine the billions of dollars Anheuser Busch had previously invested building their brand over the last century, creating goodwill with huge advertising budgets and beloved marketing campaigns such as "this Bud's for you."

Given the recent consumer attempt at cancelation of the brand, it turns out, for many customers, it no longer is "for them" as the brand successfully alienated both their older, loyal, more conservative customer base as well a very high percentage of more progressively minded Gen Z customers.

It seems leaders of companies, organizations, and brands have a few options on how to market with topics of important, yet delicate, social justice, or political issues:

Option 1. The Switzerland Approach – stay on the sidelines and hope to "stay below the radar" through concerted efforts to stay out of the fray. In many ways, this strategy sidesteps political and/or sensitive topics, even though those topics are of course important in society. Perhaps, the company or brand does not naturally relate to those areas and as such it may seem or be inauthentic to relate to these issues credibly.

Option 2. Dip a Toe in the Water Approach – taking steps to be less susceptible to drawing the ire of customers (and non-customers!). This step mostly includes hiring and training practices while improving the company's efforts around diversity, equity, and inclusion. Option 2 also includes looking at all of the brand's customer touchpoints for imagery and copywriting across their website, stores (if they have any), and all digital marketing efforts (social and print media, TV, email, and other communications channels) to ensure a diverse and inclusive cross-section of their target customers is represented. The person responsible for generating the creative content for the brand needs to be very literal (and formulaic) to ensure an appropriate balance of images/models is utilized in promotional materials. In this option, the company stops short of actually giving "voice" in its brand communications to social justice or political issues.

Option 3. Credible and Authentic Brand Building Approach – proactively building credibility as a brand that cares and develops an authentic brand position around these critical social issues. The vast majority of companies are opting for option 1, or some combination of options 1 and 2. Option 2 can include steps such as hiring executives and giving them responsibilities such as diversity, equity, and inclusion. These efforts are typically focused primarily on hiring practices and education and consequences for employees who do not follow the rules.

Option 3 is not for the faint of heart and must be authentic, sincere, and heartfelt. Do it wrong, or create one big misstep, and the brand is worse off than it would have been had it not attempted to be proactive. A billion-dollar apparel brand comes to mind that attempted to develop an authentic position on LGBTQIA+ topics and other social topics by adding a statement indicating their support of these groups on their retail storefronts only to catch the ire of highly popular comedian who torched them for not being "authentic" and not representing the customer base they were espousing they care about. Another medium-sized apparel brand had for years been taking steps to make sure a diverse range of customers were included in its marketing materials and focused its social efforts on sustainability and human ecology (healthy, safe products). It had done a wonderful job of creating a strong brand position on sustainability with a truly authentic "voice" meticulously crafted over half a century only to have its CEO make a major mistake becoming confrontational with an employee who challenged the CEO to take more steps to be in an inclusive brand by hiring more diverse employees. The CEO got into an email exchange telling this employee she was wrong – that the company was already an inclusive brand. He told her if she did not like it she could go work somewhere else.

You can imagine where this ended – the CEO was fired and the brand attempted to mitigate the negative publicity by making a substantial social donation. Fifty years of efforts as an environmentally friendly brand tarnished in a few days. Fortunately for this brand, the issue did not become viral, though it easily could have – especially the propensity for social media to be a mechanism for viral cancelation when there is a mistake or violation.

Companies, brands, and organizations cannot just wake up and "be woke." Companies and their leaders have to build the brand positioning very strategically with a range of tactics over several years, starting small and building over time. You cannot "get ahead of your skis," thinking you are farther along than you are and taking steps you have not yet sufficiently developed real credibility and authenticity as a caring and thoughtful brand. Option 3 requires very strong leadership at the top to clarify the brand's effort around social issues. CEOs and their boards must be in full alignment, with clear ownership, accountability, and initiatives passed on to key executives in the organization, primarily in Human Resources and Marketing.

Each semester, I discuss this issue with my students in one of my courses for graduating marketing majors. I ask them who has done well creating an authentic brand positioning around social issues. Further defining social issues as environmentally friendly and inclusivity, Patagonia always takes the lead on the environmentally responsible side of the social scale. And the students cite other brands as well. When we talk about inclusivity, however, these mostly 21-year-olds can name very few brands. The one, and typically only one, that rises to the top is Nike. This is not to say that no other companies are taking effort to pursue Options 2 and 3, but more a reflection that these Gen Z students (and customers for the next 50+ years) are not giving them any credit for it.

This reinforces that companies must take steps to promote diversity, equity, inclusivity, and belonging in the hiring and all of the customer/marketing touchpoints and educate all key employees to avoid making big mistakes – a clearly defensive approach. But it also suggests that developing an authentic brand position, with real credibility for social issues, is immensely difficult and expensive. Again, sincerity is paramount. The rewards to a brand like

Nike, arguably the gold standard in this space, are immense as they will continue to maintain brand relevancy, advocacy, and purchase loyalty for their younger, more progressively minded customers for years to come. Will Nike stub its toe, either fairly or unfairly as social media and word of mouth get to decide? Time will tell, but the answer is yes, probably, especially if history is any guide. But, by building such a proactive, comprehensive brand position for championing social causes (think of their campaign "everyone is an athlete"), they can weather those storms and ultimately come out stronger by adding far more new customers that appreciate them for their efforts than those they "fire" because they no longer will support the brand. Execute poorly against this increasingly critical and sensitive issue, you risk firing way more customers than you add. And if you are Bud Light, you successfully fire both core customers and new customers by alienating both constituents.

This book *Corporate Cancel Culture and Brand Boycotts: The Dark Side of Social Media for Brands*, edited by Angeline Scheinbaum and with scholarly contributions from a global team of over 20 scholarly experts in social media, takes a balanced perspective to the dire topic of corporate cancel culture (Poehlman & Scheinbaum, in press). This book is crucial to business practitioners such as CEOs, marketing managers, social media managers, brand managers, advertising executives, account managers, public relations executives, journalists, and professors/scholars alike. This book builds off of an earlier book, *The Dark Side of Social Media: A Consumer Psychology Perspective* (Scheinbaum, 2018), but with a completely different lens. As the earlier contribution focused on social media and its dark side to consumers and the psychological underpinnings of social media, this new book has a refreshed viewpoint to focus on more macro aspects – business, governments, brands, and organizations. This book will cover misinformation campaigns, the dark side of influencer marketing, corporate cancelation, human brand cancelation, corporate punishment vs. accountability, the dark side of cancel culture in sports organizations, coordinated influence operations, threats and fear with misinformation, the dark side of livestream sales on social media, and even the dark side of memes for brands. Each of these chapters can be of interest and use for leaders in the corporate world.

Adam Stone, MBA, BSME
Clemson University Professor of Practice, 2022–present
Private Equity Consultant, 2018–present
CEO Palmetto Moon, 2018–2020
CEO Hanna Andersson, 2010–2017

References

Poehlman, T. A., & Close Scheinbaum, A. (in press). Corporate cancel culture: dimensions of moral cognition in cancel culture and a catalog of corporate cancellation events. In *Cancel Culture and Brand Boycotts: The Dark Side of Social Media for Brands*. Routledge/Psychology Press, New York.

Scheinbaum, A. C. (2018). *The Dark Side of Social Media: A Consumer Psychology Perspective*. Routledge, New York.

Wood, N. T., & Allan, D. B. (2024). *This Bud Light's for You-Him/Her/Them*. SAGE Business Cases Originals, https://doi.org/10.4135/9781071934876

PREFACE: INTRODUCTION TO CORPORATE CANCEL CULTURE

Angeline Close Scheinbaum

There is clearly a dark side of social media on consumer psychology from a social and cognitive lens. However, it has become clear that there is also a dark side of social media for brands in an age of virality and cancel culture. Defined broadly, cancel culture is when a company, organization, or person (often representing a company or media outlet) is perceived of wrong-doing or offending others in a way that goes viral in the media/social media so that brand or representative is then unofficially "canceled" – losing their credibility, fan base, customers, image, relationships with stakeholders, and sales.

Our book takes a different lens. We look at the broad-scale, or macro approaches to cancel culture and related topics. What is corporate cancel culture? As introduced in this book, and in Chapter 1 (equally authored by Angeline Close Scheinbaum and T. Andrew Poehlman, colleagues at the Wilbur O. and Ann Powers College of Business at Clemson University), the phenomenon of cancel culture for companies and brands deserves its own definition. As such, in the opening chapter of this book, we define corporate cancel culture as *a phenomenon wherein consumers and other stakeholders use digital platforms to collectively withdraw support and enact social, psychological, and economic sanctions on businesses, brands, or corporations; people cancel companies or brands as an intended way to show care/prevent harm, seek fairness, loyalty/account for betrayal, show authority/subversion of the company, and establish sanctity/ degradation* (Chapter 1).

Just last year (2023), Bud Light had massive sales and stock falls as a direct result of a controversial social media influencer whose name, image, and likeness were felt to be offensive to a large and loud aspect of their established consumer base. This is a clear example of how one minor marketing decision can bring a social media firestorm to a major company. The social media outrage led the CEO to make a statement on how the brand had good intentions and that they do care about their customer base. This is just one of many examples of times when brands have suffered and social media is a catalyst for getting that brand punishment.

This is an example of the dark side of social media for brands and what can happen when consumers use social media to call for boycotts and take control of the narrative of what they think a brand should align with. This is also a unique case of an anti-influencer, where a prominent musician used his platform to express disdain and a perceived alienation. It is important to note that this marketing partnership with an influencer is not a major media investment compared to the vast media investments the brand traditionally makes in advertising such as during the Super Bowl. The brand was likely aiming for inclusivity but received backlash from parts of the consumer base that felt alienated.

While this concept of the dark side for brands was introduced in a previous book on The Dark Side of Social Media, it was only a section and primarily focused on consumer boycotts. Since then, there has been a growing interest and literature in marketing, psychology, communications, advertising, management, MIS, and economics that has highlighted the role of social media in "bringing brands down," retaliating (such as with negative consumer reviews on social media), boycotting, and social media firestorms.

As such, there is a clear need for scholars to address the dark side of social media not just for consumers (the traditional approach) but for a larger scale for companies and organizations and those who represent those brands or organizations. While most of the focus is at the brand or company level, this is happening at the macro or governmental level as well. For instance, work on social media trolls by Linvill and Warren (Chapter 4) has clearly demonstrated that consumers do not know the difference often on social media as to what posts or comments are done by authentic people or "trolls." Trolls may indeed be real people with a negative intent to cause trouble; however, their research shows that often trolls are done by artificial intelligence or bots that have been coded as a way to bring misinformation to the masses – especially during times of elections or geopolitical conflicts.

The main difference between this book and other books or studies focusing on cancel culture largely is the unit of analysis. This edited book has a unit of analysis that is broader – brands, representatives of brands, companies, organizations, and governments. Other similar volumes or books have a unit of analysis that is the consumer/individual – more specifically their mental health and consumer well-being. Collectively, our books start with a social media related problem in each chapter and call for solutions to the problem based on the data or study provided in each chapter.

It is in the spirit of inclusiveness and globality that inspires me to want to work with these esteemed scholars. The credit for the ideas, research, and energy collectively goes to the set of authors on this project (please refer to the author biographies for more details on these experts). What you will see is the true global nature of this author team. They represent universities and/or hometowns from the US, the UK, India, China, S. Korea, and Brazil. They are world-class experts and scholars of marketing, economics, communications, media studies, sports communication, parks, recreation and tourism management, and psychology. They range from graduate students to endowed professors. Despite the different countries, cultures, and ranks, we have one thing in common – a scholarly interest in social media and in making social media a better place for people, companies, and brands. We hope that this book sparks a lot of new ideas, energy, and scholarly research as well as reconsiderations by companies and their agents on best practices for social media.

This book is truly a team effort. On behalf of the author team, professors:

Hyeong-Gyu Choi,
Angeline Close Scheinbaum,
Kevin Flynn,
Sayan Gupta,
Jingyun Hu,
Kevin W. James,
Darren Linvill,
Jonathan R. Oliveira,
Janna M. Parker,
Renan Petersen-Wagner,
T. Andrew Poehlman,
Medha Reddy Edunuri
Scott R. Stroud,
Felipe Tobar,
Patrick Warren,
Kat Williams, and
Debra Zahay

PART I

Canceling Cancel Culture

How It Can Hurt People, Brands, and Sport Organizations

Angeline Close Scheinbaum

Part I focuses on the notion of "canceling cancel culture," as it can be harmful if it is not done in a way that derives social good or social justice. This idea is encapsulated by the fact that aspects of cancel culture are negative for people's well-being, companies, and for society at large.

The introduction chapter is by Angeline Close Scheinbaum and T. Andrew Poehlman, who worked together on the chapter "Corporate Cancel Culture: A Framework of Dimensions of Moral Cognition in Cancel Culture and a Catalog of Corporate Cancelation Events." In this chapter, they offer three main contributions. First, they suggest a new definition of corporate cancel culture. In the conceptual chapter, they introduce a novel topic of "corporate cancel culture." They then define *corporate cancel culture as: a phenomenon wherein consumers and other stakeholders use digital platforms to collectively withdraw support and enact social, psychological, and economic sanctions on businesses, brands, or corporations; People cancel companies or brands as an intended way to show care/prevent harm, seek fairness, loyalty/account for betrayal, show authority/subversion of the company, and establish sanctity/degradation.*

Their second contribution is that they offer a new framework, or theory. This theory has the dimensions of moral cognition in cancel culture. In that framework, it helps show and explain the purpose, triggers, emotions, and virtues associated with corporate canceling. They also have the type of cancelation as being fairness/cheating based, loyalty/betrayal based, authority/subversion based, and sanctity/degradation based. Last, and most excitingly for those who want an organized list of the companies that have been canceled (or companies that consumers attempted to cancel), they offer a list of companies that have been canceled or almost canceled. The catalog then

DOI: 10.4324/9781032670546-1

ties back to the framework with the type of cancelation and the purpose category. They rely on categorization theory.

The introduction chapter sets up work by Janna Parker, Kevin James, and Debra Zahay, who study cancel culture for both human brands as well as companies. Their excellent chapter "Cancel Culture for Human Brands and Firms: Punishment versus Accountability" gets into the motivations for cancelations, as well as some empirical work that is grounded in some items from Pew Research. Their chapter goes into details about many examples and cases of companies that have been canceled for actual things that happened, as well as some fake news examples. For instance, they note the Wayfair example that was largely based on rumors and falsehoods, but still somehow the misinformation got the company almost canceled in the minds of many consumers. A novel contribution from this chapter is that they note that canceling happens on both sides of the political aisles (progressives and conservatives).

Parker et al.'s chapter flows into a more specific area where we see cancelations in the media – the sport industry. A fascinating and detailed look into the sport industry by a global team of scholars (Felipe Tobar, Renan Petersen-Wagner, and Jonathan R. Oliveira) focuses on some classic and recent cases where social media has brought out concerns and issues in the sport context. Their chapter, "Dark Side of Social Media: Cancel Culture in Sports Organizations," gets into the teams of Real Madrid and FC Barcelona, who engaged in an unexpected mutual institutional cancelation on social media by accusing each other of having maintained and benefited from historical ties with Franco's oppressive regime.

The authors explain how the team's fan bases reacted to the allegations on social media that linked their clubs with Franco's regime. They also studied the motivations behind clubs' engagement in cancel culture and the consumer/fan stances during the conflict. The authors also noted the consequences to the economic and brand/image aspects to these clubs. They did a digital socio-psychological analysis of three videos on YouTube. This entailed over 4,000 comments.

Tobar et al. found four main themes:

Supporting official counter-canceling while Reinterpreting history;
Fans' Mockery as a counter canceling culture Reinforcement;
Fear, Repression, and Persecution: Explaining FCB's compliance with Franco's regime;
"White-washing" the history: RM's Propaganda and Manipulation.

These themes explain how fans may reject their clubs' historical associations with dark periods and figures. In doing so they mitigate cancel culture effects including sponsorship losses/non-renewals, brand damage, and declined fan support. Their chapter encourages future research into sports cancel culture. They call for scholars and sport marketers to consider the interplay of culture, political contexts, fan's collective identities, and sport team identifications inherent in the sports world. Even believed sport teams have attempted to be canceled.

1

CORPORATE CANCEL CULTURE

A Framework of Dimensions of Moral Cognition in Cancel Culture and a Catalog of Corporate Cancelation Events

Angeline Close Scheinbaum and T. Andrew Poehlman

> "Do not be deceived: Bad company ruins good morals": 1 Corinthians 15–33

It is long known that morals can be eroded or ruined by "bad company," or being around other people who are deceptive or immoral. The same may hold for companies, as consumers want to "call out" or "cancel" companies who they perceive to be immoral or who need punishing due to a perceived moral or ethical violation. The topic of cancel culture is of timely and dire importance to consumers, businesses, and society alike in the era of social media. This chapter and corresponding book are crucial because cancel culture has quickly become pervasive in modern times. As social media grows, cancel culture is a primary threat to both brand *and* corporate image, as it is now ubiquitous and often consumer controlled. Due in part to social media, there has been a clear power shift from companies to consumers, as consumers collectively have a massive voice and ability to lift a company up with positive word-of-mouth or destroy it with negative accusations and revelations.

It used to be that companies could choose the topics and times for engaging with consumers. Today, companies have no choice in the fields of engagement as consumers are constantly engaging with companies about their own topics, on their own time, and on their own preferred platforms. Consumers may actively express negative word-of-mouth, boycott, retaliate, collaboratively attack companies/brands, and now lead or participate in "cancelations" (Demsar, Ferraro, Nguyen, & Sands, 2023). And as Demsar et al. (2023) astutely note, cancelations are bad for business, and show "a clear threat

DOI: 10.4324/9781032670546-2

to established market actors (brands) and have the potential to re-organize institutional resources" (p. 232).

There are many examples of people or individuals being canceled by society, online communities, and other consumers. For instance, one of the first celebrities to become canceled was Roseanne Barr, a prominent comedian and actor (and the namesake of the television show Roseanne). In 2018, Roseanne wrote a racist tweet on social media and, as such, received a great deal of backlash from other social media users, the mainstream media, and advertisers. As a direct result, Roseanne responded via another tweet that she had taken a prescription sleeping drug (Ambien), which led to her not taking accountability for the racist tweet. As such, she shifted the blame for the racist tweet to the brand Ambien. Ambien then took to their brand's social media to tell consumers that "Ambien does not make one racist." This is an appropriate early example of cancelation because it entails social media, a canceled celebrity, and blame-shift to a company or brand. Since then, there have been many examples of celebrities, politicians, executives, or other human brands who have been canceled.

This incident is emblematic of the typical pattern observed in cancel culture scenarios. Central to this phenomenon is the involvement of an entity, be it an individual or a corporation, possessing significant social power or public influence. These entities often find themselves at the center of controversy due to actions or statements perceived as violating the norms or values of a less powerful group. This perceived violation is crucial in triggering the cancel culture mechanism. In response, the less powerful group, often marginalized or underrepresented, leverages the democratized platform of the internet to voice their dissent. The collective action taken online is a defining characteristic of cancel culture, where numbers and shared sentiment amplify the impact. This digital congregation of voices serves not only as a means of expressing disapproval but also as a tool for seeking accountability from those in positions of power. The online nature of these interactions is pivotal, as it allows for rapid dissemination of information and mobilization of support, transcending geographical and social boundaries that traditionally limited such collective actions.

As defined, cancel culture is "collective desire by consumers to withdraw support of those individuals and brands in power perceived to be involved in objectionable behavior or activities through the use of social media" (Saldanha et al., 2023). While this definition captures the broader essence of cancel culture, our focus shifts to a more specific subset: corporate cancel culture. This distinct form zeroes in on the relationship between consumers and corporate entities, rather than individuals. Corporate cancel culture emphasizes the collective action against businesses and brands, driven by consumer expectations of corporate responsibility and ethical conduct. It is not just about withdrawing support, but also about influencing corporate policies and practices, reflecting a shift in power dynamics where consumers hold corporations accountable in the public digital sphere.

The objective of this chapter on corporate cancel culture is threefold: (1) the main objective is to explicitly go beyond understanding the canceling of individual people and seriously consider the canceling companies or brands. In doing so, we aim to contribute a working definition and overview of corporate cancel culture. (2) The second objective is to provide an integrative interdisciplinary literature review synthesizing critical marketing phenomena and relevant psychological theories to explain or predict corporate cancelation. (3) The third objective is to start a scholarly conversation by providing a framework on corporate cancel culture with corresponding propositions for scholars to empirically test.

This chapter is organized as follows. We first provide a background on cancel culture with examples and definitions of cancel culture, and then we define corporate cancel culture – focusing on the unique dynamics of businesses. We then provide some secondary research insights about company cancel culture. Second, we conduct an overview of the history of cancel culture. Third, we review the consumer and psychology literature regarding how brands come to be targets for emotional attachment and backlash, as in the case of cancelation. We then introduce and synthesize relevant theories or theoretical approaches to studying cancel culture.

Background and Definitions of Cancel Culture

Industry Research and Consumer Definitions of Cancel Culture

Corporate cancelation is performed by consumers to be witnessed by other consumers, and so to define it, it is critical to consult consumer opinion on what cancel culture is. As seen in Figure 1.1, there are various consumer perspectives as to what cancel culture entails. For example, consumers define it in various ways that often relate with their political identity (i.e., liberal democrat, moderate democrat, moderate republican, conservative republican). Some of the ways that democrats explain cancel culture are "a synonym for political correctness, where words and phrases are taken out of context to bury the careers of people. A mob mentality"; "Ruining someone's life or career because a vocal minority doesn't like something that they said or did"; and "Cancel culture is a movement to remove celebrity status or esteem from a person, place, or thing based on offensive behavior or transgression." Republicans similarly have explained cancel culture with similar underpinnings, according to the industry research as collected in 2020 by the Pew Research Center (2021). By 2022, most Americans were familiar with the term cancel culture (Pew Research Center, 2022).

Next, as seen in Figure 1.2, consumers have stated that the roles of accountability and punishment in cancel culture are paramount to canceling

FIGURE 1.1 Consumer's Definitions of Cancel Culture as Reported by Pew Research: People's Definition, Gender, and Political Identification

Source: "Americans and 'Cancel Culture': Where Some See Calls for Accountability, Others See Censorship, Punishment." Pew Research Center, Washington, DC (May 19, 2021). https://www.pewresearch.org/internet/2021/05/19/americans-and-cancel-culture-where-some-see-calls-for-accountability-others-see-censorship-punishment/.

a person or plausibly a company. Accountability is related to "calling someone out," or in the case of corporate cancel culture, "calling a company out." As noted by a moderate democrat as quoted to the Pew Research, accountability is important because it is hoped to reconsider their actions in either a conscious or unconscious way. When people cancel another person or a business/brand, they may believe that they are punishing the person or company. Punishment may take the form of excluding the person or company, ostracizing, boycotting, trolling on social media, or leaving negative reviews for examples. As mentioned by a conservative republican, punishment relates to everyone being able to express their opinions and agreeing to disagree. A way to punish others is to not be willing to listen to other's ideas

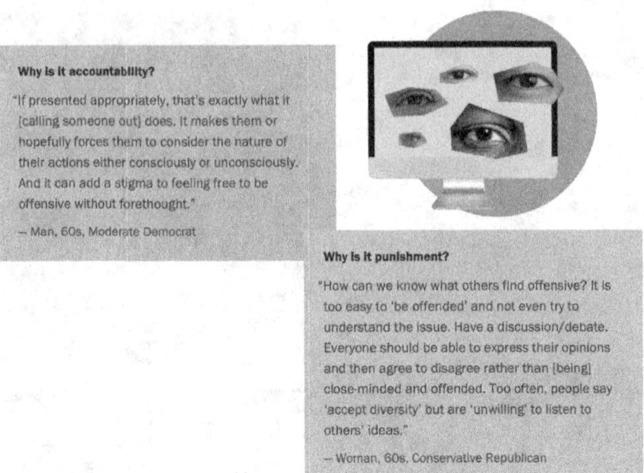

FIGURE 1.2 The Prominent Roles of Accountability and Punishment in Cancel Culture

Source: "Americans and 'Cancel Culture': Where Some See Calls for Accountability, Others See Censorship, Punishment." Pew Research Center, Washington, DC (May 19, 2021). https://www.pewresearch.org/internet/2021/05/19/americans-and-cancel-culture-where-some-see-calls-for-accountability-others-see-censorship-punishment/.

and remaining close minded to their views or seemingly offensive or immoral words or actions.

As depicted in Figure 1.3, which shows findings from the Pew Research from a study of Americans during September 8–13, 2020, a striking 60% of American adults polled say that calling out others on social media for their offensive posts is a way to hold people accountable for their actions (Pew Research Center, 2021). When asked to explain why that is, 17% of them report that it is a "teaching or learning moment." 10% of this group say that other people need to think about the consequences of what they say. The next three reasons are tied, at 6% where people say that calling out others on social media for offensive posts for accountability reasons is due to exposing social ills such as sexism or racism, the opinion that people need to think before they speak, and that it is a form of accountability (Pew Research Center, 2021).

Also from their poll, almost 40% of American adults surveyed by the Pew Research say that calling out others for their social media posts is likely to punish people who do not deserve to be punished (Pew Research Center, 2021). There are various reasons why many people think that the punishment is undeserved. Interestingly, the main reason is that people tend to consider the context in which the statement was made (18%). People also believe that others are overreacting (13%), or that it is a matter of free speech (12%).

Americans explain why they think calling out others on social media for potentially offensive posts is either holding people accountable or unjustly punishing them

Among the 38% of U.S. adults who say calling out others on social media for posting content that might be considered offensive more likely ***punishes people who didn't deserve it****, % who mention each of the following when asked to explain why in their own words*

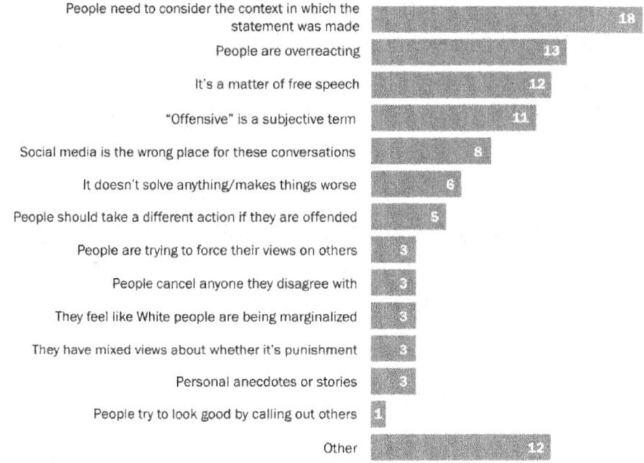

Among the 58% of U.S. adults who say calling out others on social media for posting content that might be considered offensive more likely ***holds people accountable for their actions****, % who mention each of the following when asked to explain why in their own words*

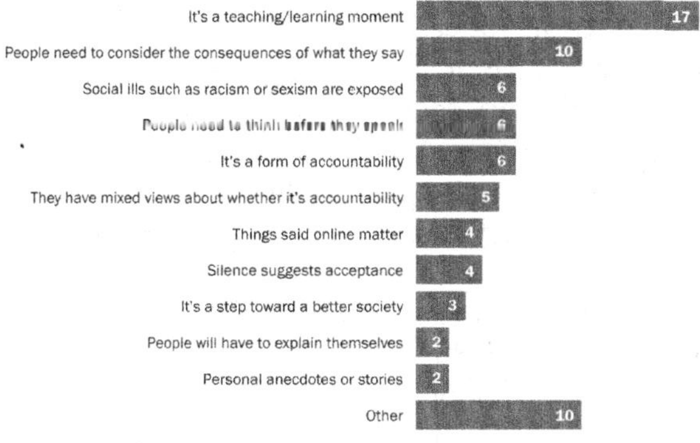

Note: Verbatim responses have been coded into categories. The 28% who received but did not give an answer for the punishment question and the 37% who received but did not give an answer for the accountability question are not shown. Including these groups, figures for each question may add up to more than 100% because multiple responses were allowed.
Source: Survey of U.S. adults conducted Sept. 8-13, 2020.
"Americans and 'Cancel Culture': Where Some See Calls for Accountability, Others See Censorship, Punishment"

PEW RESEARCH CENTER

FIGURE 1.3 Cancel Culture: Thoughts on Accountability or Unjust Punishment

Source: "Americans and 'Cancel Culture': Where Some See Calls for Accountability, Others See Censorship, Punishment." Pew Research Center, Washington, DC (May 19, 2021). https://www.pewresearch.org/internet/2021/05/19/americans-and-cancel-culture-where-some-see-calls-for-accountability-others-see-censorship-punishment/

Furthermore, the Pew Research Center found that 11% believe that the term offensive is a subjective term. In other words, a social media post can be offensive to some people, but that same post can elicit laughs or no emotional response at all from others. Last, 8% believe that social media is the wrong place for serious or heavy conversations (Pew Research Center, 2021).

These findings may be explained by theories related to moral violations and categorization theory, which can explain how consumers classify or categorize words/language used by companies (see Schmitt & Zhang, 1988), or products (Sujan & Dekleva, 1987). That is, people have the tendency to categorize people or things or organizations into categories, such as moral or immoral (Van Horen & Pieters, 2017). Upon receiving information, especially without any prior cognitions about the person or company, they may subconsciously categorize them as immoral and as such deserving of the negative social media content about them.

Academic Research in Cancel Culture

In the past five years, scholarship on cancel culture has shot up. A recent search of Google Scholar for "cancel culture" turned up approximately 11,500 hits. Figure 1.4 shows Google Scholar hits for "cancel culture" from 2010 – when there were only eight hits – to the most recent year (2023), in which there were 3,380 results for cancel culture. This exponential increase in academic interest is indicative of the growing relevance and complexity of cancel culture in contemporary society. The surge in scholarly attention mirrors the phenomenon's escalation in public discourse, reflecting an urgent need for academic exploration and understanding. The steep rise in publications, particularly in the last five years, suggests that cancel culture has evolved from a peripheral topic to a significant subject of study across various disciplines. This trend underscores the increasing recognition of cancel culture's impact on social dynamics, media, politics, and corporate behavior. The data from Google Scholar not only highlights the burgeoning academic interest but also points to the potential for a rich and diverse body of literature that can offer insights into the multifaceted nature of cancel culture and its implications for individuals, organizations, and society at large.

Google Scholar hits are an informative source of information because of Google Scholar's wide net; however, in order to understand the academic discourse on cancel culture, we turned to Scopus. Scopus is one of the world's leading and most thorough academic indexing databases and, as such, should provide a comprehensive picture of the academic literature on cancel culture. The results from this search are summarized in Figure 1.5. This search was first performed by searching Scopus for the term "cancel culture" in titles, abstracts, and keywords without any date or discipline restrictions.

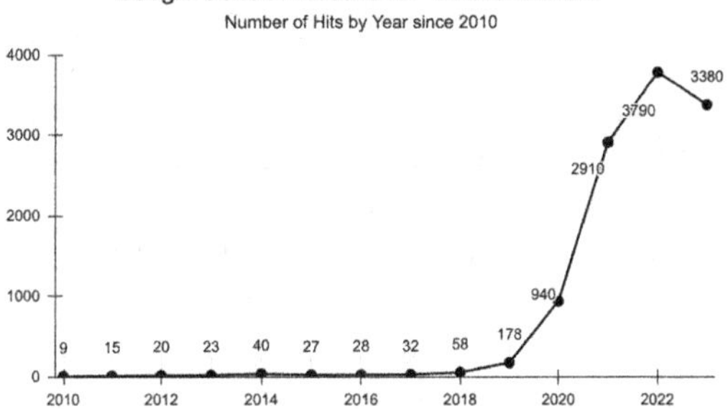

FIGURE 1.4 Google Scholar Search Results for "Cancel Culture" by Year (2010–2023).

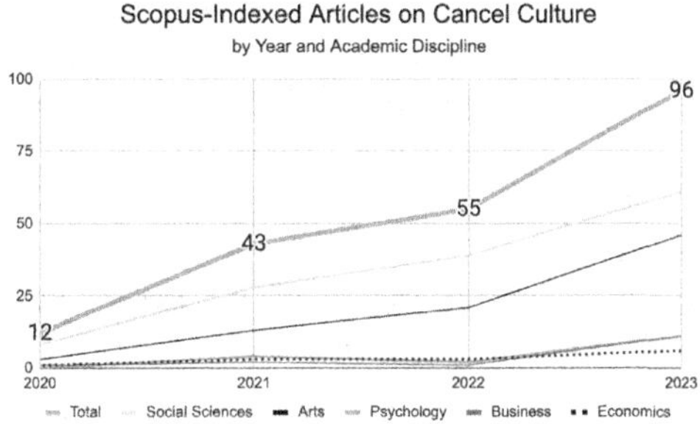

FIGURE 1.5 Scopus Search Results for "Cancel Culture" by Year and Academic Discipline.

This initial search returned 206 results with the earliest Scopus-indexed publication coming in 2020. Scopus subject areas with over 10 total papers were (in order of magnitude), Social Sciences (136), Arts and Humanities (83), Psychology (17), Business, Management and Accounting (15), and finally Economics, Econometrics, and Finance (13). Only 3 papers were found in the subdiscipline of marketing.

These findings collectively underscore the burgeoning academic interest in cancel culture, highlighting its relevance across a spectrum of scholarly disciplines. In what follows we will quickly review the extant definitions of cancel culture across different fields and attempt to arrive at a definition for corporate cancel culture that encompasses the critical concepts common across all areas of study. Despite the relatively limited exploration in marketing literature, the burgeoning interest across academic fields underscores the urgency of establishing a robust working definition of cancel culture. This section aims to traverse various disciplinary landscapes, from marketing to humanities and social sciences, to distill a comprehensive understanding and set the stage for understanding corporate cancel culture by formulating a definition that captures the essence of cancel culture in its entirety.

Academic Definitions of Cancel Culture in the Humanities Literature

The emergence of cancel culture within the business literature is still in its nascent stages, as evidenced by the production of only 28 papers over the past three years, as shown in Figure 1.5. In contrast, the Social Sciences and Humanities have been more prolific in this domain, contributing 236 papers within the same timeframe (again, see Figure 1.5). Within these disciplines, cancel culture is predominantly conceptualized as behavior of collective agency exercised by individuals with lower social power, primarily shown through social media platforms. A prominent definition from the most highly cited humanities paper on the subject (Clark, 2020) encapsulates this view:

> "Canceling" is an expression of agency, a choice to withdraw one's attention from someone or something whose values, (in)action, or speech are so offensive, one no longer wishes to grace them with their presence, time, and money.
>
> *(Clark, 2020, pp. 88–89)*

Further analysis of the literature reveals a consensus around three core elements in the definitions of cancel culture. This is succinctly summarized in the following excerpt (Tandoc, 2022, in press):

> Studies and essays that examined cancel culture offered a wide range of definitions, but three main definitional components are consistent: it involves (a) the public shaming of unacceptable behavior, and (b) withdrawal of support, which are (c) motivated by wanting to see the target persons experience some form of consequence or penalty due to their actions (e.g., losing employment, other revenue streams) or to ensure these persons are socially banished.
>
> *(Tandoc, 2022, in press)*

Additionally, Clark (2020) makes an important note regarding the inherent power dynamics at play in cancel culture, emphasizing the role of digital platforms in facilitating resistance and accountability among marginalized groups:

> The rapid mobilization in digital resistance and accountability practice among otherwise disempowered peoples compel us to identify who or what defines the disputed concept of the public sphere, who sets the rules of engagement, and thus what is considered "talking back" to dominant discourses.
>
> *(Clark, 2020, p. 89)*

These humanities-based definitions do tend to entail the element of resistance, accountability, social power, a power shift to the disempowered, offensiveness, marginalization, penalty, and shaming. As they are more humanities based, these lenses do not entail the notion of consumption and the brand or company aspect as the object of cancelation. The emerging marketing literature does.

Academic Definitions of Cancel Culture in the Marketing Literature

As noted and seen in the relatively low percentage of papers on the topic in business-related journals, the business literature on cancel culture is still emerging. However, in this short time (since 2020), business or consumption-related work on cancel culture converges on "Cancelation" as an act of supporting withdrawal of a company, firm, or organization on behalf of consumers, who turn to social media to express this dissent. For instance, supporting a withdrawal may simply not shopping there anymore and spreading negative WOM about the firm or brand as a moral signal. One recent paper in business (Saldanha et al., 2023) defines cancel culture from this "withdrawal of support" aspect as:

> A collective desire by consumers to withdraw support of those individuals and brands in power, perceived to be involved in objectionable behaviour or activities through the use of social media.
>
> *(Saldanha et al., 2023)*

However, cancelation is more than withdrawing support, and that view is in line with Demsar et al. (2023) who accurately explain how cancelation is related to, but distinct from similar concepts in business such as boycotting, spreading negative WOM, and retaliating against companies or brands. Demsar et al. (2023)'s perspective in the marketing literature expands the scope of cancelation, emphasizing its nature as a deliberate and collective action by consumers. This view underscores the role of social media as a platform for public mobilization and the intent to enact market change as a form of retribution for perceived transgressions:

> We define a cancellation as deliberate collective action on part of consumers – today typically performed on social media – which attempts to force market change through calling for the cancellation of a brand in retribution for an irreparable transgression.
>
> *(Demsar et al., 2023)*

To sum, the fundamental essence of cancel culture, as identified in both the humanities and marketing literature, revolves around the dynamics of power and the public forum of online discourse. It is characterized by individuals, often perceived as having less social power, leveraging digital platforms to challenge and hold accountable those in positions of greater power.

In the context of corporate cancel culture, this dynamic takes on a specific form. It involves the collective action of consumers and public stakeholders, who use social media and other online platforms to call out and withdraw support from businesses, brands, or corporations. This withdrawal is not merely a passive act but a deliberate and strategic response to perceived transgressions or objectionable behavior by these corporate entities. The goal is often twofold: to enforce accountability and to drive change within the market or corporate practices.

Therefore, we propose the following definition for corporate cancel culture:

> Corporate Cancel Culture is a phenomenon wherein consumers and other stakeholders use digital platforms to collectively withdraw support and enact social, psychological, and economic sanctions on businesses, brands, or corporations; People cancel companies or brands as an intended way to show care/prevent harm, seek fairness, loyalty/account for betrayal, show authority/subversion of the company, and establish sanctity/degradation.

History of Cancel Culture

Canceling began as a term 1991 when Nino Brown, a drug dealer in a movie called "New Jack City," told his subordinates to "cancel" his girlfriend. The term went seemingly dormant until 2009, when Lil Wayne – a rap artist from New Orleans – referenced the line in a song, referencing "canceling" his girlfriend. In 2014, the term gained steam, particularly in African American media and social media (Florini, 2014), when it was used in the reality show, Love and Hip Hop. In one 2014 episode, cast member Cisco Rosado told his romantic interest Diamond Strawberry while in a fight that she is "canceled."

Like so much of American culture, cancel culture started as a loose trope in African American society without the same connotations it has today. Like so much of American culture, cancel culture started as a loose trope in African American society without the same connotations it has today. Initially, the term "canceling" was used more colloquially, often in interpersonal contexts within the community. However, its meaning and scope began to evolve significantly with the advent of social movements, particularly those amplified by social media.

The #MeToo movement, emerging prominently on social media in 2017, marked a pivotal point in the evolution of cancel culture. It provided a platform for collective action versus sexual harassment and sexual assault, particularly in the entertainment industry and corporate environments. The movement empowered individuals, especially women, to publicly call out and "cancel" high-profile figures (typically but not always men) who had abused their power. This was not just about personal grievances; it became a broader societal statement about holding powerful individuals accountable.

Similarly, the #BlackLivesMatter movement, which gained renewed momentum in 2020 following the tragic death of George Floyd, utilized the concept of canceling as part of its broader strategy for social justice. It called for the cancelation of institutions, brands, and public figures that perpetuated systemic racism. This movement underscored cancel culture's potential as a tool for societal change, extending beyond individual accountability to encompass institutional and corporate responsibility.

While the initial surge in cancel culture was predominantly associated with progressive, left-leaning social movements, its mechanisms, and effectiveness have transcended political boundaries. Recent trends indicate that right-wing and conservative groups are also harnessing the power of cancelation to further their causes. This shift is exemplified by instances such as the ant-trans backlash against Bud Light, reflecting a broader pattern where conservative voices are increasingly engaging in cancelation campaigns.

This development aligns with findings from recent studies (Demsar et al., 2023; Witkowski, 2021) that note that the institutional aspect of cancelation of opponents often embeds alternative perspectives around social topics (e.g., race, gender), sexuality, abuses of power, and/or corporate greed. The basic point of cancelation remains similar across the political spectrum. These trends underscore a goal for scholars to understand cancel culture as a politically agnostic mechanism. A goal is that the conversation is made to bring markets together and further open societal discourse with important societal conversations, regardless of roots in a particular political origin (Demsar et al., 2023). However, due to the mixing-up of cancelation discourse with left-wing political views, there are similar actions stemming from right-wing causes that tend to receive different labels, such as boycotts or brand trolling.

A helpful review of how cancel culture is distinct from similar labels in the space of consumer resistance is provided by Demsar et al. (2023), as they note that negative word-of-mouth, sabotage, revenge, retaliation, collaborative attacks, boycotting do have some commonalities of the concept of cancelations. Similarly, marketing scholars have pointed out that there is an important distinction between attitudinal consumer resistance and behavioral consumer resistance, and much of the work we focus on in this chapter is behavioral consumer resistance (Tinson, Close, Tuncay Zayer, & Nuttal, 2013). Note that Demsar et al. (2023) also accurately frame this as active consumer resistance, which generally entails a consumer behavior that transcends attitudes. Consumer resistance theory has also been expanded to entail specific forms of behavioral resistance in the marketplace in the form of gift-resistance, retail-resistance, and market-resistance (Close & Zinkhan, 2007, 2009). Here, we focus on the behavioral (or active) aspect of consumer resistance where both companies/brands and in some cases retailers or even markets are actively resisted to the point of cancelation.

Social media platforms have played an indispensable role in the proliferation and power of cancel culture. Platforms like YouTube, Twitter, Instagram, and TikTok have become arenas where calls for cancelation are not only made but can rapidly gain traction and global visibility. The democratization of these platforms means that anyone with a following can initiate a cancel campaign, transforming cancel culture from a phenomenon primarily associated with social movements to a more ubiquitous method of public policing for behavior.

This evolution signifies a shift in cancel culture's application, from being a part of social movements to a regular mechanism for scrutinizing and influencing the actions of companies and individuals on a day-to-day level. Importantly, cancelations arising from movements like #MeToo and #BlackLivesMatter often stemmed from "exogenous triggers," where external events or societal shifts led to a reevaluation and condemnation of past or ongoing behaviors. Conversely, cancel culture has also increasingly responded to "endogenous triggers," where internal actions or failures within a company, such as a CEO's controversial personal conduct, spark a cancelation. These endogenous triggers underscore the growing expectation for continuous ethical behavior and social responsibility from corporate entities and public figures, reflecting a dynamic where both external societal movements (exogenous triggers) and internal actions (endogenous triggers) can precipitate a cancel culture response.

Figure 1.6 depicts the regional interest in the term cancel culture. As noted by analytics from Google searches by region, the countries where consumers are searching the term include the Philippines, Singapore, the United States, Canada, and Australia. Furthermore, and shown in the bottom part of Figure 1.6, the surge of searches of cancel culture occurred in 2020 and 2021. Interestingly, this time period had some overlap with the COVID-19 global pandemic.

People Getting Canceled: Celebrities, Professionals, and Academics

While there have been too many calls for cancelation of people to list, there has been some effort to chronicle cancelation, at least of people. While some want "cancellation of cancel culture," others have found ways to chronicle and display a list or database of those who have been accused of making a moral violation to some extent. One such endeavor is an anonymously maintained online database at canceledpeople.org, which chronicles individuals who have faced cancelation. The anonymity of the site's administrators underscores the profound impact and often contentious nature of cancel culture, particularly in sectors like academia where the stakes of public scrutiny

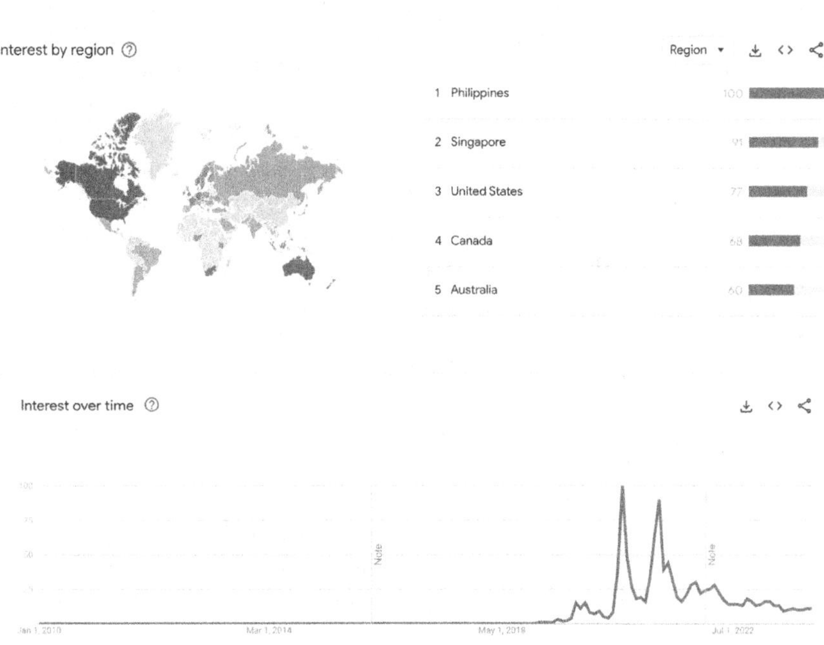

FIGURE 1.6 Depiction of The Regional Interest in The Term Cancel Culture via Google Searches of "Cancel Culture" over Time (2010–2023).

are high. This database categorizes cases based on stringent criteria, including loss of employment, coordinated efforts to silence and shame, and significant damage to reputation. This database serves as a valuable resource for understanding the scope and nature of cancel culture, particularly how it manifests in the lives of various individuals.

So far, the types of people who have been canceled seem to fall into three general categories: celebrities (people with immense social power in the modern world who often covet their social status and use it in hopes to influence culture), professionals (those who have a profession that is seen as giving them some social power or standing), and academics (scholars within academic community).

Celebrities Getting Canceled

Celebrities often become targets of cancelation due to their high social power and the public nature of their personas (see Marwick & Boyd, 2011 for a full treatment). These public personas are meticulously crafted through a blend of personal revelations and direct fan engagement, fostering a sense of intimacy and authenticity with their audience. However, this heightened visibility and perceived closeness can swiftly lead to their downfall when their actions or statements are publicly condemned. For instance, Roseanne Barr's career faced a significant setback due to her racist tweets. Similarly, Chrissy Teigen, known for her active social media presence, encountered backlash and professional repercussions over allegations of online bullying. Kanye West, another prominent figure known for his outspoken nature, has faced cancelation for his controversial remarks on race and politics. These instances underscore the delicate balance celebrities maintain on platforms like Twitter, where the line between personal expression and public persona blurs. Their experiences highlight how the very tools that build their celebrity status can also precipitate their fall from public favor.

Professionals Getting Canceled

Cancel culture has also reached into the professional ranks where the connection between the social power of private individuals, their free speech, and right to continued employment are murkier issues. In May 2020, Amy Cooper, the "Central Park Karen," was terminated from her role as an insurance portfolio manager at Franklin Templeton Investments, after a viral video showed her threatening to spuriously report a Black birdwatcher to the police.

Similarly, Adam Rapoport, former editor-in-chief of Bon Appétit, resigned in June 2020 following the emergence of a brownface photo and allegations of a racially discriminatory work culture. This revelation, coupled with public accounts from staff members about unequal treatment and pay disparities, particularly affecting employees of color, led to his resignation. Sometimes individuals need not hold traditional positions of power but be merely seen as representatives of power as in the case of a janitor at Smith College, who was attacked on social media for calling security on a young Black woman for being in a closed lounge. The incident led to widespread backlash and the janitor being placed on leave. However, a subsequent investigation found no evidence of discrimination.

Academics Getting Canceled

That janitors at universities find themselves targeted for cancelation at Universities is evidence of the pervasiveness of cancel culture in academia. An analysis of recent academic cancelation incidents (Verstynen, 2022) revealed a pattern of academic professionals facing severe repercussions for expressing viewpoints that involve contentious issues surrounding gender and race, leading to institutional actions such as suspensions or terminations, accompanied by public censure. The National Association of Scholars (NAS) documented 291 instances of cancelation at universities in the United States and Canada. This data underscores the extent to which cancel culture has infiltrated higher education, often manifesting as a response to perceived transgressions against contemporary ideological tenets. The resultant disciplinary actions highlight the precarious nature of academic discourse in the current sociopolitical climate, where the pursuit of intellectual inquiry is increasingly entangled with the demands of conforming to societal expectations.

For any academic, the rapid expansion of cancel culture can be alarming. Likewise, for corporations, the rise of cancel culture presents concern. While academic cancelations often stem from individual expressions or actions that conflict with prevailing societal norms, corporate cancel culture operates on a different dynamic. In the corporate realm, cancel culture typically targets the broader policies, practices, and cultural ethos of a company, rather than individual transgressions.

Companies Getting Canceled: Corporate Cancel Culture

Companies Getting Canceled

Firms have long been held to account by the public. The idea of societal protest of business practices goes back at least centuries. In the 20th century, as business gained more power in society, boycotts and protests became more and more prevalent. This social force likely peaked with the consumer protection movement and Ralph Nader in the late 1960s and early 1970s, but an undercurrent of mistrust and active protest has remained a constant in life inside of developed countries. In fact, the field of public relations spawned because of the consistent need to manage public perceptions of companies, corporations, and celebrities. However, in recent years, as the barriers to mass public communication have lowered, companies have found themselves increasingly in the crosshairs of angry consumers. In fact, recent work by Desmar et al. (2023) situates this issue in terms of consumer resistance and anti-consumption (Lee, 2022), which was first conceptualized in the marketing literature as a "resistance against a culture of consumption and the marketing of mass-produced meanings" (Penaloza & Price, 1993, p. 123).

However, this is not the only existing marketing literature important to understand cancel culture. The vastness of the literature on corporate social responsibility (see Agudelo, Jóhannsdóttir, & Davídsdóttir, 2019 for a recent review) and corporate branding (see Fetscherin & Usunier, 2012) both speak to the amount of interest businesses have in shaping their public image. While these streams of research primarily arose in the pre-social media age, the ubiquitous and profitable use of online, social media platforms by companies today necessitates a shift in focus. Academics and managers alike must transition from corporate strategies rooted in one-to-many communication styles to those that accommodate many-to-one interactions. This shift calls for a focused exploration of "cancel culture" in academic literature, moving beyond the broad and potentially outdated focus on shaping public opinion.

Consumer Intention and Effects of Corporate Cancelation: A Categorization Theory Perspective

Categorization theory may help explain a mechanism of consumer intention and intended effects of corporate cancelation. The theory has been employed in consumer research (e.g., Sujan & Dekleva, 1987) in brands and products, but not in the context of cancelations or boycotts. It should be stated that the effects of cancelation on corporations are not trivial. Italian luxury brand Dolce & Gabbana were "canceled" upon their entry into the Chinese market for advertising that offended Chinese consumers. This happened at a particularly inopportune time, as the market for luxury goods was exploding in 2018 and has since reached fever pitch. Advertising that was "meant as a joke" as displayed an ostensibly confused Chinese woman trying to eat pizza with chopsticks (the ad campaign also included other cultural mismatch malapropisms). As a result, Dolce & Gabbana had lost 98% of its market share by 2020.

Another story lies in a member of Planet Fitness not being happy with the gym's LGBTQIA+ friendly policy of transgender members using the locker room of the gender they identify with. A female member was offended by a transgender woman who was shaving in a towel in the women's locker room. The offended woman took a photo and complained to the managers, who noted that the other member was in line with their inclusive corporate policy. The offended woman was not happy with this response/their corporate policy and then took to social media (Facebook) to share her side of the story, how she felt offended, and in doing so triggered an outpouring of media attention to Planet Fitness. While some were supportive of their inclusive policy, other social media users called for a boycott of the gym, and a literal cancelation of the gym memberships (Smith, 2024).

There were clear economic and reputational consequences to the brand due to the call for corporate cancelation. The company value was $5.3 billion on March 14, 2024 and down to $4.9 billion on March 19, 2024, which is a $400 million reduction that correlates with the company's policy and decision to cancel the offended customer's gym membership after she shared a photo of the other member shaving in the female locker room (Smith, 2024). It is curious what the intentions of the shade and loud social media posts and calls for gym cancelations (literal cancelations) were, but there were clear effects to the company. As a popular artist, Taylor Swift, says about LGBTQIA+

advocacy, some may shade others who are different, and this transcends to some not wanting to patronize or give business to companies who have different stances on social topics. The song, *You Need To Calm Down*, suggests that people who have issues with other people's gender identity should take a seat, restore peace, and not act on their desires to yell about the people they hate, as shade does not make others less gay (Swift, 2019).

Some people do not want to calm down and instead want companies with different political or social stances dragged, canceled, boycotted, or "taken down." Indeed, consumers intend their actions to have these types of effects. As seen in Figure 1.7, Porter Norvelli (2022) surveyed consumers to assess the outcomes they would desire if they engaged in company cancelation. Unsurprisingly, the most popular desire is to get a company to "change its ways" (38%). This is followed by specifically desiring companies to change political stances (27%), and a desire to have an offender within a company fired (26%). Consumers also want to send a message to companies to disassociate themselves from a particular spokesperson (22%), and about 1-in-5 desire for companies to take a reputational hit as a product of their behavior (19%). Likewise, consumers report that they would engage in cancelations to change brand imagery (18%), to get a company to take a stance on social networks (15%) and some have hopes that the company will "go away completely" (14%).

These results could again be explained by categorization theory (Sujan & Dekleva, 1987) in that consumers can subconsciously place companies into "good" or "bad" or into categories such as companies that have "ethical business practices" or "unethical business practices." We theorize per categorization theory that consumers may presume that an unethical company should "change its ways," and as such a cancelation of the company could help drive the company to more ethical or even prosocial business practices. Furthermore, when consumers categorize companies as being political on the "wrong side" (which here means that they disagree with a political stance or involvement that the company has that misaligns with their own personal views or the company has an immoral stance on a polarizing political issue, such as abortion), they are motivated to "help" by canceling the company as a way to try to drive the company to change their stance or remove their alignment with the political issue.

Similarly, consumers can categorize the employees or, more specifically, the leader of a company or the employee who was perceived to have committed a transgression (moral or legal) as "bad." As such, the consumer motivation to cancel the company is actually a motivation to have a particular employee or set of employees fired. In firing an employee, this is a perceived way to see justice, as firing someone often times ruins their reputation, financial stability of the person and their family if applicable, ability to secure future income, and the person's mental health. Firing an employee who is

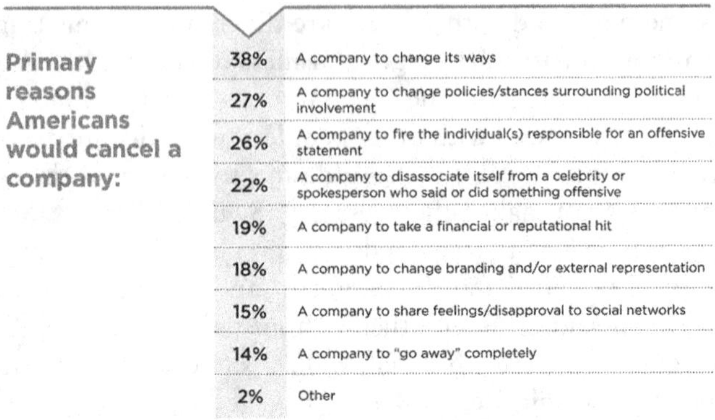

Primary reasons Americans would cancel a company:

38%	A company to change its ways
27%	A company to change policies/stances surrounding political involvement
26%	A company to fire the individual(s) responsible for an offensive statement
22%	A company to disassociate itself from a celebrity or spokesperson who said or did something offensive
19%	A company to take a financial or reputational hit
18%	A company to change branding and/or external representation
15%	A company to share feelings/disapproval to social networks
14%	A company to "go away" completely
2%	Other

FIGURE 1.7 Norvelli (2022) Survey Results of Main Reasons why American's Would "Cancel a Company"

perceived to have committed a moral violation could also extend to "firing" or disassociation of endorsers, influencers, or spokespersons who said or behaved in an offensive way.

Often times these offensive statements or behaviors are done on social media platforms, or social media is used as the communication channel to get momentum to see some drastic effects of corporate cancelations. These effects include, but are not limited to, employees or associated human brands demoted, disassociated, or fired. More drastically, companies can lose millions in the stock market or future sales, damage to brand equity, or even have to go out of business. There are downstream negative impacts to the economy and to local areas where the business employed people and suppliers to such effects of corporate cancelation, that perhaps the average consumer does not think about when they go on a cancelation effort against a company.

Catalysts Behind Corporate Cancelations: Toward a Framework for Explaining Corporate Cancel Culture

In recent years, many companies have faced public calls for cancelation. To offer a comprehensive perspective, we have collated examples from four distinct sources, each contributing uniquely to our understanding of corporate cancel culture. These sources are referenced numerically in Table 1.1 as follows: AdAge's (2020) "biggest cancels" of the year (Source 1), enzuzo.com's (2024) compilation of 18 brands impacted by cancelation movements (Source 2), an article on website EatThis, NotThat!' (Ruback & Ruback, 2024) on seven food brands that encountered public backlash (Source 3), and, finally, the most extensive list comes from Desmar et al. (2023), who documented 25 instances of corporate cancelations (Source 4). Many of these lists overlapped (as can be seen in the table), and some included instances were removed for either (a) being about an individual rather than a company or (b) the cancelation occurring prior to the advent of digital social media platforms.

In this section, we analyze the catalysts behind corporate cancelations. We start by examining the origins of both endogenous and exogenous cancelation triggers to understand how they set off the chain of events leading to corporate backlash. Following this, we explore the sources of controversy: the specific areas where companies' objectionable content arises. Next, we consider the various social issues that can lead to cancelation, drawing from recent consumer insights. Finally, we analyze the moral violations (Haidt, 2013) implicated in these instances, seeking to understand the evolutionary underpinnings of public response.

Locus of the Triggering Event

Social phenomena like online cancelation mobs do not happen in a vacuum; they happen in the context of the fast-paced, high information availability world where triggering events incite new social narratives. Triggering events have been traced to the spread of online trends more broadly and have been baked into the very concept of virality by Berger (2016) in his STEPPS model (see also Berger & Milkman, 2012). Corporations can think about these triggering events as having two loci, endogenous (that is, something to do with the company's behavior), and exogenous (something to do with the societal zeitgeist).

Endogenous Triggers

Endogenous triggers can be characterized as actions the company (or its representatives) has taken and publicly and purposefully displayed. To say it another way, these are public actions on the company's behalf that cause consumers' relationship with the company to change. For instance, in 2011, GoDaddy's CEO Bob Parsons posted photographs online of an elephant he had killed. Consumers saw this purposeful statement as changing their relationship with the brand. Other times, endogenous triggers are when an employee or the namesake of a brand does something racist, sexist, or otherwise perceived by its audience or the public at large to be immoral.

Exogenous Triggers

A more difficult issue for marketers to deal with is societal movements unrelated to their brand. In 2020, the murder of George Floyd by a police officer (Derek Chauvin) triggered a summer of racism protests, both in person and online. The resultant protests led to a larger social movement – broadly termed #BlackLivesMatter – that has been one of the largest shake-ups to modern life. Likewise, with the #MeToo social movement, these cultural moments force a reappraisal of current and past actions. They can catch companies unaware, especially if they have cultural blindspots about these issues in their organization. In 2020, many brands (like Aunt Jemima and Uncle Ben's) were called out for pre-existing issues consumers felt they should have already addressed. Some brands with perceived liabilities attempted to pre-emptively promised change because of these movements' social force. For instance, the brand "Plantation Rum" promised to change their name in 2020 because of the obvious reference to slavery; however, it dropped the promise in 2022 and, as such, could potentially be vulnerable to cancelation (Dodd, 2022).

Source of Controversy

In assessing this list of cancelations, we have identified three primary sources of controversy (though much more work is needed). Firstly, issues with brand imagery (Keller, 1993, Kotler & Keller, 2016) are a key factor, as the symbolic nature of a brand's imagery is crucial in consumer perception, and any misalignment with societal values can provoke backlash. Secondly, corporate practices (Klein, Smith, & John, 2004) are a frequent trigger for public disapproval, encompassing areas such as environmental policies, labor practices, and corporate governance, where ethical lapses can quickly escalate into calls for cancelation. Lastly, employee conduct (Blader & Tyler, 2005), including the behavior of both executives and other employees, can reflect on the entire organization and lead to broader accountability demands.

Issues That Lead to Cancelation

Naturally, any research on corporate cancelations needs to ask, "What issues cause cancelation events?" In pursuit of this understanding, Statista conducted a consumer poll to ascertain the offenses that would prompt a call for corporate cancelation. Their findings, which encompass responses where over 30% of consumers indicated a willingness to cancel a company, shed light on a specific spectrum of social issues tied to ethical violations. Notably, the offenses that garnered the highest disapproval were those involving harm to subordinates, with the mistreatment of animals (44%) marginally surpassing the mistreatment of workers (41%). Additionally, substantial proportions of consumers expressed willingness to cancel companies for corruption (40%), environmental harm (35%), the sale of unhealthy (34%) or faulty products (33%), and tolerance of racism (38%) or sexism (32%).

These insights serve as a valuable starting point for delineating the sensitive social issues that trigger corporate cancelations. In our analysis, as demonstrated in Table 1.1, we have consolidated these categories into six primary issue classifications, augmenting them with two additional categories (politics and sexual ethics) that align with documented instances of cancelation. This categorization results in a list of issues, presented alphabetically, for which consumers are known to cancel companies: (1) Animal Treatment, (2) Corruption, (3) Environmental Harm, (4) Politics, (5) Product Issues, (6) Racism, (7) Sexual Ethics and (8) Worker Treatment. It is important to acknowledge that this list, while informative, is not exhaustive. Continuous academic investigation is required to expand and refine our understanding of the diverse social issues that can precipitate corporate cancelations.

Moral Foundations

While it is important to understand specific social issues that provoke strong feelings and a desire to cancel companies, social issues sit on the surface of a deeper psychology in humans about moral violations. All cancelation happens because of perceived moral transgressions on the part of a company or one of its agents. Haidt's Moral Foundations Theory (2013) suggests that human moral reasoning is influenced by five core dimensions: Care, emphasizing empathy and the prevention of harm; Fairness, focusing on justice and equitable treatment; Loyalty, valuing allegiance to group norms; Authority, respecting established hierarchies and traditions; and Sanctity, upholding the sacredness and purity of certain values and practices (see Table 1.1 for a summary). Below, we summarize these dimensions of moral cognition and relate them to cancel culture.

Care/Harm. When companies engage in actions perceived as causing harm – be it to consumers, employees, or society at large – they often face cancelation for violating the Care dimension, as the public reacts strongly against practices that show a lack of empathy or compassion. This can be either direct physical harm (as in GoDaddy's CEO killing an elephant for sport) or ignoring an issue like domestic violence, in which people are harmed (as in Snapchat's promotion of a joke about Rihanna and Chris Brown).

Fairness/Cheating. Corporations that are seen as engaging in unfair practices, such as exploiting labor, manipulating customers, or unequal treatment of stakeholders, can trigger a backlash under the Fairness dimension, as these actions are perceived as violating the principle of equitable and just treatment. Racism, sexism, and other types of discriminatory actions are often seen as being "unfair" because they punish people for characteristics they cannot control or are irrelevant to the evaluation of people.

Loyalty/Betrayal. Companies that betray consumer trust, whether through breaking promises, shifting values, or actions contrary to their brand identity, can face cancelation due to the violation of the Loyalty dimension, as they are seen as failing to uphold commitments to their community or customer base.

TABLE 1.1 A Framework for Corporate Cancel Culture: Dimensions of Moral Cognition as Related to Cancel Culture

	Care/Harm	*Fairness/ Cheating*	*Loyalty/ Betrayal*	*Authority/ Subversion*	*Sanctity/ Degradation*
Evolutionary Purpose	To raise children and keep them from harm	To work with others for mutual benefit	To form groups that can stick together	To create and sustain positive hierarchies	To avoid disease or other harm
Universal Triggers	When a child shows signs of pain or distress	A cheater or someone who works well with a group	An external conflict that the group has to deal with together	Someone claiming authority or submitting to another	People or animals carrying disease
Modern-Day Triggers	A cute video, an animal at a rescue shelter	Being faithful to your partner, shoplifting	Any sort of organized team	Respect in the workplace for superiors	Concepts like fascism
Typical Emotions	Empathy	Frustration, thankfulness	Pride, anger at a betrayal	Esteem, terror	Revulsion
Virtues Associated	Generosity, sympathy	Objectivity	Allegiance to a group	Acquiescence	Restraint, faith

For instance, when the CEO of Goya (a Hispanic foods company) endorsed Donald Trump – who has made many inflammatory statements about Hispanics, many in the Hispanic community saw the company as prizing low corporate taxes over respect for the majority of the company's customers.

Authority/Subversion. Violations of the Authority dimension occur when companies challenge societal norms or disrespect traditional values and hierarchies, leading to cancelations as they are perceived as undermining established structures or showing a lack of respect for authority. While no companies on the list have violated this dimension (yet), any company that is seen as sidestepping legitimate laws (representing the authority of the society) will be morally sanctioned.

Sanctity/Degradation. Companies can be canceled for violating the Sanctity dimension when they engage in actions or campaigns that are seen as degrading or disrespectful to what is considered sacred or deeply valued by society, such as insensitive marketing or disregard for cultural or moral sensibilities.

In particular, sexuality is seen as a sacred issue, and inappropriate sexualization of products (as in Tampax's case) or people (as in Balenciaga's case) can lead to harsh moral judgments of corporations.

Again, Table 1.2 provides a catalog of corporate cancelation events; it lists the companies that were canceled (or at risk of being canceled by some groups), a brief summary of the reason, the source of the controversy, the locus of trigger, the issue, and the moral foundation violated. The source is listed in the last column. Recall, the sources for this Table are as follows. AdAge's 2020 'biggest cancels' of the year is Source 1. Enzuzo.com's compilation of 18 brands impacted by cancelation movements is Source 2. An article on the website EatThis, NotThat!' on seven food brands that encountered public backlash is Source 3. Again, the most exhaustive set of brands or companies is from Desmar et al. (2023), who documented 25 instances of corporate cancelations (Source 4). There are a few recent cancelations (Planet Fitness and TikTok) that had not been noted, and as such the source is noted as n/a.

Discussion

In conclusion, this chapter reviews the previous definitions of cancel culture and introduces the concept and definition of "corporate cancel culture." Recall, the proposed definition is a phenomenon *where companies or their brands are publicly sanctioned and no longer supported by consumers as due to perceived transgressions by the company, their agents, and/or their employees.* This definition is of value to companies and scholars who are interested in the topics of morality, transgressions, public relations, branding, business ethics, and categorization theory.

This chapter also provides an integrative review of the cancel culture literature and theories related to morality and moral cognition from both the humanities literature and the emerging literature in business and marketing. This literature review helped base a new conceptual framework of "Dimensions of Moral Cognition as Related to Cancel Culture," which depicts how companies or brands have or may be canceled for a variety of reasons. The framework (or matrix) notes there are different sources of controversy, loci of the trigger that got the brand or company canceled, the main issue with the cancelation, and importantly – the moral foundation violated. The chapter ends with a catalog, updated as of March 2024 (at the time of this chapter writing) of companies that have been canceled (or at least temporarily canceled to have to cause a rebrand). The catalog came from compiling four sources that have provided some lists of companies or brands that have been canceled. These lists were compiled from AdAge, Enzuzo.com, a website called EatThis, NotThat!', and the most comprehensive and only academic source of Desmar et al. (2023), who documented 25 examples of corporate cancelations. The present contribution is not only a synthesis of these lists

TABLE 1.2 A Catalog of Corporate Cancelation Events with Controversy Source, Locus of Triggers, Issue, and Moral Foundation Violated

Brand	*Reason Summary*	*Controversy Source*	*Locus of Trigger*	*Issue*	*Moral Foundation Violated*	*Source*
Amazon	Corporate policies and history affected bid to locate HQ in NYC	Corporate Practices	Endogenous	Worker/ Customer Treatment	Fairness, Care	2
Apple	Planned product obsolescence	Corporate Practices	Endogenous	Corruption	Fairness, Loyalty	2
Aunt Jemima	Branding perceived as racist, now rebranded as Pearl Milling Company	Brand Imagery	Exogenous	Racism	Fairness	2, 3, 4
Balenciaga	Child sexualization in brand imagery	Brand Imagery	Endogenous	Sexual Ethics	Sanctity	2
Bon Appetite	Employee complaints workplace conditions	Corporate Practices	Endogenous	Worker/ Customer Treatment	Fairness, Loyalty	4
Bud Light	Partnership with transgender influencer	Brand Imagery	Endogenous	Sexual Ethics	Loyalty, Sanctity	2, 3
Chick-fil-A	Support for conservative political issues	Corporate Practices	Endogenous	Political	Fairness, Loyalty	4
Chicos	Racially stereotypical branding	Brand Imagery	Exogenous	Racism	Fairness	4
Coon cheese	Brand imagery with racist connotations	Brand Imagery	Exogenous	Racism	Fairness, Sanctity	4
"Cops" TV Show	Racial profiling in the show's policework	Corporate Practices	Exogenous	Racism	Fairness	4
CrossFit	Canceled a pride-themed workout	Corporate Practices	Endogenous	Sexual Ethics	Fairness	4
Dilbert	Creator went on YouTube rant calling Black Americans a hate group	Employee Conduct	Endogenous	Racism	Fairness, Loyalty	2
Dolce & Gabbana	Insensitive ad campaign in China; Subsequent racist messages	Brand Imagery	Endogenous	Racism	Fairness, Loyalty	4

Dove	Ad implying Whiteness (as opposed to Blackness) equates to cleanliness	Brand Imagery	Endogenous	Racism	Fairness, Loyalty	2
Facebook (Meta)	Mishandled customer data, didn't take privacy seriously, Cambridge Analytica scandal, deaths on Facebook live	Corporate Practices	Endogenous	Worker/ Customer Treatment	Fairness, Loyalty, Sanctity	2
GoDaddy	Founder filmed himself shooting an elephant	Employee Conduct	Endogenous	Animal Treatment	Loyalty, Care	2
Goodyear Tires	Donald Trump false accused of banning MAGA hats	Corporate Practices	Exogenous	Political	Fairness	1
Goya	Hispanic brand CEO publicly supporting Donald Trump	Employee Conduct	Endogenous	Political	Loyalty	1, 2, 3
H&M	Ad showing a Black child in a hoodie with possibly racist slogan	Brand Imagery	Endogenous	Racism	Fairness, Loyalty	4
Hachette Book Group	Publishing of Woody Allen memoir post his sexual abuse scandal	Corporate Practices	Endogenous	Sexual Ethics	Sanctity	4
Harry Potter	Author (JK Rowling) alienated some audience with trans-related postings and disdain for the media saying "people who menstruate" rather than the term women	Employee Conduct (Views)	Exogenous	Political	Care	2
Heineken	Ad showing Black people passed by with the slogan "lighter is better"	Brand Imagery	Endogenous	Racism	Fairness	2
Hershey	Partnership with transgender influencer	Brand Imagery	Endogenous	Sexual Ethics	Loyalty, Sanctity	3
Jo Malone	Replacing a Black actor in a Chinese ad without his knowledge	Corporate Practices	Endogenous	Racism	Fairness, Loyalty	1, 4
L'Oréal Paris	Firing a Black Transgender model for facebook post on racism	Corporate Practices	Endogenous	Racism	Fairness, Care	1
M&M's	Changing brand imagery to be more politically correct	Brand Imagery	Endogenous	Sexual Ethics	Loyalty, Sanctity	3

(*Continued*)

TABLE 1.2 (Continued)

Brand	*Reason Summary*	*Controversy Source*	*Locus of Trigger*	*Issue*	*Moral Foundation Violated*	*Source*
Martin's Potato Rolls	CEO support for far-right politician	Employee Conduct	Endogenous	Political	Loyalty	3
NBA	NBA-affiliated person supporting Hong Kong protests	Employee Conduct	Endogenous	Political	Loyalty	4
Netflix "Cuties"	Sexualization of young girls	Brand Imagery	Endogenous	Sexual Ethics	Sanctity	4
New Coke	Redid the formula of the popular soft drink with an unwanted product change/ didn't listen to customers in lieu of sales seeking	Corporate Practices	Endogenous	Worker/ Customer Treatment	Care	2
Nike	Planning to release a shoe featuring objectionable flag	Brand Imagery	Endogenous	Racism	Loyalty	4
Oatly	Allowing investment from companies that conflict with brand values	Corporate Practices	Endogenous	Environmental Harm	Loyalty	1, 3, 4
Planet Fitness	Reaction and social media rant by a member to corporate Policy on transgender gym members in locker rooms matching their gender identity	Corporate Practices	Exogenous	Political	Loyalty, Sanctity	n/a (too recent)
Roseanne (TV Show)	Namesake actor did a racist tweet and then blamed a drug brand (Ambien); TV show rebranded without her to The Conners	Employee Conduct	Endogenous	Racism	Loyalty, Care	2

Snapchat	Ad campaign making light of domestic violence	Brand Imagery	Endogenous	Sexism	Care	4
Soul Cycle Equinox	CEO hosted Donald Trump fundraisers	Employee Conduct	Endogenous	Political	Loyalty	4
Starbucks	BLM apparel banned, then sold with SBUX branding	Corporate Practices	Endogenous	Racism	Fairness	4
TikTok	US legislators at the state and federal level accusing social media platform of privacy issues especially as being owned by foreign adversary	Corporate Practices	Endogenous	Worker/ Customer Treatment	Loyalty, Sanctity, Fairness	n/a (see book foreword)
Tampax	Product sexualization on social media	Brand Imagery	Endogenous	Sexual Ethics	Sanctity	2
Uncle Ben's	Racially stereotypical branding	Brand Imagery	Exogenous	Racism	Loyalty, Sanctity	4
Urban Outfitters	Brand positioning as an ally with a history of cultural appropriation	Corporate Practices	Exogenous	Racism	Loyalty	2
Washington Redskins	Racially stereotypical branding	Brand Imagery	Exogenous	Racism	Fairness, Loyalty, Sanctity	4
Wonderful Company	Corporate policies regarding water usage	Corporate Practices	Exogenous	Environmental Harm	Loyalty	2
Yeezy	Namesake posted anti-Semitic content on social media and wearing of racist "white lives matter" shirt	Employee Conduct	Exogenous	Racism	Loyalty, Care	2

but explaining them in the context of the proposed framework here (controversy source, locus of trigger, issue, and the moral foundation violated).

As a limitation of this chapter is that we only look at companies, and not human brands, future research on the cancelation of human brands will be helpful for scholars and those interested in cancel culture. For future research, as we provide a framework for scholars, there is ample room to extend or test aspects of this framework with empirical research on corporate cancel culture.

NOTE: The authors have made equal contributions to this chapter.

References

22 Cancel Culture Examples: Brands That Have Been Cancelled. (2024, March 27). Brianna Ruback. https://www.enzuzo.com/blog/cancel-culture-examples

AdAge (2020, December 18). *The 9 Biggest "Cancels" of 2020*. Ad Age. https://adage.com/article/year-review/9-biggest-cancels-2020/2299066

Baronavski, S. A., Mcclain, C., Auxier, B., Perrin, A., & Ramshankar, M. (May 19, 2021). *Americans and 'Cancel Culture': Where Some See Calls for Accountability, Others See Censorship, Punishment*. Pew Research Center. https://www.pewresearch.org/internet/2021/05/19/americans-and-cancel-culture-where-some-see-calls-for-accountability-others-see-censorship-punishment/

Berger, J. (2016). *Contagious: Why things catch on*. Simon and Schuster.

Berger, J., & Milkman, K. L. (2012). What makes online content viral?. *Journal of Marketing Research*, 49(2), 192–205.

Blader, S. L., & Tyler, T. R. (2005). How can theories of organizational justice explain the effects of fairness? In J. Greenberg & J. A. Colquitt (Eds.), *Handbook of Organizational Justice* (pp. 329–354). Lawrence Erlbaum Associates Publishers.

Clark, M.D. (2020). Drag them: A brief etymology of so-called "cancel culture". *Communication and the Public*, 5(3–4), 88–92.

Close, A. G., & Zinkhan, G. M. (2007). Consumer experiences and market resistance: An extension of resistance theories. *Advances in Consumer Research*, 34, 256.

Close, A. G., & Zinkhan, G. M. (2009). Market-resistance and Valentine's Day events. *Journal of Business Research*, 62(2), 200–207.

Demsar, V., Ferraro, C., Nguyen, J., & Sands, S. (2023). Calling for cancellation: Understanding how markets are shaped to realign with prevailing societal values. *Journal of Macromarketing*, 43(3), 322–350.

Dodd, O. (2022). *Alexandra Gabriel Gives Update on Plantation Name Change*. CLASS.November24.https://classbarmag.com/news/fullstory.php/aid/856/Alexandre_Gabriel_gives_update_on_Plantation_name_change.html

Fetscherin, M., & Usunier, J.-C. (2012). Corporate branding: An interdisciplinary literature review. *European Journal of Marketing*, 46(5), 733–753.

Florini, S. (2014). Tweets, tweeps, and signifyin': Communication and cultural performance on "black twitter". *Television and New Media*, 15(3), 223–237. https://doi.org/10.1177/1527476413480247

Haidt, J. (2013). Moral psychology for the twenty-first century. *Journal of Moral Education*, 42(3), 281–297. https://doi.org/10.1080/03057240.2013.817327

Keller, K. L. (1993). Conceptualizing, measuring, and managing customer-based brand equity. *Journal of Marketing*, 57(1), 1–22. https://doi.org/10.2307/1252054

Klein, J. G., Smith, N. C., & John, A. (2004). Why we boycott: Consumer motivations for boycott participation. *Journal of Marketing*, 68(3), 92–109. https://doi.org/10.1509/jmkg.68.3.92.34770

Kotler, P., & Keller, K. L. (2016). *Marketing Management* (15th ed.). Pearson Education.

Latapí Agudelo, M. A., Jóhannsdóttir, L., & Davídsdóttir, B. A. (2019). A literature review of the history and evolution of corporate social responsibility. *International Journal of Corporate Social Responsibility*, 4(1), 1. https://doi.org/10.1186/s40991-018-0039-y

Lee, M. S. (2022). Anti-consumption research: A foundational and contemporary overview. *Current Opinion in Psychology*, *45*, 101319.

Marwick, A. E., & Boyd, D. (2011). I tweet honestly, I tweet passionately: Twitter users, context collapse, and the imagined audience. *New Media & Society*, 13(1), 114–133. https://doi.org/10.1177/1461444810365313

Penaloza, L., & Price, L. L. (1993). *Consumer Resistance: A Conceptual Overview*. ACR North American Advances.

Pew Research Center. (2021). *Americans and 'Cancel Culture': Where Some See Calls for Accountability, Others See Censorship, Punishment*. E.A. Vogels, M. Anderson, M. Porteus, C.

Pew Research Center. (2022). *A Growing Share of Americans Are Familiar with 'Cancel Culture'*. E.A. Vogels, June 19. https://www.pewresearch.org/short-reads/2022/06/09/a-growing-share-of-americans-are-familiar-with-cancel-culture/

Ruback, B., & Ruback, B. (2024, March 12). *7 restaurant chains that are struggling in 2024*. Eat This Not That. https://www.eatthis.com/restaurant-chains-struggling-2024/

Saldanha, N., Mulye, R., & Rahman, K. (2023). Cancel culture and the consumer: A strategic marketing perspective. *Journal of Strategic Marketing*, 31(5), 1071–1086.

Schmitt, B. H., & Zhang, S. (1998). Language structure and categorization: A study of classifiers in consumer cognition, judgment, and choice. *Journal of Consumer Research*, 25(2), 108–122.

Smith, R. (2024). *Planet fitness stock tumbles as boycott calls grow*. Newsweek, March 21. https://www.newsweek.com/planet-fitness-boycott-stocks-market-cap-social-media-1881788

Sujan, M., & Dekleva, C. (1987). Product categorization and inference making: Some implications for comparative advertising. *Journal of Consumer Research*, 14(3), 372–378.

Swift, T. (2019). You need to calm down [Song]. On *Lover*. Republic Records.

Tandoc Jr., E. C., Tan Hui Ru, B., Lee Huei, G., Min Qi Charlyn, N., Chua, R. A., & Goh, Z. H. (2022). # CancelCulture: Examining definitions and motivations. *New Media & Society*, 26(4), 1944–1962.

Tinson, J., Close, A., Tuncay Zayer, L., & Nuttall, P. (2013). Attitudinal and behavioral resistance: A marketing perspective. *Journal of Consumer Behaviour*, 12(6), 436–448.

Van Horen, F., & Pieters, R. (2017). Out-of-category brand imitation: Product categorization determines copycat evaluation. *Journal of Consumer Research*, 44(4), 816–832.

Verstynen. (2022). The real face of cancel culture, inside higher education. March 9. https://www.insidehighered.com/views/2022/03/10/confronting-real-face-cancel-culture-opinion

Witkowski, T. H. (2021). Broadening anti-consumption research: A history of right-wing prohibitions, boycotts, and resistance to sustainability. *Journal of Macromarketing*, 41(4), 610–625.

2

CANCEL CULTURE FOR HUMAN BRANDS AND FIRMS

Punishment versus Accountability

Janna M. Parker, Kevin W. James and Debra Zahay

When President Obama participated in a live interview with Yara Shahidi, a Harvard undergraduate, which was broadcast on YouTube, he addressed the overall topic of activism. "If I tweet or hashtag about how you didn't do something right or used the wrong verb, then I can sit back and feel pretty good about myself, cause, Man, you see how woke I was? I called you out. That's not activism." (President Barack Obama, YouTube, October 30, 2019). The social media clip with the President's quote became a takeaway for many Americans because both liberal and conservative politicians, political experts, and celebrities agreed with his point on social media (Chiu, 2019).

The Origins of Cancel Culture

Since 2014, as stories of online campaigns to "cancel" a person or a firm continue to appear on social media or are reported by news channels, both the media and academics have investigated what is referred to as "cancel culture" or "call-out culture." Proponents of this phenomenon claim that it is a form of activism based on social justice that includes not only calling out undesired behavior but also calling for boycotts of brands. Opponents argue that it is a form of mob bullying since canceling may target a firm or an individual, often before an opportunity is given to explain or defend the current or past behavior.

When did cancel culture begin? Many have claimed different references in pop culture as being the beginning of the use of "canceling" to refer to an individual. A Vox article (Romano, 2020) traces the use back to a quote in the movie New Jack City, when a character played by Wesley Snipes says,

DOI: 10.4324/9781032670546-3

"Cancel that b****. I'll buy another one." By 2015, the term "cancel" was used on Black Twitter to refer to someone you disapproved of, and according to Romano, it could be a joke or a serious reference. Others say that the use of "cancel" to refer to disapproval of a person started on March 17, 2014, Suey Park, a journalist, was offended by a satirical Tweet sent by Stephen Colbert about NFL owner Daniel Snyder launching the Washington Redskins Original Americans Foundation. Colbert's tweet – "I am willing to show #Asian community I care by introducing the Ching-Chong Ding-Dong Foundation for Sensitivity to Orientals or Whatever" (Watercutter, 2016). Park's response was to tweet, "The Ching-Chong Ding-Dong Foundation for Sensitivity to Orientals has decided to call for #CancelColbert. Trend it," which referred to canceling his TV show; however, some of his fans threatened to the point that Park's safety was of concern to Colbert. He asked his fans to stop harassing Park. While Park's tweet did not yield the desired results, the cultural phenomenon of social media "canceling" is still prevalent a decade later.

While cancel culture is now frequently addressed by reporters and pundits, politicians, and even celebrities as aggressive online behavior that is damaging to the target, public shaming, which is a component of cancel culture, is not a new phenomenon. While some have tried to tie the roots of cancel culture back to historical periods such as when people were put in stocks, the Salem witch trials, or even the French Reign of Terror, those punishing individuals derived their punitive power from "the state" (Mishan, 2020). When people refer to cancel culture, this phenomenon takes place online, and any individual can cancel a person or firm with the intent that their cancelation will go viral. It entails a form of punishment, similar to how customers can "punish" companies for their lack of corporate social responsibility (Valor et al., 2022).

What Is Cancel or Call-Out Culture?

As a body of work in the academic literature began to evolve, multiple definitions were developed across the disciplines, with the majority of early research coming from the social sciences, such as psychology, linguistics, communications, and even business, for which we provide a brief review later in this chapter. Predating the use of the word canceling, which is also used for private individuals who are not a human brand, the term collaborative brand attack (CBA) describes "a joint, event-induced, dynamic, and public offenses from a large number of Internet users via social media platforms on a brand that are aimed to harm it and/or to force it to change its behavior" (Rauschnabel et al., 2016, p. 381). While a CBA can be considered a form of canceling, it leaves out perceived transgressions of false rumors. Tandoc et al. (2022) reviewed several cancel culture definitions across disciplines.

They identified three consistent components of the definitions: (1) the public shaming of unacceptable behavior, (2) withdrawal of support, and (3) a motivation to see consequences or a penalty that could be financial or social. New definitions have been conceptualized since this review, but even the new conceptualizations that we found followed this same approach.

Defining the concept is not limited to the realm of academia. The online platform dictionary.com defines cancel culture in the website's Pop Culture Dictionary as,

> the popular practice of withdrawing support for (*canceling*) public figures and companies after they have done or said something considered objectionable or offensive. *Cancel culture* is generally discussed as being performed on social media in the form of group shaming.
>
> *(Dictionary.com, 2020)*

A comparison of this definition to those developed by academics reveals that many of the definitions are similar to the findings by Tandoc et al. (2022). The website continues with a much shorter history, similar to that of Mishan (2020).

Why Do People Participate in Cancel or Call-Out Culture?

Multiple entities have asked this question, including the press, think tanks, industry, and academics. From September 8–13, 2020, the Pew Research surveyed 10,093 adults in the United States to ask them if they had heard of cancel culture (38% had never heard of it). For those who had heard of it, two follow-up open-ended questions requested that participants write in their own words: (1) What cancel culture means and (2) How they felt about calling others out on social media. Pew reported that respondents were divided on whether it was holding people accountable (58%) or punishment for those who do not deserve it (38%). A relationship was found between political ideology and cancel culture opinions, with Republicans being more likely to see it as punishment (56%) and Democrats being more likely to see it as holding someone accountable (75%) (Vogels et al., 2021). The Pew Research study provided guidance on the empirical portion of this research, which will be further described in the methodology section.

However, the Pew Research was not the only research organization examining cancel culture from the perspective of individuals. Only a couple of weeks after the Pew survey, the 2020 Statista Global survey included a section on cancel culture (Figure 2.1). Since many movements can become a global phenomenon, the same survey was given to participants in the United Kingdom and Germany. However, the only details provided in the public report are that in the United Kingdom, respondents had a similar opinion

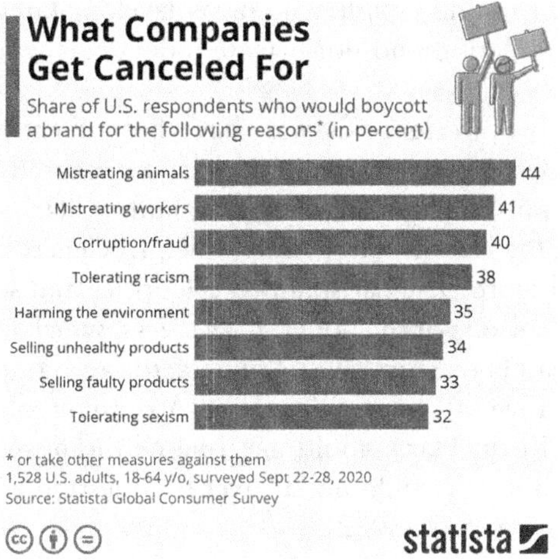

FIGURE 2.1 What Companies Get Canceled for

Source: https://www.statista.com/chart/25283/us-adults-who-would-boycott-a-brand-reasons/.

as those in the United States. In contrast, in Germany, respondents ranked worker mistreatment, environmental harm, corruption, health concerns around products, and racism (Buchholz, 2021).

Additionally, another study by YPulse on Call-Out Culture Trends reveals three main differences between European Gen Z and Millennials and those from North America when it comes to canceling brands or influencers (a human brand). YPulse found that young North Americans (72%) are more likely to think cancel culture has gone too far, but only 63% of young Europeans think it has. For canceled brands, young North Americans are more forgiving than young Europeans, with 71% of Europeans believing a brand can make a comeback compared to 83% of North Americans and 26% of North Americans who boycotted a brand made it a permanent change vs. 33% of Europeans (YPulse, 2023).

Canceling Brands: Human Brands and Firms

For this work, we relied on long-accepted definitions of a brand and its extension of a human brand. For this research, we use McDonald et al.'s (2001) definition of a *brand* as "an identifiable product, service, person, or place augmented in such a way that the buyer or user perceives relevant, unique added values which match their needs most closely." A *human brand* is a term that refers to any well-known persona who is the subject of marketing communications efforts (Thomson, 2006). Human brands can be celebrities, CEO brands, person brands (e.g., Martha Stewart or Calvin Klein), social media influencers, professional athletes, etc. For this cancel culture research, we only focus on firms and people who have developed into a human brand as an object of cancelation and not private individuals who can also be the target of a cancelation.

A Google search of "celebrities who have been canceled" will result in a long list of articles. In our search, names that appeared included Chrissy Teigen, Johnny Depp, Will Smith, Jeffrey Star, James Charles, Jake and Logan Paul, Kanye West, the Kardashian Family, Ellen DeGeneres, Armie Hammer, Demi Lovato, and more. The list spanned celebrities and social media influencers. In a recent episode of the podcast *Smartless,* which is hosted by actors Jason Bateman, Sean Hayes, and Will Arnett, actor and comedian Kevin Hart appeared on their Live in Los Angeles show. A running joke throughout the episode was that Kevin Hart would ask one of the hosts a question, and many times, they said they could not answer his question because they might get canceled (Bateman et al., 2022).

One of the most well-known cancelations of a celebrity in recent years is that of Ellen DeGeneres, as explained by McRady (2019). Most people trace it back to 2020 when, at that time, one current and ten former employees of the show claimed that Ellen's "be kind" mantra was fake and that the workplace was toxic due to producers and managers. However, they asserted that Ellen was ultimately responsible because the show had her name on it (Yandoli, 2020). Suddenly, former guests and others started talking about how rude Ellen was to them. Warner Bros. Entertainment launched an investigation, and three executive producers were fired (Kubota, 2021). Ellen's ratings were down, and even though her contract had been renewed for three years, in 2021, she announced that the next season would be the 19th and last season. In an interview with Savannah Guthrie on the TODAY show, Ellen was asked if she felt like she was the target of cancelation, and not only did Ellen say she was, but that the whole situation seemed to be orchestrated and coordinated (Kubota, 2021).

This all came after Ellen's first cancelation on social media when, in 2019, she was criticized for a photo that showed her talking and laughing with former President George W. Bush at an NFL game. After being criticized online for being friendly with someone who had a different viewpoint on LGTBQIA+ issues and many called a war criminal, Ellen addressed the situation on her show. In a four-minute monologue, she talked about the importance of being kind even to those with whom you disagree on serious issues. The backlash was immediate, and other celebrities commented on her situation from differing viewpoints. While there is no proof of a coordinated attack, Ellen had 16 successful years as an Emmy-winning daytime talk show host with good ratings until 2019.

Firms, or company brands, have also been the target of cancelations. Over the years, Starbucks has been the center of many controversies and calls for boycotts that predate the use of the term "cancel." For this overview, only a few of the more well-known cancelations are listed. In 2013, CEO Howard Schultz asked gun owners to please not bring guns into stores in open carry states. He announced Moms Demand Action for Gun Sense, a group with over 100,000 members at the time, and wrote an opinion piece on CNN.com calling for Starbucks to impose a ban (Brownstone, 2013). The group had urged people to #SkipStarbucks on Saturdays until the gun policy change was made. After Schultz's request, the group changed the hashtag to #CelebrateStarbucks. Another frequent target of conservatives is the Starbucks holiday cup, resulting in numerous boycotts by those who claim that Starbucks started a "war on Christmas" each time the company updated the holiday cups for their diverse customer base. While a brief history from 2015 to 2018 is available (Sugar, 2018), this controversy and boycott are frequently revived.

The most recent call for a boycott of Starbucks was after the start of the Middle East War between Israel and Gaza. Workers United, the union organizing group helping local Starbucks stores unionize, sent out a tweet in support of Gaza using the Starbucks logo, and Starbucks sued the group for using the Starbucks logo. This dispute has led to the vandalizing of some store locations by protesters from both sides: Pro-Gaza and Pro-Israel. On Twitter, supporters from both sides have called for a boycott and accused Starbucks of supporting killing Jews and Palestinian genocide. Starbucks CEO released a letter saying that the company

> condemns 'unleashed violence against the innocent, hate and weaponized speech, and lies,' he noted that 'escalating protests' had led to vandalism at many stores. Protesters, he said, 'had been influenced by misrepresentation on social media of what we stand for'.
>
> *(Harpaz, 2023)*

Even politicians tweeted that Starbucks should be boycotted. In this situation, Starbucks attempted to avoid controversy, and the reason for the lawsuit was misrepresented.

Sometimes, a brand cancelation occurs due to lies spread online, as was the situation for the online retailer Wayfair. In the summer of 2020, QAnon conspiracy theorists spread a rumor that Wayfair listed overpriced items on its website as a means to traffic missing children through the website. These conspiracy theorists found outdated, missing children's posters that had names that matched the names Wayfair gave to specific products (Figure 2.2). None of the children featured in these conspiracy posts were still missing. Meanwhile, concerned citizens continued to report these children as missing. After several months, Wayfair and the Department of Homeland Security were able to debunk the lies spread online. However, the actual damage was not done to Wayfair, according to Jessica Contrera, an investigative reporter

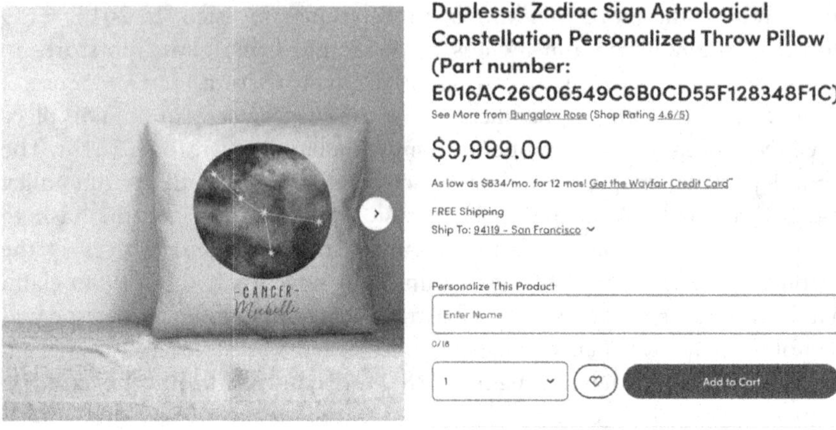

FIGURE 2.2 Wayfair Pillow Mistakenly Listed for $9,999.00 and Falsely Associated by Social Media Users with Missing Child

Source: https://www.washingtonpost.com/dc-md-va/interactive/2021/wayfair-qanon-sex-trafficking-conspiracy/ and https://twitter.com/washingtonpost/status/1471580494252830721.

for *The Washington Post.* She interviewed the victims and their families and discovered that with all of this negative attention, the children experienced severe emotional trauma (Contrera, 2021).

Additionally, due to the calls to the National Human Trafficking Hotline, victim advocates could not get through when trying to assist real victims of human trafficking. When attempting to submit an online request, it could take weeks to get a response due to the volume of reports of the Wayfair conspiracy. Local law enforcement, Homeland Security, and other local, state, and federal agencies, as well as nonprofits, were inundated with these calls, which wasted resources (Contrera, 2021). False rumors can have unintended consequences beyond hurting the intended target.

Cancel culture has become a phenomenon with a serious societal impact. The research question that guides this work asks: does an individual's political ideology and social justice attitudes determine whether they see cancel culture as holding an individual or firm accountable or whether it is solely meant to punish?

Literature Review and Theoretical Framework

Canceling and Call-Outs: Are the Concepts the Same?

Are cancel culture and call-out culture the same concept? Depending on the source, the answer varies. Typing this question into Google will result in various articles or blog posts with numerous opinions, such as the concepts are the same, are different, or that while initially the terms were for different concepts, now the words can be used interchangeably, as President Obama did in his 2019 YouTube interview (Obama Foundation, 2019).

Defining Canceling, Call-Outs, and Cancel Culture

The academic research into canceling, call-outs (calling out), and cancel culture is multidisciplinary, which provides both richness and some confusion as multiple definitions have been posited. Clark, a professor of media studies, wrote an essay on the etymology of cancel culture and defined "cancelling as an expression of agency, a choice to withdraw one's attention from someone or something whose values, (in) action, or speech are so offensive one no longer wishes to grace them with their presence, time, and money" (Clark, 2020, p. 88) and then using an educational background in journalism and media studies, proceeds to provide a brief history of canceling. Clark refers to blacklisting and boycotting as canceling's analog antecedents, although others, such as Mueller (2021), state that for brands, boycotting is part of canceling. Clark continues to explain "that 'reading' another individual-giving them a dressing down that uses colorful and descriptive language .... begat calling out (which begat canceling) .... has been perfected by Black women like our grandmothers would dress someone down (which began calling out)" or "when Black women or grandmothers would let us know what they see" (Clark, 2020, p. 88).

Another commonly used definition for cancel culture was derived by Eve Ng, whose educational background includes a Ph.D. in communication and another PhD in Linguistics as well as Feminist Studies. Ng suggests that cancel culture is,

> The withdrawal of any kind of support (viewership, social media follows, purchases of products endorsed by the person, etc.) for those who are assessed to have done something unacceptable or highly problematic, generally from a social justice perspective, especially to alert sexism, heterosexism, homophobia, racism, bullying, and related issues.
>
> *(Ng, 2020, p. 623)*

In the social sciences, researchers have used the definitions from both Clark and Ng. Mueller (2021) investigated psychological predictors of cancel culture and used Clark's definition as the basis for his attempted scale development. Clark's definition is often cited, but researchers in different disciplines continue to work on developing a universally accepted definition. For their research into political ideologies, cancel culture, and self-construal, Cook et al. (2021) used the definition by Ng (2020). They stated that cancel culture is also known as call-out culture.

In the introduction, the origin of the term "cancel" as it is used today was briefly explored, and Twitter is considered the original social media platform for canceling (e.g., Watercutter, 2016; Romano, 2020). Researchers in communications, public relations, and marketing began investigating canceling as it has implications for firms and human brands. After reviewing the current definitions in the literature and conducting qualitative interviews, Tandoc et al. (2022) argue that canceling is more than mob behavior despite its overlap with other online misbehaviors, such as trolling (Golf-Papez & Veer, 2022).

As more brands were canceled on social media and in the press, Saldanha et al. (2022) defined cancel culture from a marketing perspective as the "*collective desire by consumers to withdraw support of those individuals and brands in power, perceived to be involved in objectionable behavior or activities through the use of social media*" (Saldanha et al., 2023, p. 1072); however, the authors differentiate canceling from boycotting due to the public shaming that occurs online. Additionally, cancel culture is different from consumer activism due to the use of digital platforms that enable the cancelation to be widespread and empower traditionally marginalized groups. As pointed out in the article, one of the key differences between a boycott and cancel culture is that for a boycott, the backlash is to attempt to elicit behavior change by the company, whereas, in cancel culture, the primary motivation is to spread negativity toward the focal company. Most recently, Costa and Azevedo (2024) explain the importance of antecedents to cancel culture.

Brand Transgression: Perceived or Actual?

Cancel culture has also been explained as a social media-driven event where one-time brand or product users stop using the product because the entity has encountered a problem or been involved in a perceived scandal (Ramto & Farajallah, 2022). Brands that are the target of a CBA are often the result of perceived unethical behavior, which should be considered a subjective opinion as the behavior may not be a legal violation or even a violation of a widely accepted social norm (Rauschnabel et al., 2016). Thus, "the issue of 'unethical behavior' is often identified and, at least from the viewpoint of the attackers, 'validated' by groups such as non-governmental organizations (NGOs), interest groups, or other social communities" (Raushnabel et al., 2016, p. 387).

Perceived or actual transgressions can equally serve as a trigger for cancelation by a like-minded group of consumer activists. Through the lens of institutional theory, which seeks to analyze how "various actors create, maintain, or disrupt both markets and marketing practices, leading to transformative change," Demsar et al. (2023, p. 325) propose a four-stage model for brand cancelation. The authors also posit that there are five macro-categories of social justice movements around political ideology, race, gender and sexuality, abuse, and corporate greed, that when consumers perceive a violation, will trigger the first stage, which is transgression evaluation. It is at this stage that the transgression is deemed irreparable or not.

At stage two, those who perceive a transgression to have occurred will then mobilize others to cancel the brand, and those with an opposing view will try to diffuse the cancelation. The third stage is when the brand chooses a response type by taking proactive action, apologizing, passively ignoring, or actively ignoring. The fourth and final stage is market realignment, with the brand choosing to either comply with the institutional logistic changes required by the movement behind the cancelation by making fundamental changes regarding policies, branding, etc., or even firing those involved or upper management. The other option is to ignore the reasons for the cancelation. Both approaches can have an impact on both markets and societal values.

Demsar et al. (2023) primarily categorize transgressions from a perspective of social justice that includes political ideology; thus, one could suggest that there is an inherent liberal bias. While institutional theory is an interesting lens through which to analyze cancel culture and its impact on markets, it has an implied assumption that the evaluation stage will be based on legitimate cultural cognitive forms. However, in the case of cancel culture, cancelation can occur with incorrect information or even intentional lies about a firm or human brand. Since canceling firms and human brands have occurred from groups of all political ideologies, it is often based on subjective opinion rather than facts or even on outright false rumors. Next, we review herd behavior theory, which is the theoretical basis for our conceptual model and the empirical analysis.

Cancel Culture Participants Following the Herd

Herd behavior is "everyone doing what everyone else is doing, even when their private information suggests doing something quite different" (Banerjee, 1992, p. 798). This reliance on observation of the behavior of others rather than using their information for decision-making is an inefficient use of information that results in a loss of equilibrium in the markets. While herding behavior theory was proposed in the economics literature (Banerjee, 1992) since then, it has been applied in other disciplines, including cognitive psychology and neuroscience (e.g., Raafat et al., 2009), social collective behavior on social media networks (Kong et al., 2023), and social media (e.g., Mattke et al., 2020).

In popular culture, "following the herd" is a common expression used to describe behavior in which people make decisions based on the actions of others and, according to Raafat et al. (2009), can be applied to various situations such as fashion trends, stock market bubbles, and even mob violence. The authors conceptualize a model of herding behavior that understands how members align based on the *mechanisms of transmission* of the thought or behavior and the *patterns of connections*. They define herding as "a form of convergent social behavior that can be broadly defined as the alignment of thoughts or behaviors of individuals in a group (herd) through local interactions and without centralized coordination" (Raafat et al., 2009, p. 420). There are two approaches to herding: (1) pattern-based focus on patterns of interaction in which people are merely units of the pattern and (2) transmission-based, further broken down into mentalizing (rational processing) and non-mentalizing (social or emotional contagion) facets.

Online crowd behavior can be positive when collective intelligence occurs, such as when an online false rumor is debunked when some individuals verify the accuracy. Then, the rumor is defused, but herd behavior undermines collective intelligence (Pröllochs & Feuerriegel, 2023). When people act based on social or emotional contagion rather than rational processing, they may become so identified with the group or the cause that they lose their sense of individualization. This identification can even lead to collective or mob behavior, such as "canceling," a form of the non-mentalizing transmission-based approach to herding behavior (Raafat et al., 2009).

Does Political Ideology Impact Perceptions of Cancel Culture Behavior?

In the 2020 Pew Research study on cancel culture, differing opinions on whether it was punishing a person wrongly or holding a person accountable were strongly associated with the individual's political ideologies (Vogels et al., 2021). When conducting interviews for item generation, respondents were asked about their political affiliation and again when the items were used in a survey (Mueller, 2021). T-tests revealed a significant difference between those leaning liberal and those leaning conservative. Politicians from both political parties and political pundits from both liberal and conservative views have complained publicly about the other side's participation in cancel culture while claiming moral high ground. When investigating cancel culture and political affiliation, Cook et al. (2021) conducted a literature review that covered political affiliation and research related to moral decision-making, cultural identity, online aggression, self-construal, and the role of self in reactions to violence and honor as it relates to aggression. Reviewing these constructs is outside the scope of this research; however, we recommend reading their review for those researching in this area.

Canceling and Social Justice Attitudes

The first definitions of canceling and cancel culture were based on social justice (e.g., Clark, 2020; Ng, 2020). In the last few years, as the research into cancel culture has moved beyond social science (e.g., Mueller, 2021) into communications (e.g., Tandoc et al., 2022), it seemed clear that an investigation of cancel behavior must also include a study of the respondents' social justice attitudes. After reviewing existing social justice definitions, Torres-Harding et al. (2012) found that social justice was "consistently described as a value or belief, encompassing the idea that people should have equitable access to resources and protection of human rights. In addition, definitions of social justice typically involve power" (Torres-Harding et al., 2012, p. 78). They posit that participation, collaboration, and empowerment are essential elements of social justice work and that its purpose is to eliminate social oppression and promote wellness.

Social justice attitudes are linked to action. Torres-Harding et al. (2012) developed a multi-dimensional social justice scale based on the theory of planned behavior (Ajzen, 1991), which included attitudes, social norms, perceived behavioral control, and behavioral intentions related to social justice. Note that the definitions of canceling and cancel culture conceptualized by Clark (2020) and Ng (2020) have components of social justice. Demsar et al. (2023) describe five categories of brand transgressions that are based on social justice issues. Some suggest that canceling is an appropriate method for implementing a social justice campaign (Bouvier, 2020), while others have measured social justice attitudes when studying cancel culture (e.g., Mueller, 2021; Tandoc et al., 2022).

Is Cancel Culture Accountability or Punishment?

Both accountability and punishment exist in the realm of societal norms. These societal norms can exist in organizational environments such as businesses or in family units such as raising children or parenting. Accountability can be defined from a business organizational standpoint as being answerable to how poorly or well an individual carries out his or her responsibility. Accountability has two parts: an action will be "evaluated by" an audience and the potential exists for reward or punishment for the action (Hall et al., 2007). Within the youth justice literature, accountability is when the individual is aware of their actions and responsible for the negative consequences (Forst et al., 1992). Other scholars break down accountability into two parts: "informative" accountability and "coercive" accountability (Murthy, 2008). From this perspective, informative accountability is the information that the infraction happened. An example of this would be to inform an employee that a problem has occurred in the workplace that is under investigation. *Coercive accountability* implies that the person being accused is capable of being punished, and the parties accusing the defendant of the punishment are capable of delivering the punishment. This often occurs in a legal setting, such as a court of law, or in an organizational setting, such as a business setting, where an employee gets terminated for cause.

Punishing, on the other hand, is often seen as an institutional function where punishing someone is part of institutional authority to provide all members of the organization rewards and consequences depending on the behavior (Priyambodo et al., 2023). In the consumer marketing literature, customers willingness to punish is defined as "the consumer's motivational state to act negatively and penalize another entity that is caused by the consumer's perception that the entity's actions do not support the consumer's empowerment to affect movement toward his or her personal goals" (Sweetin et al., 2013; Duman & Ozgen, 2018).

Cancel culture is a relatively new phenomenon in marketing academic literature. Cancel culture has been explained as a social media-driven event where one-time brand or product users stop using the product because the entity has encountered a problem or been involved in a perceived scandal (Ramto & Farajallah, 2022). As pointed out in the article, one of the key differences between a boycott and cancel culture is that for a boycott, the backlash is to attempt to elicit behavior change by the company, whereas, in cancel culture, the primary motivation is to spread negativity toward the focal company.

The Pew Research work on cancel culture asked respondents to describe cancel culture from an accountability perspective versus a punishment perspective (Vogels et al., 2021). An examination of the quotations in the publicly available research leads to the conclusion that accountability can be about calling out behaviors, saying something about behaviors, making a teaching moment, or bringing attention to an action. Punishment, on the other hand, is blocking, censoring, causing a termination, chastising, or attacking. In the methodology section, more details regarding the Pew Research study are provided, as this work was used for developing scale items used in this work.

Why Do People Engage in Cancel Culture Behavior?

After reviewing the literature associated with cancel culture, we propose the following conceptual model (Figure 2.3) of Perceptions of Cancel Culture Behavior based on the Herding Behavior model proposed by Raafat et al. (2009). In this model, the outcome of attitude toward social justice is at the consumer level. A moderator is political ideology, with a spectrum from liberal to moderate to conservative that could intensify a consumer's attitude toward social justice and how that can lead to an opinion of a company being held accountable and or being punished.

Pew Research Study on Cancel Culture

In September 2020, the Pew Research conducted an online survey ($n = 10{,}093$) with adults in the United States. The study was part of a more extensive

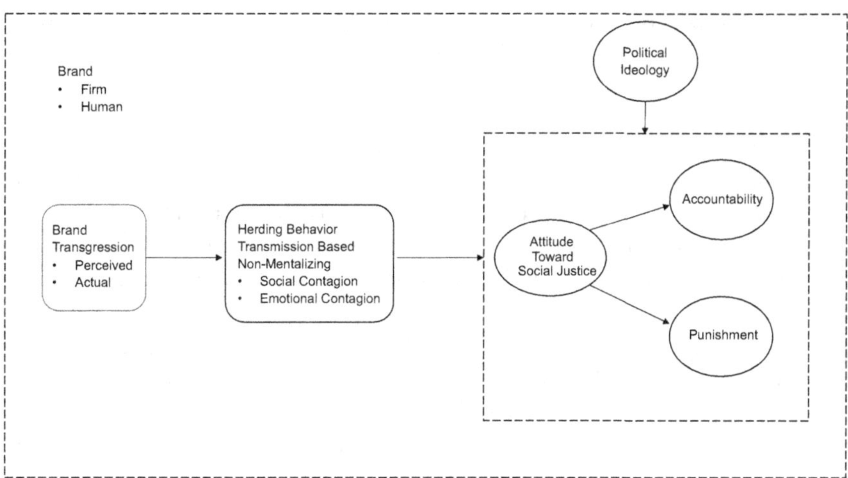

FIGURE 2.3 Conceptual Model of Perceptions of Cancel Culture Behavior (Consumer Level)

survey for the ongoing American Trends panel, Wave 74, September 7–13, 2020. One section of the survey focused on cancel and call-out culture. The cancel culture questions were presented one at a time. The first question asked, "How much, if at all, have you heard about the phrase cancel culture?" Only those who answered "a fair amount" (22%) or "a great deal" (22%) were presented with the following questions. The open-ended question asked, "In your own words, what do you think cancel culture means?" The survey also asked another question of all respondents, "In general, when people publicly call out others on social media for posting content that might be considered offensive, are they more likely to"... with three randomized options (Hold people accountable for their actions, Punish people who did not deserve it, No answer). Depending on their selection, those who chose the accountability option (n = 6,093) were asked, "Please explain why you think calling out offensive content on social media is more likely to hold people accountable for their actions." Those who selected the punishment option (n = 3,518) were asked, "Please explain why you think calling out offensive content on social media is more likely to punish people who didn't deserve it." Open-ended questions were coded into categories with the percentage of respondents for each category reported.

In the survey, respondents also indicated their political ideologies from Democrat to Republican and Independent as well as conservative to liberal values. This information was used to categorize respondents. In addition to the article and findings published on the website (Vogels et al., 2021), the Pew Research follows a policy of data transparency with data sets, coding processes, and surveys available for downloading (Pew Research Center, 2020).

Our purpose in reporting this information from the Pew Research is to provide the background for the items generated for this study.

Methods

For this study, a questionnaire was designed based on the cancel culture finding reported by the Pew Research. A review of the literature revealed the lack of a cancel culture scale with adequate reliability and validity, as the only instrument widely available is a scale proposed by Mueller (2021) that lacks reliability and validity. Therefore, we examined the publicly available qualitative interviews (Vogels et al., 2021) to derive questions from the online panel survey. Specifically, we systematically reviewed the coded categories derived from the respondents who had heard of cancel culture. We followed best practices when deriving the survey items from the Pew Research findings to test for further analysis (Churchill & Iacobucci, 2006). The derived items are available in Table 2.1.

Demographics

Data were collected using Prolific, a nationally known data provider. The sample size for the factor analysis is 344 (n = 344). The largest age range is

TABLE 2.1 Items Generated from the Pew Research Data

Variable Name	*Items Generated from the Pew Research Data*
Cancel Pew1	Society should hold firms and individuals accountable for what they say and do by calling them out on social media.
Cancel Pew2	Society should censor offensive speech.
Cancel Pew3	Canceling is restricting freedom of speech.
Cancel Pew4	It's important to call out those individuals and firms that make racist or sexist statements.
Cancel Pew5	We should not honor significant historical figures whose personal lives or actions violate today's cultural values.
Cancel Pew6	Calling a person or firm out on social media for past statements or behavior holds them accountable even if the person or firm has changed.
Cancel Pew7	Calling people and firms out on social media mostly punishes those who don't deserve it.
Cancel Pew8	People who call out others on social media are trying to force their views on others.
Cancel Pew9	People try to look good by calling out others.
Cancel Pew 10	Calling a person or firm out on social media for offensive speech should be considered a teaching moment for the individual and society.

25–34 (37%), followed by 35–44-year-olds (20%) and 18–24 (17%). Gender is split evenly, with 172 male respondents. The largest percentage of informants report is liberal or somewhat liberal. Most of the sample reports were employed full time (43%) or part time (17%). 51% report never being married, while 25% report being married. The sample is predominantly white (71%), followed by black (11%), Asian (7%), and Hispanic (7%). From an education perspective, the largest percentage has a bachelor's degree (35%), followed by some college but no degree (26%). From an income perspective, the largest money range is $25k–49,999 (25%), followed by $50k–74,999 (21%), then less than 25k (16%).

Factor Structure

When the items in Table 2.1 were used in exploratory factor analysis (EFA), a three-factor solution emerged. Further purification was found to create more cross-loadings. From the Pew Research report, we expected to find that cancel culture would have at least two parts. Those would be to punish and to hold them accountable. Indeed, we can see that factor 1 does include PW1, which states that society should hold firms and individuals accountable for what they say and do by calling them out on social media. Based on the highest loading item in factor 1, we can see that calling out or holding accountable for racist or offensive statements is of high priority. The third item, calling people out as a teaching moment, also corresponds to holding them accountable. The final to discuss for this scale is PW 6, which states that holding accountable is important even if the person or firm making the statement has changed. Scale reliability for these five items is represented by a Cronbach's alpha equal to .763.

The second factor comprises three items: calling people and firms out on social media mainly punishes those who do not deserve it, people who call out others on social media are trying to force their views on others, and people try to look good by calling out others. This factor does include a punishment component as well as an item regarding a narcissistic view of the person calling out the firm (Pew 9). This scale has elements of bullying behavior, such as forcing views on others and punishing people who do not deserve it for the sake of the person who is calling out the firm. This corresponds to the definition of spreading hate. Scale reliability for these five items is represented by a Cronbach's alpha equal to .656.

The third factor only has two items; however, these are strongly loaded. These items have to do with restricting speech and censorship. Scale reliability for these two items is represented by a Cronbach's alpha equal to .698. Factor loadings are in Table 2.2.

TABLE 2.2 Factor Loadings

Pew Item	*Factor 1*	*Factor 2*	*Factor 3*
PW 4 Racist or sexist	.732	–.130	.204
PW 1 Society holds account	.715	–.216	–.031
PW 10 Calling out teaching	.709	–.060	.275
PW 5 Historical figures	.576	–.209	.393
PW 6 Calling out accountable	.552	–.229	.144
PW 9 Calling out looks good	–.024	.803	–.276
PW 8 Calling out forcing views on others	–.337	.767	–.154
PW 7 Calling out punishes	–.426	.567	.054
PW 2 Censor offensive speech	.272	–.025	.851
PW 3 Restrict freedom of speech	–.113	.295	–.785

Discussion

Returning to the Pew survey, we expected the factors to center around accountability, punishment, censorship, as well as sensitive topics like causing harm to others. Our findings do suggest that the first factor, which is slanted toward accountability or holding others accountable, represents 40% of the percentage of variance explained. This corresponds to the Pew findings where most respondents, regardless of political party, viewed cancel culture as holding another accountable. The types of comments most subject to canceling include racist or sexist comments foremost, as well as historical figures. Indeed, for our data, the suggestion is that the most significant percentage of the explanatory power of the three concepts is holding others accountable.

The second factor does not perfectly correspond to the punishment literature, but it does include punishment. This factor can be described as a narcissistic element where the individual who is calling out the company or band has something to gain. This factor also includes forcing opinions on someone else and unnecessarily punishing others. Based on this definition, the punishment element is seen as reluctant and possibly unnecessary for the gain of the person calling out the behavior. Interestingly, this factor corresponds with the Pew research findings where cancel culture relates to mean-spirited actions taken to cause harm to others (12%) and people canceling anyone they disagree with (9%).

The final factor is censorship, which represents 10% of the variance explained. The Pew survey also shows that censorship of speech or history is the second largest group (14%) behind accountability. Interestingly, in the Pew research, Conservatives are more likely than Liberals to believe that cancel culture equates to censorship.

Our items correspond well to the Pew survey. The Pew survey also asserted and found evidence that political ideology would play a role in responding to cancel culture. One example is the belief that cancel culture is a form of censorship. To test this on our scale, we next break our sample down by political ideology, specifically liberals and conservatives, to examine how the groups answer the survey items.

Sample Demographics

The sample includes more liberal responses than conservatives; thus, we reduced the sample size from the larger data set to conduct T-tests to empirically test for differences in answering the above questions based on political ideology. To arrive at a balanced sample, we recorded the conservative variable to include conservative and somewhat conservative into the same variable now labeled conservative. Then, we randomly selected 139 of the liberal responses to arrive at a balanced sample for further analysis.

The sample size for conservatives is 127, while the sample size for liberals is 139. Independent sample T-tests were run to measure survey items that were consistent with the Pew Research questions. The largest age bracket is 25–34 (33%), followed by 35–44 (21.8%). Males represent 50% of the sample, with 133 total, while women have a sample size of 120, with 12 people being nonbinary and one respondent preferred not to disclose gender. 83 respondents report working full-time, 56 report working part-time, and 27 respondents are students. 83 respondents reported being married, while 126 reported never being married. The sample is heavily represented by white people (frequency is 195), with blacks being the second largest group with 24 respondents. Regarding education, the largest group in the sample has a bachelor's degree (33%), followed by some college with no degree (28%). The largest group, from an income perspective, earns between 25k and 49,999k (25%), followed by 50k and 74,999k (20%).

Results

Independent T-tests were run to assess if people with different political ideologies reacted differently to the Pew survey items. For the question society holds accountable, we see that liberals agree more with the statement than do conservatives (L: $\bar{x}$ = 3.98, SD = .82; C: $\bar{x}$ = 3.12, SD = 1.01; p = .025). Conservatives tend to agree more with the statement regarding restricting speech than the liberals (L: $\bar{x}$ = 3.3, SD = 1.2; C: $\bar{x}$ = 4.22, SD = .84; p = .001). Liberals tend to agree more with the statement regarding racist or sexist items than do conservatives (L: $\bar{x}$ = 4.47, SD = .64; C: $\bar{x}$ = 3.37, SD = 1.2; p = .001). Liberals tend to agree more with the statement regarding historical figures than do conservatives (L: $\bar{x}$ = 3.79, SD = .945; C: $\bar{x}$ = 2.04, SD = 1.13; p = .026). Conservatives tend to agree more with the statement regarding calling out punishes than do liberals (L: $\bar{x}$ = 2.44, SD = 1.08; C: $\bar{x}$ = 3.17, SD = .87;

TABLE 2.3 Perception Differences by Political Ideology

Variable	*Conservative Mean/SD*	*Liberal Mean/SD*	*t-Score/ Significance*
Society holds account (Pew 1)	3.12/1.01	3.98/.82	7.5/.025
Restrict free speech (Pew 3)	4.22/.84	3.3/1.2	7.21/.001
Racist or sexist (Pew 4)	3.37/1.20	4.57/.64	10.4/.001
Historical figures (Pew 5)	2.04/1.13	3.79/.945	13.6/.026
Calling out punishes (Pew 7)	3.17/.87	2.44/1.08	6.04/.001
Calling out forcing views on others (Pew 8)	3.75/.98	2.57/1.11	9.08/.042
Calling out looks good (Pew 9)	4.1/.82	3.41/1.1	5.71/.001

p = .001). Conservatives tend to agree more with the statement regarding calling our forces than do liberals (L: $\bar{x}$ = 2.57, SD = 1.11; C: $\bar{x}$ = 3.75, SD = .98; p = .042). Finally, conservatives tend to agree more with the statement calling out look good than liberals (L: $\bar{x}$ = 3.41, SD = 1.1; C: $\bar{x}$ = 4.1, SD = .82; p = .001). See Table 2.3 for the means and significance levels. Perception differences of the results by political ideology are in Table 2.3.

Multivariate Analysis

Using the original sample (n = 344), a multivariate analysis of covariance (MANCOVA) was conducted using the three dimensions of the canceling behavior items as the dependent variables, political ideologies and age as fixed factors, and social justice attitudes as covariates. Social justice attitudes were measured using the 11 items from the Torres-Harding et al. (2012) social justice attitudes dimension of the multidimensional social justice scale. Items were evaluated with a 5-pt. Likert-type scale with 1 = strongly disagree and 5 = strongly agree. Reliability for the 11 social justice items is represented by a Cronbach's alpha equal to .944.

The skewness value is −653 for accountability, −.210 for punishment, and −.169 for censorship, which are all within the accepted range (Hair et al., 2010); however, the kurtosis values (alpha = .05) for accountability (.511) and punishment (.189) fell within the accepted range, but censorship (2.1380) did not. To test for equality of error variances, Levene's Test was not significant. Thus, this condition was met; however, the Box's M test was significant, thus violating assumptions of covariance. Additionally, the adjusted R^2 for censorship was only .033, so we removed censorship as it only had two items, and the kurtosis value was not within the accepted range. We proceeded without censorship, resulting in both Box's M and Levene's Tests not being significant.

All multivariate tests (Pillai's Trace, Wilks Lambda, Hotelling's Trace, and Roy's Largest root) show that the covariate of social justice attitudes

TABLE 2.4 Tests of Between Subjects Effects

	Accountability				*Punishment*		
	df	*F*	*Sig.*	*M(SD)*	*df*	*F*	*Sig.*
Covariate							
Social Justice Att.	1	37.394	<.001		1	2.877	n.s.
Main Effects							
Political	4	9.542	<.001		4	8.523	<.001
Age	5	1.308	n.s.		5	.484	n.s.
Adjusted R-Squared Values							
Accountability R^2 =	.356						
Punishment R^2 =	.158						

and the main effect of political ideology are significant across all dependent variables ($p < .001$); however, age is not significant, and neither is the interaction, which the interaction was not expected to be significant. Social justice attitude was only significant for accountability, whereas political ideology affected both accountability and punishment. Table 2.4 has the tests of between subjects effects.

The T tests indicated differences between those who lean conservative and those who lean liberal. A comparison of the means that evaluated the social justice attitudes for all political ideologies (n = 344) provided further support that there is a difference. A comparison of the means for the five categories indicates that social justice attitudes did differ based on political ideologies with the following values: conservative (n = 15, M = 3.78, SD = .48), somewhat conservative (n = 45, M = 3.90, SD = .54), moderate (n = 72, M = 4.08, SD = .62), somewhat liberal (n = 80, M = 4.43, SD = .51), and liberal (n = 132, M = 4.59, SD = .59). The ANOVA results are significant model (F = 24.667, df = 4, $p < .001$) and the R^2 is .22.

Discussion

As seen from Tables 2.3 and 2.4, political ideologies affect how respondents answer the scale items. Examining the differences as they pertain to the factors, we find that for the first factor, accountability, of the five items, differences emerge for three of the items. Liberals agree more with holding others accountable than do conservatives. Similarly, we see that liberals are more likely than conservatives to hold accountable for racist or sexist comments and to condemn political figures than are conservatives. Interestingly, if change has occurred or considering calling out a teaching moment, no significant differences between the two groups emerged.

Regarding factor 2, we can see that conservatives tend to believe that punishment is less warranted than liberals on all items. The three items in the factor are significantly different, with all the items being higher for conservatives. This indicates that conservatives see the punishment aspect as less justified.

Lastly, of the two censorship items, conservative respondents view canceling as restricting free speech. The definitions proposed for canceling and cancel culture all have some element of social justice, which aligns with our findings that those who view cancel culture as holding an entity or person accountable are likely to believe in social justice values whereas those who view cancel culture as punishment do not. There is not just one side of the political aisle that is engaging in and propagating cancel culture.

General Discussion

Cancel culture, as a phenomenon in the business realm, is gaining attention from both an academic perspective and a business strategy perspective. However, a Google search will suggest that the study of public relations has existed since the beginning of the 20th century. While public relations can be defined as promoting the positive aspects of the company to stakeholders, the task of restoring a suffering brand is a traditional public relations function that is not new (Hunt et al., 2021). Social media technology and the subsequent rapid consumer adoption are the catalysts behind the power shift in the company and consumer interaction (Saldanha et al., 2022). Practitioners suggest that due to the close relationship between cancel culture and social media, it is crucial that brands have not only a comprehensive social media policy but also a crisis response plan (Nierman, 2022).

Prior to social media, the power was with the company or brand as a service failure would typically be handled by customer service and be a one-on-one interaction between the company and the injured consumer. If a CEO or firm representative said something scripted or unscripted that could be deemed offensive, even if it was on the news, a firm only had to wait for another firm representative to be the focus of the news cycle. With social media and especially YouTube, video clips live on forever.

In 2010, the United Breaks Guitar YouTube video emerged (Carroll, 2009) as an example of customers fighting back publicly from actual wrongdoing using social media as a vehicle to correct a wrong in a very public setting (Barker et al., 2013). Also, in 2010, the British Petroleum tragedy that claimed 11 lives and sent millions of gallons of oil onto the Gulf Coast happened, while a live stream video shared and counted the amount of oil pouring into the ocean over social media. The public was further enraged when an interview video of the CEO went viral in which he was asked how long before the oil spill would be contained. He responded by saying he wanted it over soon because he wanted his life back. Within six weeks of the explosion, a "Boycott BP" Facebook group had nearly 95,000 members, with additional smaller groups calling for a boycott (Neuman, 2010). These early examples of social media activism or "canceling" illustrate a societal shift in which customers fight back by using social media to demand change and accountability.

Fast forward to today, where an actual or perceived indiscretion by a brand, a person, or a firm can cause groups to utilize social media to demand cancelation. One of the differences from the previously mentioned examples is that canceling is not trying to make the object of the cancelation change behavior or correct a wrong, but rather to either punish or hold the object of the cancelation accountable. Canceling involves not only shaming the object but also utilizing the power imbalance created by social media's herding behavior function, often in the name of social justice (Tandoc et al., 2022), with the goal being to withdraw support for the brand being canceled (Saldanha et al., 2023). In the recent cancelation of Starbucks, the firm continued to make news headlines, and in December 2023, the firm lost $11 billion in value, which was mainly attributed to the boycotts (Fabino, 2023). This serves as an example of the cancelation of a brand that one could argue committed a perceived brand transgression, as there are vocal supporters and opponents for both sides.

The conceptual model of Perceptions of Cancel Culture Behavior presented in Figure 2.3 attempts to piece together the objects that can be canceled, which can be a brand that is a firm, or a human. Next, the herding behavior made possible through social media drives cancelation through social and emotional contagion. The extent to which punishment or desire for accountability occurs is thought to be a function of the attitude toward social justice. Further, as found by the Pew Research Center (2020), people with differing political views can change both their attitude toward social justice and the desire to punish or hold them accountable. While our research explores both scale development for a cancel measurement derived from the Pew Research and the effects of social justice and politics, much more work in the Cancel literature is needed.

Future Research

The first area of germane for the study is how an object of a cancelation recovers from being canceled. While work has emerged exploring how to recover from negative online reviews (see Nazione & Perrault, 2019), suggesting caring perceptions and taking action in the form of an apology mitigated the problem better than doing nothing or deleting the review.

However, canceling differs from a service failure complaint online as the transgression is not related to the product functionality or warning others about the product functionality but rather an actual or perceived indiscretion relating to race, gender, corporate greed, or a politically sensitive topic (Demsar et al., 2023). Therefore, the strategy for change and revitalization becomes more complicated.

Some literature has emerged suggesting strategies such as preemptively engaging with activists can help mitigate brand decay (Chen, 2023); still, other work suggests that the reason for canceling and the response varies based on the reason for canceling and who is being canceled (Len-Ríos et al., 2015). Based on this work, future research is needed based on whether the canceled object is a brand, a human, or a firm. Taken a step further, Len-Ríos et al. (2015) suggest that when a human is, the cancel target recovery will vary based on whether the human is a celebrity or politician. Canceling objects involves contagion, which can occur without rational thought, driven by herding behavior, and can change based on political ideologies and attitudes toward canceling, will benefit from future research regarding who or what is the object of the cancelation.

A second area requires validating and testing the cancel scale developed here in other situations. We suggest that the scale presented here to measure accountability and punishment is preliminary at best, and further refinement and purification are necessary. Developing psychometrically valid scales will be necessary to understand the nuances involved in canceling brands, people, and firms.

A third area for future research involves model testing. Our research focused on how political ideology affects both the cancel objectives and the attitude toward social justice. However, the herding behavior and the contagion elements remain ripe for future research. It is crucial for future research to consider the moderating effect of contextual factors. This could involve experimenting with manipulating the object of cancelation or studying the actual process of cancelation and recovery. Such research would be invaluable for guiding brand managers, marketers, public relations specialists, as well as celebrities, politicians, and influencers through the intricacies of the canceling process.

Limitations

The first limitation here involves the typical issues involved with cross-sectional survey research. Cancelation and recovery will need longitudinal data to examine potential changes in attitudes toward the focal object during the cancelation and recovery process. This will help determine what strategies are effective and at what time during the process. It can vary based on whether the cancel goal is for accountability or punishment.

A second limitation involves the fact that canceling involves contagion, which can occur without rational thought. This makes measuring why canceling is happening and how to correct canceling difficult. Perhaps survey research would be limited based on the lack of rationality. Future research could explore grounded theory or perhaps in-depth interview research featuring laddering to best drill down why canceling is happening and how to best combat the canceling, given the various factors discussed here.

A third limitation in cancel culture research involves limited theoretical testing and potential divergent paths for theoretical development. Image Repair Theory proposes a process from damage to recovery, and stress response to negative reviews could enhance organizational attractiveness (Kollitz et al., 2022). This is in line with mainline service recovery literature where a marketer can turn the negatives into a positive, but only one time (Maxham III & Netemeyer, 2002). However, as discussed, cancel culture and negative online reviews differ. Other work suggests that counterinsurgency theory, derived from military intelligence strategies, could be a viable theory to view cancel culture response (Chen, 2023).

A possible promising theory to build on is the Institutional Theory Perspective (Demsar et al., 2023). This theory has the potential to examine both the actors doing and being canceled, as well as the reason for cancelation and the subsequent marketing reaction to the cancelation together under a framework. As stated in the author's article, this chapter examines the macro perspective of cancelation while understanding how the affected participants respond to the social pressure for change. Still, other work applies the theory of planned behavior and power theory to predict, explain, measure, and account for cancel behavior (Tandoc et al., 2022; Saldanha et al., 2023).

While utilizing previous theories derived from other areas is applicable and useful, cancel culture and the marketing implication would benefit from either a unification of theory or a theory explicitly developed to explain cancel culture (Hunt, 2014). Our study presents a comprehensive framework for theory testing that incorporates various elements of the cancel process and multiple actors involved in the process. However, we recognize the need for further development, refinement, and unification of this framework to facilitate the navigation of the cancel process by both researchers and practitioners.

This project was funded in part by the Direct Selling Education Foundation.

References

Ajzen, I. (1991). Theory of planned behavior. *Organizational Behaviour and Human Decision Processes*, *50*(2), 179–211.

Banerjee, A. V. (1992). A simple model of herd behavior. *The Quarterly Journal of Economics*, *107*(3), 797–817. https://doi.org/10.2307/2118364

Barker, M. S., Barker, D., Bormann, N. F., Neher, K. E., & Zahay, D. (2013). *Social Media Marketing: A Strategic Approach* (p. 330). Mason, OH: South-Western Cengage Learning.

Bateman, J., Hayes, S., & Arnett, W. (Hosts). (2022, February 12). Kevin Hart: Live in Los Angeles [Audio podcast episode]. *Smartless*. https://www.smartless.com/episodes/episode/21a59fa9/kevin-hart-live-in-los-angeles

Bouvier, G. (2020). Racist call-outs and cancel culture on Twitter: The limitations of the platform's ability to define issues of social justice. *Discourse, Context & Media*, *38*(8), 100421. https://doi.org/10.1016/j.dcm.2020.100431

Brownstone, S. (2013, September 18). Starbucks Says You Can't Bring Guns into Its Stores, Unless You Want To. *Fast Company*. https://www.fastcompany.com/91025986/19-ceos-died-on-the-job-leaders-work-life-balance

Buchholz, K. (2021, July 9). What Companies Get Canceled For. *Statista*. https://www.statista.com/chart/25283/us-adults-who-would-boycott-a-brand-reasons/

Carroll, D. (2009, July 6). United Breaks Guitar. *Sons of Maxwell*. https://www.youtube.com/watch?v=5YGc4zOqozo

Chen, S. (2023). A counterinsurgent (COIN) framework to defend against consumer activists. *Journal of Brand Management*, *30*(4), 275–301. https://doi.org/10.1057/s41262-022-00297-3

Chiu, A. (2019, October 31). 'He Is Right on All Counts': Obama Finds Rare Bipartisan Support by Bashing 'Woke' Shaming. *The Washington Post*. https://www.washingtonpost.com/nation/2019/10/31/obama-woke-shaming-bipartisan-support-yang-coulter-gabbard/

Churchill, G. A., & Iacobucci, D. (2006). *Marketing Research: Methodological Foundations* (Vol. 199, No. 1). New York: Dryden Press.

Clark, M. D. (2020). Drag them: A brief etymology of so-called "cancel culture." *Communication and the Public*, *5*(3–4), 88–92. https://doi.org/10.1177/2057047320961562

Contrera, J. (2021, December 16). A QAnon Con: How the Viral Wayfair Sex Trafficking Lie Hurt Real Kids. *The Washington Post*. https://www.washingtonpost.com/dc-md-va/interactive/2021/wayfair-qanon-sex-trafficking-conspiracy/

Cook. C. L., Patel, A., Guisihan, M., & Wohn, D. Y. (2021). Whose agenda is it anyway: An exploration of cancel culture and political affiliation in the United States. *SN Social Sciences*, *1*(9), 237. https://doi.org/10.1007/s43545-021-00241-3

Costa, C., & Azevedo, A. (2024). Antecedents and consequences of the "cancel culture" firestorm journey for brands: Is there a possibility for forgiveness? *Journal of Marketing Management*, *40*(3–4), 289–312. https://doi.org/10.1080/0267257X.2023.2266465

Demsar, V., Ferraro, C., Nguyen, J., & Sands, S. (2023). Calling for cancellation: Understanding how markets are shaped to realign with prevailing societal values. *Journal of Macromarketing*, *43*(3), 322–350.

Dictionary.com. (2020, July 31). What Does Cancel Culture Mean? *Pop Culture Dictionary*. https://www.dictionary.com/e/pop-culture/cancel-culture/

Duman, S., & Ozgen, O. (2018). Willingness to punish and reward brands associated to a political ideology (BAPI). *Journal of Business Research*, *86*, 468–478. https://doi.org/10.1016/j.jbusres.2017.05.026

Fabino, A. (2023, December 5). Starbucks Loses $11 Billion in Value Amid Boycotts. *Newsweek*. https://www.newsweek.com/starbucks-market-loss-boycotts-strikes-red-cup-day-1849713

Forst, M. L., Crim, D., & Blomquist, M. E. (1992). Punishment, accountability, and the new juvenile justice. *Juvenile and Family Court Journal*, *43*(1), 1–9. https://doi.org/10.1111/j.1755-6988.1992.tb00714.x

Golf-Papez, M., & Veer, E. (2022). Feeding the trolling: Understanding and mitigating online trolling behavior as an unintended consequence. *Journal of Interactive Marketing*, *57*(1), 90–114. https://doi.org/10.1177/10949968221075315

Hair, J., Black, W. C., Babin, B. J., & Anderson, R. E. (2010). *Multivariate Data Analysis*. Upper Saddle River, NJ: Prentice Hall.

Hall, A. T., Bowen, M. G., Ferris, G. R., Royle, M. T., & Fitzgibbons, D. E. (2007). The accountability lens: A new way to view management issues. *Business Horizons*, *50*(5), 405–413. https://doi.org/10.1016/j.bushor.2007.04.005

Harpaz, B. (2023, December 20). Why Is Starbucks Being Targeted by Activists for both Israel and Gaza? *Forward*. https://forward.com/fast-forward/574222/starbucks-protests-israel-gaza-union-boycott/

Hunt, S. D. (2014). *Marketing Theory: Foundations, Controversy, Strategy, and Resource-Advantage Theory*. London: Routledge.

Hunt, C. S., Mello, J. E., & Deitz, G. D. (2021). *Marketing*. McGraw-Hill.

Len-Ríos, M. E., Finneman, T., Han, K. J., Bhandari, M., & Perry, E. L. (2015). Image repair campaign strategies addressing race: Paula Deen, social media, and defiance. *International Journal of Strategic Communication*, *9*(2), 148–165.

Kollitz, R., Ruhle, S., & Wilhelmy, A. (2022). How to deal with negative online employer reviews: An application of image repair theory. *International Journal of Selection and Assessment*, *30*(4), 526–544.

Kong, Y. X., Wu, R. J., Zhang, Y. C., & Shi, G. Y. (2023). Utilizing statistical physics and machine learning to discover collective behavior on temporal social networks. *Information Processing & Management*, *60*(2), 103190.

Kubota, S. (2021, May 13). 'It Was Too Orchestrated': Ellen DeGeneres Opens Up about Personal Attacks in TODAY Exclusive. *TODAY*. https://www.today.com/popculture/ellen-degeneres-opens-about-personal-attacks-today-exclusive-t218281

McRady, R. (2019, October 8). Ellen DeGeneres Addresses Negative Backlash after She Sat Next to George W. Bush at NFL Game. *ET*. https://www.etonline.com/ellen-degeneres-addresses-negative-backlash-after-she-sat-next-to-george-w-bush-at-nfl-game-133972

McDonald, M. H., De Chernatony, L., & Harris, F. (2001). Corporate marketing and service brands-Moving beyond the fast-moving consumer goods model. *European Journal of Marketing*, *35*(3/4), 335–352. https://doi.org/10.1108/03090560110382057

Mattke, J., Maier, C., Reis, L., & Weitzel, T. (2020). Herd behavior in social media: The role of Facebook likes, strength of ties, and expertise. *Information & Management*, *57*(8), 103370.

Maxham III, J. G., & Netemeyer, R. G. (2002). A longitudinal study of complaining customers' evaluations of multiple service failures and recovery efforts. *Journal of Marketing*, *66*(4), 57–71.

Mishan, L. (2020, December 29). Notes on the Culture: The Long and Tortured History of Cancel Culture. *The New York Times*. https://www.nytimes.com/2020/12/03/t-magazine/cancel-culture-history.html

Mueller, T. S. (2021). Blame, then shame? Psychological predictors in cancel culture behavior. *The Social Science Journal*, 1–14. https://doi.org/10.1080/03623319.2021.1949552

Murthy, K. V. (2008). Corporate Governance in Banks-An Eclectic Approach. (November 18, 2008). https://papers.ssrn.com/sol3/papers.cfm?abstract_id=1303415

Nazione, S., & Perrault, E. K. (2019). An empirical test of image restoration theory and best practice suggestions within the context of social mediated crisis communication. *Corporate Reputation Review*, *22*, 134–143.

Neuman, S. (2010, May 25). As BP Backlash Grows, So Do Calls for Boycott. *NPR*. https://www.npr.org/2010/05/25/127110643/as-bp-backlash-grows-so-do-calls-for- boycott

Ng, E. (2020). No grand pronouncements here...: Reflections on cancel culture and digital media participation. *Television & New Media*, *21*(6), 621–627.

Nierman, E. (2022, August 31). Why Social Media, Cancel Culture, and Crisis Management have Become Intertwined. *Fast Company*. https://www.fastcompany.com/90781299/why-social-media-cancel-culture-and-crisis-management-have-become-intertwined

Obama Foundation. (2019, October 13). President Obama in conversation with Yara Shahidi and Obama Foundation Program Participants. Available at https://www.youtube.com/watch?v=Ioz96L5xASk&t=3548s

Pew Research Center. (2020, September 8–13). American Trends Panel Wave 74 Data Set Download. *Pew Research Center*. https://www.pewresearch.org/science/dataset/american-trends-panel-wave-74/

Priyambodo, B., Wijaya, A. F., & Riyadi, B. S. (2023). The analysis of performance accountability system for government agency: A punishment theory perspective. *International Journal of Membrane Science and Technology*, https://cosmosscholars.com/phms/index.php/ijmst/article/view/1289/748

Pröllochs, N., & Feuerriegel, S. (2023). Mechanisms of true and false rumor sharing in social media: Collective intelligence or herd behavior?. *Proceedings of the ACM on Human- Computer Interaction*, 7(CSCW2), 1–38.

Raafat, R. M., Chater, N., & Frith, C. (2009). Herding in humans. *Trends in Cognitive Science*, *13*, 420–428.

Ramto, O. B., & Farajallah, M. (2022). Risks of Cultural Marketing in the Era of Cancel Culture, *International Journal of Advanced Research in Economics and Finance*, 4(4), 74–87.

Rauschnabel, P. A., Kammerlander, N., & Ivens, B. S. (2016). Collaborative brand attacks in social media: Exploring the antecedents, characteristics, and consequences of a new form of brand crises. *Journal of Marketing Theory and Practice*, 24(4), 381–410.

Romano, A. (2020, August 25). Why We Can't Stop Fighting about Cancel Culture. *Vox*. https://www.vox.com/culture/2019/12/30/20879720/what-is-cancel-culture-explained-history-debate

Rauschnabel, P. A., Kammerlander, N. and Ivens, B. S. (2016), Collaborative brand attacks in social media: Exploring the antecedents, characteristics, and consequences of a new form of brand crises. *Journal of Marketing Theory and Practice*, *24*(4), 381–410. https://doi.org/10.1080/10696679.2016.1205452

Saldanha, N., Mulye, R., & Rahman, K. (2022). Cancel culture and the consumer: A strategic marketing perspective. *Journal of Strategic Marketing*, https://doi.org/10.1080/0965254X.2022.2040577

Sugar, R. (November 2, 2018). How Starbuck's Annual Holiday Cup Became a Battleground for the Heart and Soul of America. *Vox*. https://www.vox.com/the-goods/2018/11/2/18052550/starbucks-holiday-cup-explained-2018-controversies

Sweetin, V. H., Knowles, L. L., Summey, J. H., & McQueen, K. S. (2013). Willingness-to-punish the corporate brand for corporate social irresponsibility. *Journal of Business Research*, *66*(10), 1822–1830. https://doi.org/10.1016/j.jbusres.2013.02.003

Tandoc, Jr., E. C., Ru, B. T. H., Huei, G. L., Charlyn, N. M. Q., Cha., R. A., & Zhang, H. G. (2022). #cancelculture: Examining definitions and motivations. *New Media & Society*, https://doi.org/10.1177/14614448221077977

Thomson, M. (2006). Human brands: Investigating antecedents to consumers' strong attachments to celebrities. *Journal of Marketing*, *70*(3), 104–119. https://doi.org/10.1509/jmkg.70.3.104

Torres-Harding, S. R., Siers, B., & Olson, B. (2012). Development and psychometric evaluation of the social justice scale (SJS). *American Journal of Community Psychology*, *50*, 77–88. https://doi.org/10.1007/s10464-011-9478-2

Valor, C., Antonetti, P., & Zasuwa, G. (2022). Corporate social irresponsibility and consumer punishment: A systematic review and research agenda, *Journal of Business Research*, *144*, 1218–1233. https://doi.org/10.1016/j.jbusres.2022.02.063

Vogels, E.A., Anderson, M., Porteus, M., Baronavski, C., Atske, S., McClain, C., Auxier, B., Perrin, A., & Ramshankar, M. (2021, May 19). Americans and 'Cancel Culture': Where Some See Calls for Accountability, Others See Censorship, Punishment. *Pew Research Center*. https://www.pewresearch.org/internet/2021/05/19/americans-and-cancel-culture-where-some-see-calls-for-accountability-others-see-censorship-punishment/

Watercutter, A. (2016, February 22). Here's What Happened to the Woman Who Started #CancelColbert. *Wired*. https://www.wired.com/2016/02/cancelcolbert-what-happened/

Yandoli, K. L. (2020, July 16). Former employees Say Ellen's "Be Kind" Talk Show Mantra Masks a Toxic Work Culture. *Buzzfeed News*. https://www.buzzfeednews.com/article/krystieyandoli/ellen-employees-allege-toxic-workplace-culture

YPulse. (2023, July 25). NA vs WE: Young Consumers See Cancel Culture Differently. *YPulse*. https://www.ypulse.com/article/2023/07/25/we-na-vs-we-young-consumers-see-cancel-culture-differently/

3

DARK SIDE OF SOCIAL MEDIA

Cancel Culture in Sports Organizations

Felipe Bertazzo Tobar, Renan Petersen-Wagner and Jonathan R. Oliveira

The assertion that sports and politics should not intertwine has been proved unpractical and unrealistic as they are inevitably interconnected as influential structural elements of contemporary society (Tobar, 2023). The vision that sports serve as a "microcosm of the larger political ecosystem" (Hartzell, 2023, p. 31) reflecting political tensions, conflicts, and ideologies is not new, being manifested in notable examples such as Hitler's political exploitation of Berlin in 1936 Olympics to promote the Nazi ideology or apartheid-era South Africa's ban from international sports events due to their internal racial segregation policies (Rademeyer, 2000). However, the relationship between sports and politics has gained prominence with the emergence of the digital age revealing new power relations and stakeholders attempting to force societal and sporting structural changes (Lee Ludvigsen & Petersen-Wagner, 2022a). The powerful omnipresence of social media has amplified the use of sports as a platform for political purposes evidencing how sports are an "unarguably battleground for political power struggles over issues of contemporary ideological importance that continue to influence the identities, communities, and material conditions of our lives" (McClearen, 2023, p. 27).

The promotion of cancel culture in sports due to political ideology has been a feature of diverse Western social media platforms – Facebook, Instagram, Twitter, TikTok, and YouTube – revealing how these digital spaces are important vehicles for investigating and influencing the relationship between sports and politics (Lee Ludvigsen & Petersen-Wagner, 2022b). Recent events, such as when former football player Colin Kaepernick was mocked for a tweet calling the United States' Independence Day holiday a "celebration of white supremacy" (Choe, 2020) or the organized boycott of the FIFA Qatar 2022 World Cup by Human Rights groups accusing the host country of being a

DOI: 10.4324/9781032670546-4

symbol of "modern-day slavery" and an unsafe place for the LGBTQIA+ community (Dun et al., 2022), have demonstrated the power of social media in fostering political expression and activism while evidencing the influence of the outcomes of those digital discussions to future implementation of new policies by sports organizations.

In contemporary Spain, which is still influenced by the outcomes of the Spanish Civil War (1936–1939) and the dictatorship of General Francisco Franco (1939–1975), Real Madrid Club de Fútbol (hereafter RM) and Futbol Club Barcelona (hereafter FCB), the two most followed sports organizations globally across the five most popular social media platforms (Instagram, Twitter, Facebook, TikTok, and YouTube) (CIES Football Observatory, 2023; Best YouTube Channels by Football Clubs, n.d.), recently engaged on a series of institutional mutual cancelation on social media platforms related to the historically dark and sensitive discussion of which club should be considered the "club of the regime" (Grez, 2023). Although gaining an ever-growing relevance in media outlets, the phenomenon of cancel culture in sports has been overlooked in academic studies. This chapter, divided into three sections, intends to expand discussions over such a relevant topic by analyzing how these "world-class brands" (Mañas Viniegra, 2018) promoted and managed a mutual institutional canceling, what were the practical consequences of economic and brand/image perspectives for them and their fan bases' reactions regarding the allegations of their clubs being linked to Franco's regime.

By conducting a historical literature review, the first section looks at the political impacts and influences of the Spanish Civil War and Franco's regime over FCB and RM until current times and how these events and periods were decisive in forging distinctive collective identities and a long-term dissonance among these two clubs related to their histories linked to Franco's regime. We also have acknowledged how the new platform media environment has given space to digital activism and the spread of a culture of cancelation ever more popular in sports. In the second section, we discuss the results of the conducted thematic analysis (Braun & Clarke, 2006) and critical discourse analysis (Fairclough, 2010) of three institutional videos (and their comments and replies) posted on YouTube by FCB, RM, and Marca Newspaper. The story of the data revealed a total of four themes that evidenced support for the official counter-canceling by RM of rewriting history; mockery as a predicted mechanism to reinforce official counter-canceling; the use of fear, repression, and persecution narratives as a response to counter-canceling; and the accusation of "fake news" to disbelief and reject links with Franco's regime by FCB and its supporters. In the third section, the chapter discussed how these findings could be comprehended on the light of different psychological theories such as image repair theory (Benoit, 2015), cognitive dissonance theory (Festinger, 1957), confirmation bias (Peters, 2022), and collective identities and team identification (Alabarces, 1998; Chun & Sagas, 2022).

Among other significant conclusions, this chapter reveals how football supporters, due to mechanisms of collective identity preservation, share the tendency to deny historical links of their clubs with dark pasts and consequently minimize the often-harmful practical consequences of cancel cultures such as sponsorship losses, damages to institutional brands and images, and reduction or loss of fan base support.

Literature Review

The Spanish Context – FC Barcelona and Real Madrid CF

The Spanish Civil War and Franco's regime have left deep-seated divisions within Spanish society that persistently influence perceptions and recollections of these eras (Gunther et al., 1986). An understanding of the historical context of the Spanish Civil War and Franco's regime, yet summarized in this literature review, is therefore crucial not only to grasping historical and current political dynamics in Spain but to facilitate the comprehension of the conflicts that directly involve FCB and RM, two sports organizations responsible for "football's biggest global rivalry" (Fitzpatrick, 2012), which extends the sporting field with intense political character (Oliveira & Capraro, 2020). Football, in particular, due to its popularity among Spaniards, continues to be intentionally explored as a vehicle of nationalism and regionalism identities discourses, political values, and cultures (Shobe, 2008; Oliveira & Capraro, 2020) and naturally constitutes a mirror of Spain's ongoing struggle to deal with dissonant interpretations of the official narratives and historical occurrences involving the Spanish Civil War and Franco's regime (Tobar, 2023).

The Spanish Civil War: Impacts on FC Barcelona and Real Madrid CF

The civil conflict, undoubtedly one of "Spain's darkest chapters" (Keeley, 2023), involved the Nationalist forces led by General Francisco Franco Bahamonde (1907–1975) and the Populists ("Popular Front"), a coalition of conservative republicans, anarchists, socialists, communists, and syndicalists (Williams, 1990). While the Nationalists received substantial support from Mussolini and Hitler's military forces (Whealey, 2004), the Populists, initially led by President Azaña and several prime ministers, established an alliance with the USSR throughout the civil war (Farràs, 2021). The military *coup d'etat* allegedly intended to ensure the existence of a unified and conservative Spain amid widespread dissatisfaction among right-wing groups, including Catholics, landowners, monarchists, the bourgeoisie, and the military, which were discontent with recent structural changes promoted in Spanish Second Republican (1931–1936) such as agrarian reform, universal suffrage, the abolition of divorce, the separation of Church and State, and the subordination of the military to the civil power (Leal, 2014). The war resulted in an estimated 540,000 deaths, 500,000 prisoners across 188 concentration camps on both sides (García, 2022), and 200,000 individuals into exile (Pichel, 2019).

The cities of Madrid and Barcelona were under Populist control throughout the three-year conflict. Following the seizure of public and private institutions (e.g., industries, banks, newspapers, and religious schools), RM was seized by the Popular Front (Martialay, 2017) while FCB avoided the seizure of anarchists from the National Confederation of Labor (CNT) after creating an employee's committee with legitimacy before the CNT to run the club (Díaz, 2016). RM, once a historically traditional club with conservative members, many from the military or affiliated with the Spanish Confederation of Autonomous Rights (CEDA) (Expósito, 2020), was led by Colonel Juan José Vallejo on behalf of the Workers' Cultural Sports Federation (Expósito, 2020), and later by Colonel Antonio Ortega Gutierrez, who was affiliated with the Communist Party of Spain and at that point in June 1937, acting as the new General Director of Security by Prime Minister Juan Negrin (Martialay, 2017). At the hands of Populist forces, RM's Vice-President Gonzalo Aguirre was assassinated at the beginning of the conflict, and Santiago Bernabéu, whose name is after the club stadium nowadays, was heavily persecuted before escaping to France in 1938 to join later the Nationalist troops (González Calleja, 2014).

During the civil conflict, RM played only two official friendly matches in September and October of 1936, being forced to close its official activities in November 1936 after FCB opposed the idea of allowing its rival to relocate and participate in the still-alive Catalunya Championship, located in a safe region controlled by the Populists (Expósito, 2020). Football activities continued at RM's Old Chamartín stadium through matches between sports battalions created to defend the Republican liberty, lining up famous boxers, cyclists, bullfighters, basketballers, and footballers, including all RM players (Real Madrid C.F., 2002a). One of the three sports battalions located at the stadium was "the Josep Sunyol Sports Batalion," named after FCB President and Catalan Deputy for the Catalan Republican Left (ERC), assassinated on August 6, 1936, by Franco's troops at the beginning of the civil war when acting on behalf of Joan Casanovas, Catalan parliament's President (Martialay, 2017). On the other hand, FCB continued competing, including winning the Mediterranean League, a competition reserved for clubs from the Republic zone – Catalunya, Valencia, and Murcia – that could still travel safely within Spain (Díaz, 2016). When football was impracticable in the country due to the war, FCB embarked on a tour to Mexico and the United States to raise funds for the club and promote Republican propaganda in contribution to war efforts (Quiroga, 2015; Díaz, 2016; Vogel, 2017). Unlike the club's headquarters bombed in 1938, the *Les Corts* stadium was not impacted.

In January 1939, the FCB and *Martinenc* reserve teams played the last match before the invasion of Franco's army into Barcelona (Tomàs, 2023).

The Political Influences of Franco's Regime over FC Barcelona and Real Madrid CF

Franco's regime has exercised different influences across decades over Spanish football. During early Francoism (1939–1951), the principles of brutal repression and irreconciliation of the *Falange Española Tradicionalista* (FET) y de las *Juntas de Ofensiva Nacional Sindicalista* (JONT), or in English "Spanish Traditionalist Phalanx and Assemblies of the National-Syndicalist Offensive," the regime's only legal party, directly impacted Spanish football development (Tobar, 2023). Football became a tool of mass indoctrination, ideological propaganda, and national integration (Rieck, 2021). Since the first months of Franco's regime, Colonel Troncoso, President of the Spanish Football Federation, carried out depurations within every football club located at the defeated side to eliminate what was considered "sporting undesirables and those who have proven to be against to the spirit of the savior movement of Spain" (Martialay, 2017, p. 346). For instance, RM and the Sports Battalion's captain Quesada was suspended for six months, despite sustaining he had no choice but to join the Popular Front in the conflict (Real Madrid C.F., 2002a). Following the purging process within FCB, a friendly match was played against Athletic Bilbao, symbolizing "the new Barcelona freed from Marxism and separatism" (Quiroga, 2015, p. 69). Beyond the imposition of at least two members of the FET in club's boards and the designation of new presidents (e.g., in 1940, General Moscardó appointed Enrique Piñeyro Queralt, a Catalan who was commander of Franco's army as FCB's new president, and in 1943 Santiago Bernabeu, former RM player and army caporal of Franco's troops was selected RM's new president) (Shobe, 2008; Martialay, 2017), from 1940, teams had their names Hispanicize/nationalized (e.g., Football Club Barcelona became Club de Fútbol Barcelona and Athletic Club Bilbao became Atlético de Bilbao) (Masià, 2014). Furthermore, across all official matches, players were forced to perform the Roman (aka fascist) salute and sing the Falangist anthem, "Cara al sol" (Quiroga, 2015).

From the Spanish transition period (1975–1978), historians have sustained that in the aftermath of war, the dictatorship intended to forge a Castilian-centered Spanish nation annihilating any vestige of regional identity by stripping regional institutions, language, political ideology, and cultural symbols (see Solé, 1986; Conversi, 1997), which included the fate of football clubs like FCB and Athletic Bilbao from Catalunya and the Basque region, respectively, where independence movements were highly nurtured pre-1936 (Burns, 1999). However, recent historiography (Quiroga, 2015, 2020; Núñez Seixas, 2009; Arias, 2018, 2021a) has challenged such interpretation. Following the influence of German and Italian dictatorships, interested in fostering the regime's popularity and promoting its regionalized Spanish nationalism, the Francoist nation intentionally gave space for the existence of expressions of local and regional identities though subordinated to the main Spanish national identity (Quiroga, 2015, 2020). In this point, remembering the existence of friendly matches between the regional teams of Castile and Catalonia throughout the 1940s, the use of the Catalan language and illustrations of Catalan flags (*Senyeras*) in FCB's official magazine since the mid-1950s, and the exploration of Catalan symbolism through folk music and dances during FCB's stadium inauguration in 1957, Quiroga (2015, 2020) demonstrates how the dictatorship "pursued the manipulation rather than eradication of regional identities" (p. 509) to "create a new regionalized idea of Spain" (p. 67).

In the difficult post-war period, RM and FCB, like every other club, incorporated and followed the new regime's orders and values (Rieck, 2021). Quiroga (2015, 2020) found clubs that dominated the domestic competitions in the first regime's decade, like Atletico Aviación (a club born out of the merger between Atletico Madrid and the Aviación Nacional--the sports section of the Air Army) won five Spanish leagues (1939–40, 1940–41, 1949–50, 1950–51). Athletic Bilbao won five Spanish Cups (1943, 1944, 1945, 1950 and 1955), and FCB won five Spanish leagues (1944–45, 1947–48, 1948–49, 1951–52, 1952–53), and four Spanish Cups (1942, 1951, 1952, 1953). These wins gained the attention of Franco's cabinet. Considered a middle-table club that was almost relegated in 1947–48 in the Spanish League, since the beginning of Franco's regime, RM had only conquered two Spanish Cups (1946 and 47) (aka Generalissimo Cup), and two league titles (1953–54 and 1954–55), being considered irrelevant in the eyes of the regime (Tobar, 2023). For instance, according to Rieck (2021), Franco only granted one audience to RM before 1955. Importantly in this discussion was the identification by Arias (2021a), who pointed out that Franco was a "supporter" of all the football clubs as they served the regime's political interests of solidifying Spanish nationalism domestically and internationally. It was notably the international success of RM from 1955 when it started winning its five-straight European Cup (1955–1959) that contributed to the notion of RM as the regime's club, particularly during late Francoism (1959–1975), in which Spain was still in large part rejected in a democratic Europe (Espinosa, 2014).

As Franco's regime was based on centralized nationalist narratives, and RM, located at Spain's capital, presented an ideal model of a centralist Spanish identity, the club "became Spain" when playing internationally (Rieck, 2021). In these geopolitical circumstances, RM coincidentally became the best team globally, with popularity across Europe rivaling the Beatles (Gifford, 2023). Quiroga (2015) informs how RM's president and players did not identify with the idea of representing Franco but were conscious of the imposed responsibility. In its centennial book, RM defends that the club always understood the importance of nurturing institutional and personal relationships with politicians from all spectrums, "especially when Spain have lived under authoritarian or dictatorial regimes, notably in the long years of Franco's government, when the instituted power intended to direct or control every social activity, including sports" (Real Madrid C.F., 2002b, p. 659). Therefore, Rieck (2021), who rejects the thesis of Franco's interference – personally or directly – in RM, instead of calling it "Franco's Club," characterizes it as the "Ambassador of Spain."

It is precisely from this political and symbolic association that emerges what Vogel (2017) pointed out as "Catalan Narratives." Created and diffused by FCB supporters' pro-Catalunya independence, who naturally nurtured anti-Francoism sentiments (Oliveira & Capraro, 2020), these narratives explore the historical aspirations of democracy, autonomy, and independence from a centralized Spain through football, pejoratively associating RM with Franco's regime. Authors such as Burns (1999), Shobe (2008), Kassing (2019), and Usall (2021) list on and off-field episodes to support the thesis that RM was the regime's club and FCB, its victim. For instance, the 11-1 victory of RM against FCB in Madrid on the return leg of the 1943s Spanish Cup, where police and FET agents entered the away locker room to allegedly intimidate FCB's players, was considered an extension of the civil war conflict (Quiroga, 2015).

Also, the hiring of Argentinian star Alfredo Di Stefano in 1953 from Colombian professional team Millonarios Fútbol Club by RM was criticized by allegations of Franco's interference and ignited senses of injustice and privilege toward the capital's club (Shobe, 2008). Further, the mistake committed by referee Emilio Guruceta in 1970 (who awarded a penalty to RM against FCB for a foul outside the penalty area in a Spanish Cup clash) (Burns, 1999) are examples used to sustain the historical narrative of RM favoritism. According to Shobe (2008), the latter episode was significant because, in the eyes of Catalans, it confirmed the long-term persecution from central Spain against FCB and Catalunya and was decisive in pushing certain club directors to reawake the club as the bearer of Catalunya's identity and promote acts of resistance. In this point, in 1971, the club advocated for the use of Catalan in schools; in 1972, it started making stadium announcements in the Catalan language as well as flying the Catalan flag over the stadium; in 1973 reclaimed the club's Catalan name; in 1974 during the 75th anniversary organized a festival of Catalan music at the Palau Blaugrana; and in 1975 reclaimed Catalan as its official language (Shobe, 2008; Usall, 2021).

Quiroga (2015, 2020), while recognizing FCB as a symbol of Catalan identity, which followed a contemporary social process that saw in late Francoism legislation changes allowing independence to associations and higher tolerance to the diffusion of regional identities, also sustained that club's board of directors, which included members of the center-right nationalist political party Democratic Convergence of Catalonia, did not see incompatibility between Spanish and Catalan identities as they were in favor of the existence of a federalized Spain that recognizes Catalunya's singular identity. Quiroga (2020) cites two episodes associated with the celebrations of the 1973–74 Spanish League to justify his views. First, Agustí Montal's declarations to Mundo Deportivo newspaper about his expectation to transform the club into "the symbol of Catalonia and the best Spanish embassy abroad" (p. 75), and, secondly, the picture in Barcelona's official magazine of the Camp Nou parade in which fans were waving Catalan and Spanish flags in "an explicit expression of loyalty of the club to Franco's regime" (p. 75). Quiroga (2015, 2020), thus, sustains that the

> Catalan identity associated with F. C. Barcelona did not necessarily imply anti-Spanish sentiment, nor was Barça's institutional support for the dictatorship an obstacle for directors and supporters to turn FCB into the standard-bearer of the anti-centralist and pro-democratic struggle in the world of football.
>
> *(Quiroga, 2020, p. 75)*

Indeed, FCB, along with most of the dictatorship, demonstrated close alignment with higher instances of the regime. For decades, the club was "the ideological driving force of a local Francoism which became Catalanised" (Quiroga, 2020, p. 72), honoring the "Spanish Caudillo" through public recognitions as well as regular visits at its official palace (Arias, 2021a, 2021b, 2023; Oliveira & Capraro, 2020). According to Oliveira and Capraro (2020), the club that created the image of a Catalan institution persecuted by the centralized government has benefited from the relationships with Franco's regime. Oliveira and Capraro (2020) initially remind when the club were only able to sign Hungarian striker Ledislao Kubala in 1950, who was banned by FIFA (Féderation Internationale de Football Association) for fleeing Hungary (under control of the Soviet Union) at the request of the local federation, after using connections within Franco's regime.

Oliveira and Capraro (2020) also pointed out that in 1962, in imminent bankruptcy by facing a debt of 230 million pesetas (Spanish currency of the time) derived from the inauguration of FCB's new stadium (Camp Nou) in 1957, the Council of Ministers and General Francisco Franco intervened to allow the reclassification (once considered a green area) and selling of the *Les Corts* stadium, which curiously retained its Catalan name under Franco (Quiroga, 2020). About this episode, Arias (2018) reproduced the letter sent by former FCB President Enrique Llaudet toward Franco, in which, on behalf of the club, he extends "gratitude for offering such constant help in all orders." Furthermore, in 1971, FCB was granted approximately 43 million pesetas from Franco's regime as non-refundable funds. These funds were allocated for the construction of the Palau Blaugrana, a multi-sport complex, along with new ice rinks. As documented by Arias (2023) through official records, Franco was accorded the title of Honorary President at the inauguration of these facilities.

The Catalan club, which throughout the regime had at its presidency two members of the FET and JONS, Miró-Sans (1953–1961), responsible for leading the construction of Camp Nou in 1957, and Llaudet (1961–1968), in charge of solving the club's financial troubles by requalifying the Les Corts area in 1962 (Arias, 2021b) has given three different distinctions to General Franco – all withdrew in 2019. First, in 1951, Franco was awarded a diamond and gold club's badge of honor by former president Agustí Montal Galobart on the final of the Generalissimo Cup of that year. In 1971, the second distinction consisted of a gold medal former president Agustí Montal Costa awarded at the Royal Palace of El Pardo in gratitude for the Caudillo's personal support in constructing the Palau Blaugrana multisport complex. The third and last award happened in 1974 due to the FCB's 75th anniversary, in which Franco received from Agustí Montal Costa the commemorative gold medal (García-Soler, 2019). Arias (2023) informed that the same gold medal was given on the same day to Minister Secretary General of the Movement Jose Utreta Molina, who, in turn, conceded later to FCB a golden plaque symbolizing the highest possible distinction in Spanish sport.

According to the Spanish Newspaper *El Plural*, in 2003, the club could withdraw Franco's medals. However, FCB's president Joan Laporta during his first term (2003–2010) said, "the badge cannot be withdrawn from Franco because it does not appear in the minute books and because Barça was pressured to give it to him." In total, historical documents from the Archive of the Civil House of the Head of State in the *Palacio de Oriente* and photos from the Alcalá Archive and La Vanguardia Española newspaper evidence over 160 visits from 42 different FCB's presidents and directors across the 44 years of Franco regime either for exclusive sporting purposes or acting due to political interests and demands (Arias, 2023). These historically hidden connections between FCB and Franco's regime give legitimacy to Quiroga's (2020) observation of how football clubs did not have a permanent identity adapting to the different demands from Franco's political regime and historical and cultural contexts across decades. On this point, Quiroga (2020) argues that FCB did not exhibit a pro-Catalanist stance toward independence following Franco's death. According to Kassing (2019), it was only when Joan Laporta, a former member of the Catalan Solidarity for Independence Party, assumed the presidency of FCB in 2003 that the club initiated a revival of its Catalan pro-independence identity by embracing Catalan language and symbols.

As reviewed so far, football's historical and political significance is intrinsically connected with the political realm in Spain and is extensive and particularly associated with the rivalry between FCB and RM, which produces and reproduces national and regional identities and discourses (Shobe, 2008). In contemporary Spain, debates and accusations between fans of these clubs regarding the roles of their respective teams during the Spanish Civil War, particularly throughout Franco's regime, continue to surface, including on social media platforms, highlighting antagonistic narratives surrounding a dissonant past.

Media Effects in a Platform Society – Cancel Culture and Sports

In a media environment where traditional media organizations have ceded their hegemonic power in the communication process (see Jenkins, 2006), we are witnessing the emergence of new stakeholders who can control the message by *controlling* their own channels/media, reverberating what McLuhan (1964) once considered as the medium being the message. In a way, platformization (van Dijck et al., 2018), and more specifically platformization in the cultural industries (Poell et al., 2022), have provided new places for individuals and organizations to bypass traditional media such as television and newspaper, and connect directly with their audiences. Moreover, in this new platform media environment where algorithms take prominence over traditional gatekeepers such as editors and journalists (see Petersen-Wagner and Lee Ludvigsen, 2023), *all* become content producers by either posting new content, or engaging with posted content through viewing, liking, commenting, and therefore feeding the algorithm.

Amongst the transformations stemming from platformization it is possible to highlight how those new places such as the distinct social media platforms become spaces of autonomy where individuals are *free* to congregate and communicate (from similar Latin roots to *community*) their hopes and outrages toward specific events (see Castells, 2015). These new forms of digital activism are not only reflected on political issues such as the ones described by Castells (2015) in his book but also transcend to other spaces such as sport. For instance, football fans have YouTube to vent their frustration toward the video-assistant-referee during the 2018 FIFA Men's World Cup (Petersen-Wagner and Lee Ludvigsen, 2022b). Other forms of digital activism can be seen when football fans campaigned against the increase in ticket prices in the English Premier League (Cleland et al., 2017), the historical change in campaigning that is more politically orientated in terms of "project identities" (Fitzpatrick & Hoey, 2022), the safe stand movement in the English Premier League (Turner, 2022), and broadly a movement against modern football, and its associated *malaises* as commercialization and securitization (Lee Ludvigsen, 2019, 2023).

Therefore, social media platforms become democratic spaces where ordinary people can have a voice and engage in discussions about critical social issues (Jackson et al., 2020). Typically, social media platforms such as Twitter, Facebook, Instagram, YouTube, and others can also act as the propelling force of the culture of cancelation. "Cancel culture" refers to the widespread movements started on the internet that seek to address abuses of power, discrimination or misconduct of individuals, groups of people or institutions on social media platforms (Lewis & Christin, 2022). If, on one hand, such online movements have promoted political correctness toward a social change agenda, on the other, internet cancelation has also sparked severe criticism due to its pushbacks on the liberal discourse that threats public debates (Lewis & Christin, 2022). On the other hand, there is a tenuous and grey line in online public judgments between those comments or posts seeking social justice coherently and those that might go too far undermining any counterargument, debate, or opposing thought. Internet movements require carefulness and critical rationale to promote social justice without depleting public debate and dialogue.

In the sports world, cases of cancel culture have dramatically grown in recent years. Athletes, managers, and even sports organizations have experienced cancelations for various reasons on social media platforms. For instance, in 2019, the Houston Astros baseball team was involved in a sign-stealing scheme scandal during the 2017 and 2018 seasons. The scandal generated severe adverse public reactions from fans, other teams, sponsors, media, and organizers, triggering player suspensions, a $5-million fine, and two managers fired (Edouard, 2021). In the same year, Daryl Morey, the general manager of the Houston Rockets, expressed his support for pro-democracy protesters in Hong Kong via Twitter, stating, "Fight for Freedom. Stand with Hong Kong." The statement resulted in a massive backlash from the Chinese government and various Chinese sponsors and partners, weakened diplomatic relations with the Chinese market, leading to a financial drawback for the team, suspension of NBA broadcasts in China, and the cancelation of sponsorship deals (Escobar, 2021).

There are also examples of athletes themselves being canceled, or temporarily canceled by fans, brands, and sport organizations alike. For instance, in 2022, tennis star Novak Djokovic faced not only a wave of negative public sentiment on social media but also deportation from Australia due to his refusal to get vaccinated for COVID-19 when he attempted to participate in the Australian Open Grand Slam (Duncan, 2023). This was during the times when Djokovic was also attending social outings with friends or other tennis players that some perceived as wrong and branded as "superspreader events." Similarly, Aaron Rodgers (a famous quarterback formerly with the GreenBay Packers) was also vocal about not wanting to get the COVID-19 vaccine. While he was not fully "canceled," he certainly was the subject of much discussion, and much of it was negative and may have harmed part of his reputation. Even the FIFA World Cup, the world's premier football event, has not been immune to online backlash. The organizers of the FIFA Qatar 2022 World Cup have had to contend with social media boycott campaigns due to concerns about human rights, the working conditions of immigrants, the criminalization of the LGBTQIA+ community, and the societal role of women in the host country (Dun et al., 2022).

Despite the substantial growth of cancel culture cases in sports, the concept of cancel culture remains untapped in the academic field of sports. Our search for related studies in prominent databases such as "Scopus," "Web of Science," and "SPORTDiscus" yielded limited results. One of the few contributions we found was a study by Sailofsky (2022), which analyzed Twitter reactions to a scandal involving two ice hockey players, Brendan Leipsic (formerly of the NHL Washington Capitals) and Jeremy Leipsic (formerly of the University of Manitoba Bisons), and other individuals in which a private conversation was leaked in May 2020 containing misogynistic and vulgar remarks about women. The study concluded that while most responses expressed disapproval of the players' behavior, a minority not only considered it acceptable but also claimed that the punishments suffered by the athletes were unjust, arguing that cancel culture went too far. Another notable study was conducted by Mesler et al. (2022), which examined the responses of athletes and brands to public calls for their cancelation due to perceived misconduct. The study suggested that the image of brands associated with athletes facing public cancelation is in a precarious position between standing with the athletes' side or the furious public.

These studies represent a recent scientific breakthrough in a topic with still plenty of perspectives to investigate. For instance, how does cancel culture manifest between rival institutions? What strategies do sports organizations employ to "cancel" each other? How do individuals, collectives with shared identities, and sports organizations react to institutional cancelation and counter-cancelation practices? This study addresses this newly emerging phenomenon of institutional canceling, of which we did not find publications in the literature, by focusing on the unfolding practices of "canceling" and "counter-canceling" between FCB and RM, both of which have been accusing each other of ties to the dark regime of Franco. Our study, therefore, is driven by the following three research questions:

1 How did the fans of FCB and RM respond to the mutual canceling practices between these clubs?
2 What were the institutional positions and motivations of FCB and RM in engaging with and navigating the cancel culture related to their associations with Franco's regime?

3 From an economic and brand image perspective, what were the tangible repercussions for FCB and RM due to their participation in institutional canceling related to their associations with Franco's regime?

Methods

Subscribing to the digital turn in the social sciences (see Marres, 2017), we have taken social media platforms as important places where socializations unfold. Among the different social media platforms available to professional sport for further spectacularizing, YouTube because of its historical technological affordances that prioritize horizontal videos can be considered a current alternative and future substitute for the most important medium to sport: television (see Lee Ludvigsen & Petersen-Wagner, 2022a). Historically the relationship between YouTube and professional sport has been recognized as involving remediation (see Deuze, 2006) where shorter content format was re-created based on the most valuable asset in sport/media, the live game, and match. Nevertheless, in the past decades, organizations related to sport such as international and national federations, leagues, brands, athletes, clubs, and broadcasters have recognized YouTube as an important medium for curating content that is both remediated from other media and also originally produced for this specific platform (Lee Ludvigsen & Petersen-Wagner, 2022a, 2022b; Petersen-Wagner & Lee Ludvigsen, 2022a, 2023; McCarthy, 2021). Moreover, distinctly from television where consumption is predominantly *passive* – in the sense that viewers are unable to directly interact back with the sender or with other viewers through the same medium – another technological affordance that YouTube allows users to perform is to *actively* consume through liking and commenting on videos, in a way affording moments for collective action (Petersen-Wagner & Lee Ludvigsen, 2022b; McCarthy, 2022). Therefore, YouTube's comments area becomes a place of significant value for understanding how to socialize or in this chapter's case – of canceling and counter-canceling – takes place.

As such, to comprehend how canceling has taken place in terms of RM and FCB institutional videos in relation to its association with the Franco regime, and the aftermath in terms of media coverage on Marca, we have employed YouTube Data Tools (Rieder, 2015) to connect to YouTube's Application Programming Interface (API v3) (YouTube, 2023a) and automatically scrap all comments from the three videos (see YouTube, 2023b, 2023c, 2023d). On 9th June 2023, we collected a total of 4,070 first-level comments and replies (262 on FCB's video, 2,899 on RM's video, and 909 on Marca's video), that went through a first stage data cleaning where one of the authors identified comments related to the research topic (*Franco, Franquismo, and Regime*). This data-cleaning process yielded a total of 243 comments and replies that became the center of our analysis. Those comments were predominantly in

Spanish, with a few in English and one in Catalan. For the presentation of results below, we have translated all comments to English and noted which ones were originally in another language.

On a second stage, we have employed a thematic analysis (Braun & Clarke, 2006) where four themes were identified. Those four themes related to (i) supporting the official counter-canceling by RM and re-writing history; (ii) mockery to reinforce official counter-canceling; (iii) fear, repression, and persecution as a response to counter-canceling; and (iv) accusing RM of whitewashing the history. While the four themes appeared predominantly on RM and Marca's videos, the first two are assumed to be written by RM supporters, and the final two are assumed to be written by FCB supporters. On a final moment, we have approached those themes through critical discourse analysis (Fairclough, 2010) as we understand that on a basic level words are powerful instruments in struggles for recognition (see Honneth, 1996), which we recognize to be potentialized in contexts of identity politics and cancel culture (Lewis & Christin, 2022).

Results

The Original Content – Analysis of the Videos Posted by FCB, RM, and Marca Newspaper

This investigation thoroughly examines three videos – two of institutional nature from FCB and RM, and one from Marca (Spanish Newspaper) – and their content that expose a series of attacks and counterattacks targeting the institutional reputation of RM and FCB, and the comments and replies left by users on those YouTube videos. These exchanges of assaults stem from accusations of intimate ties and preferential treatment by the authoritarian regime led by Francisco Franco in the 20th century. The conflict sparked during FCB's President Joan Laporta's April 17, 2023, press conference (YouTube, 2023b). In response to allegations made by the Barcelona provincial prosecutor's office, Laporta convocated journalists to publicly defend the club over the charges of persistent corruption in Spanish football. Specifically, FCB was accused of committing crimes of continuous false administration and continued falsification of commercial documents. These charges were related to allegedly illicit payments exceeding 7.3 million euros (equivalent to $7.8 million) directed toward José María Enríquez Negreira, a former vice president of the Spanish Referee Committee from 2001 and 2018. This committee holds the authority to assign referees and assistants for league and national competitive matches in Spain. The payments were allegedly made to secure FCB favorable referee decisions during matches, disguised under the guise of "technical video assessments" of referees' performances and disciplinary criteria (Grez, 2023).

Throughout the two-hour media conference streamed live on FCB's YouTube Channel and now available for on-demand consumption (YouTube, 2023b), which was watched by 114.847 thousand viewers by July 2, 2023, Laporta not only defended the club and what he quoted as the "sentiments of millions of Barcelona fans around the world" but presented hundreds of documents and accused the charges of an "illegal defamation campaign," a species of "public lynching" or a "smear campaign loaded of fake news" against the club's image and values. Laporta also directly attacked RM, which has asked to be included in the trial suggesting that the club was hindered with title losses during the period in which FCB allegedly paid Negreira. RM's stance was heavily criticized by Laporta, sustaining – without evidence (Grez, 2023) – that Spain's capital club has historically linked with refereeing favoritism and considered the club of Franco's regime:

> I want to refer to the presence of a club in the trial. A club that, on its own, appears as a private prosecutor in the trial. A club that says they feel negatively impacted in sporting terms. This club is the Real Madrid. A club that, as we all know, has been historically favored when it comes to refereeing decisions. Historically and currently. Whatever the reasons are, they have been favored. We all know that they have been favored by refereeing decisions. A club considered the team of the regime due to their proximity to power. I think it is worth remembering that, for seven decades, most of the presidents of the collective were, in consecutive terms, ex-socios, ex-players, or ex-directors of Real Madrid. The fact that this club presents itself and alleges to feel damaged in the greatest part of history seems to me like the biggest act of cynicism without any precedence, and I am confident that the judicial system will unmask it.
>
> *(YouTube, 2023b)*

Causing surprise over the sporting media (Martin & Southby, 2023), in a timely response on the same day, RM posted on its social media platforms – Facebook, Instagram, Twitter, and YouTube – a four-and-a-half-minute video titled "¿Cuál es el equipo del régimen?" (Which is the team of the regime?) (Real Madrid, 2023). The video can be accessed here: https://www.youtube.com/@realmadrid. It is important to note that this video was in Spanish without any English translation (YouTube, 2023c). By July 2, 2023, the video had garnered 254,443 views on RM's YouTube channel. The video, accompanied by dramatic classical violin music, begins by presenting Joan Laporta's accusations against RM at his press conference as the club of Franco's regime. These accusations are immediately juxtaposed with the video's bold title displayed in capitalized letters against a dark background.

The subsequent segments of the video comprise a series of statements supported by historical images and documents, drawing connections between

FCB and the Spanish dictator Francisco Franco. The first accusation presented in the video focuses on Camp Nou, FCB's stadium's inauguration in 1957. The video asserts that the stadium was inaugurated by Jose Solis Ruiz, the Minister Secretary-General of the Movement. As historical footage of the stadium's inauguration is shown, a narrative voiceover from NODO's ("News and Documentaries" – a state-controlled series of cinema newsreels) recounts the event in the following terms:

> The great stadium is going to open its doors, but before it does, here on its green grass, the auxiliary bishop of Barcelona, Doctor Jubany, will preside over a solemn mass. A religious ceremony that is the vivid feeling of spirituality and will serve to honor this man-made construction. The Minister Secretary-General of the Movement, Mr. José Solís Ruiz, on behalf of the Head of the State, will inaugurate the stadium of FC Barcelona. The minister is accompanied by the National Delegate for Physical Education and Sport, Mr. Elola. A beautiful symphony of color where the blue and garnet colors of this historic club merge perfectly with the red and yellow of the Spain flag, creating the ideal setting for this memorable act. It is handed to the members of the board of directors so they can pay homage when the president of FC Barcelona, Mr. Miró-Sans, raises aloft the Spanish flag to mark the field's official opening. In perfect synchrony, the national anthem of Spain is played, as if to salute the Spain flag, which unites every man in Spain.
>
> *(YouTube, 2023c)*

RM's second accusation revolved around FCB's alleged act of awarding Franco the Gold and Diamond Club Badge. The video supports this claim by highlighting recorded scenes of the ceremony; however, it does not specify the date when this event occurred. Subsequently, the video asserted that FCB named Franco an Honorary Member in 1965, again presenting recorded scenes featuring former FCB presidents and the Spanish dictator. Continuing their response, RM's video further claimed that FCB awarded Franco a medal on three separate occasions, followed by scenes of an official visit where FCB players can be seen shaking hands with the dictator. Another accusation by RM was that FCB was saved from bankruptcy three times thanks to Franco's reclassification of land. To substantiate this allegation, the video displays newspapers from that era with headlines reading "Franco clears Barcelona's debts" and "A Third Reclassification of Land." It also features a copy of Decree 2735 of 1965, including the name of Franco, responsible for one of the land reclassifications associated with FCB's stadium area. Moreover, photographs of players making the fascist salute before matches and in front of FCB's stadium, where a memorial displaying the regime's official motto, "*Caidos Por Dios y Por La Patria. Presentes*!" (Fallen for God and the Homeland. Here in Attendance!), are shown. Additionally, footage of Franco being applauded at Camp Nou was included (YouTube, 2023c)

RM's video also intended to demonstrate FCB's favoritism under the regime by emphasizing that "FC Barcelona won 8 leagues and 9 Spanish cups during Franco's regime." The video displayed images of Franco and his wife, Carmen Polo, presenting trophies to FCB captains at the stadium's tribune of honor. Furthermore, the video argued that, during Franco's regime, RM had to wait 15 years to secure a league title, despite omitting that the club had won the Spanish Cup in 1946 and 1947. To support this claim, the video included highlights of matches between RM and FCB in which FCB successfully scores goals against RM. In the last part of the video, RM highlighted the challenges the club faced during the Civil War, stating that "Real Madrid was dismantled" with assassinated, detained, or exiled players during that period. To provide further context, the video presents a historical narration from Santiago Bernabeu's documentary that delves into the state of RM immediately after the conflict:

> In 1939, Real Madrid was in a critical situation. The official headquarters had been destroyed in a bombing. The club's trophies had been stolen. The stands of the Chamartín Stadium had been stripped of all wood. Only five players remained from the original squad. The rest of the players had been exiled or detained by those who achieved victory.
>
> *(YouTube, 2023c)*

RM's video concludes with a quote from the legendary player and President Santiago Bernabéu whose name is after the club stadium: "*When I hear that 'Real Madrid has been the team of the regime,' I want to sh*t on the father of the person who says it.*" As this affirmation resounds, the video juxtaposes it with images portraying Franco once more welcoming FCB's delegation in the official state palace and presenting trophies to FCB captains at stadiums. The video finally ends with a final counterattack against FCB by reiterating the video's title, firmly asserting RM's stance that it was its main rival, the club of Franco's regime (YouTube, 2023c).

The third and last video analyzed in this study was published by Marca Newspaper on its YouTube channel on the same day (YouTube, 2023d). The Marca Newspaper is particularly known for its extensive coverage of the daily activities of football clubs like RM and Atlético Madrid. Established in 1938, in the nationalist-held city of San Sebastián, it is currently based in Madrid and has several international editions, broadening its reach beyond Spain (Marca, n.d.). The video's content was a full reproduction of RM's video, and 83.825 viewers watched it by July 2, 2023. FCB did not respond to RM's video, preferring to remain silent and make its history department available to its members and the public. FCB's stance was followed by the two main Catalan newspapers covering the club daily – "The Mundo Deportivo" and "SPORT." While SPORT did not publish a single video about the conflict, the Mundo Deportivo reproduced Laporta's press conference video. However, it only garnered five comments, none mentioning Franco and his regime (YouTube, 2023e). This latter newspaper engaged indirectly with RM's accusations as it posted a video defending the titles conquered by FCB in the 20th century that are currently under scrutiny due to the Negreira case. They even launched a campaign symbolized by the hashtag #TheShieldIsNotStained (YouTube, 2023f). Once more, none of the commentaries have displayed Franco and his regime. This lack of engagement and the absence of mentions to Franco in those videos and comments released provided the rationale for our decision to exclude the Catalan press from our study.

Discourse Analysis of User Comments across the Three Videos

Discourse analysis of user comments across all three videos sheds light on the growing presence of football fandom within online communities (Petersen-Wagner, 2017a, 2017b; Petersen-Wagner & Lee Ludvigsen, 2022b; Woods & Lee Ludvigsen, 2022) and its entanglement with local politics, as rival fans reinforced, including through mutual mockery and cancelation, distinct institutional versions of the Spanish past linked with the Spanish Civil War and Franco's regime promoted by their respective clubs. Significantly, results revealed strong support for RM's official response (aka counter-canceling) against FCB, which was seen as a legitimate and long-awaited reaction to the ongoing social, cultural, political, and sporting accusations (aka canceling) made by the so-called "Catalan Narratives" (Vogel, 2017) linking RM's historical successes to Franco's regime. This type of fan support reflects the broader processes and mechanisms of group identification and identity preservation inherent in sports, notably in football (Porat, 2010). On the other side, FCB fans have responded to RM's video in two distinct ways, undermining its value and credibility by reducing offensiveness of the acts through notions of fear, repression, and persecution, and accusing the rival club of whitewashing its own historical links with the Franco regime. Inasmuch those comments are not *official communication* by the clubs themselves, but as their institutional regime is of associative clubs, it is possible to argue that the strategies employed by FCB's fans reflect those presented by Benoit (2015) in terms of public relations, crisis management, and image repair. While many fans acknowledged the accuracy of the video's content but justified the club's support and awards to Franco and his regime (and vice-versa) by highlighting the coercive nature of the dictatorial era (Richards, 2013), suggesting that the club, as an ideological rival of the regime, was compelled to praise and honor the "Spanish Caudillo," other considerable groups of supporters accuse the video of manipulating and distorting history, labeling it as a form of "fake news."

Supporting Official Counter-Canceling While Reinterpreting History

Initially, as seen below, RM supporters' comments strongly support the video released by their club, in absolute jubilation to finally be able to counterattack and dispute the claims spread by Catalans and FCB fans of Franco's ownership and influence over the RM's sporting success throughout the dictatorship period.

Supporter #1: *"Finally, the TRUTH is being said. FC ROBALONA was the most favored team during Franco's era, winning the most leagues during Franco's rule and being the most corrupt." (Originally in Spanish)*

Supporter #2: *"They showed evidence of who the club of Franco is. This narrative generated since the 1950s has ended, the truth always comes to light. Greetings." (Originally in Spanish)*

Supporter #3: *"Barcelona's Franco lie has come to an end. They should come up with another one." (Originally in Spanish)*

Supporter #4: *"Don't remove this video, this video is great. Let them eat their words. Enough with saying that Madrid is the team of the regime. It's not just Laporta who says it, but also the separatists, who are far from reality." (Originally in Spanish)*

Supporter #5: *"Real Madrid didn't honor Franco, didn't name him an honorary member, and didn't save him from bankruptcy three times. Barcelona did. So, it's strange that being the team of the regime, as the Barcelona president says, Madrid didn't do it. Don't you think? The lie of Barcelona being anti-Franco has come to an end. They were only 'anti-Franco' after Franco's death, like all the cowards and miserable ones. But while Franco was alive, they honored him to obtain favors." (Originally in Spanish)*

Within these comments, the vital element of identity formation – "the other" (Alabarces, 1998) – and the consequent emergence of a dichotomy between "us" and "them" emerged (see also Giulianotti & Armstrong, 2001). Drawing from social identity theory , which examines identity from a collective viewpoint and focuses on how people position themselves relative to ingroups and outgroups, RM supporters by responding positively to RM's video demonstrated a predictable exercise of differentiation from FCB supporters, particularly considering the new evidence surrounding Franco's regime. The "Madridistas," as the supporters of RM are called in Spain (Oliveira & Capraro, 2020), established new notions of truth and falsehood over Spanish football during Franco's dictatorship after the disclosure of RM's video. In other words, RM supporters detach FCB (and its supporters) from the "righteous" side of history, i.e., one of an untouchable and clean example of resistance to Franco's regime, attempting to finally debunk and counter-cancel the "Catalan Narratives" (Vogel, 2017) while rewriting what for them is a crucial version of a common past that continues to influence their personal and group identities as RM supporters. As identified in the following theme, aligned with patterns observed in the literature, the comments and responses from RM supporters led to the formation of groups' discriminatory practices, the creation of stereotypes, and the development of social prejudices against "the other" (in this case, FCB) (Chun & Sagas, 2022).

Fans' Mockery as a Counter Canceling Culture Reinforcement

The use of derogatory language and mocking statements toward FCB has been prevalent among supporters of RM. This mockery reinforced the counter-canceling effect promoted by RM's video while boosting attacks on FCB's reputation and fan base. RM supporters have played with words to create a new stereotype and associate FCB with Franco's regime, using terms such as "Barçaregimen" and "Francolona." One called the club "Basuralona," a term to convey a lack of moral integrity toward FCB, as "basura" in Spanish means "trash." Furthermore, it was possible to identify mockery aimed at the world-famous FCB's motto "More than a club," which is currently embraced by FCB as a historical symbol of political resistance toward Franco's persecution and in defense of Catalan identity and culture as well as to convey the club's social influence in Catalunya (Oliveira & Capraro, 2020). Other supporters ironically refer to Franco as FCB's "sugar daddy" and the "son of Negreira and grandson of Franco" to accuse the club of receiving tangible and intangible benefits on and off the field throughout its history.

Supporter #6: *"Greetings to the 'Barcaregimen'!" (Originally in Spanish)*
Supporter #7: *"F. C Francolona" (Originally in Spanish)*
Supporter #8: *"Shameless Franconalona" (Originally in Spanish)*
Supporter #9: *Of course, during Franco's regime, which saved them from bankruptcy. And now, it's the separatist Andorran regime of Negreira. Different regime, same corruption. Simply Basuralona. (Originally in Spanish)*
Supporter #10: *"Barcelona is more than a club, home of Francoism." (Originally in Spanish)*
Supporter #11: *"Sons of Negreira and grandsons of Franco." (Originally in Spanish)*

Other supporters have developed distinct tactics of mockery to diminish FCB's reputation and brought to the counter-canceling movement historical facts uncovered on RM's video as evidence of FCB's gratitude and recognition toward Franco during his rule. In this point, comments from RM supporters copied and pasted official communications published in the Catalan newspaper *La Vanguardia* during the 1950s and 1960s, where former FCB presidents expressed their honor to be in the presence of Franco and aligned the club with the values of the "Spanish Caudillo." The controversial Law of Historic Memory enacted in 2007 during the Spanish Socialist Workers Party (PSOE) term also was brought up to provoke FCB. The Spanish Law 5 of 2007 intended the recognize the victims of the Spanish Civil War who "fought for the defense of democratic values, including the members of the Republican Police Corps, the Communist International Brigade members, and the militia fighters," and the persecution and violence committed by Franco's regime during its dictatorship regime. As this law also called for the prohibition of public celebrations of Franco's memory and the removal of symbols associated with his figure from public spaces (Tobar, 2023), one supporter, in a mocking tone, suggested that Camp Nou, FCB's stadium, which was allegedly inaugurated thanks to the support of Franco's regime, should also face the same fate and be demolished.

Supporter #12: *"His Excellency the Head of State receives CF Barcelona at El Pardo. The Generalissimo warmly congratulates the president of Barcelona for those magnificent victories... The very cordial interview concludes with the Barcelona president expressing the club's recognition and support for the person of the Caudillo. La Vanguardia Española, 27/11/1952." (Originally in Spanish)*

Supporter #13: *"Through these words and through La Vanguardia, I deeply and publicly thank the Caudillo, on behalf of the Football Club Barcelona, for the honor he bestows upon us with his presence at our stadium in the grand Cup Final (Enrique Llaudet, president of CF Barcelona). LVE, 26/6/1966." (Originally in Spanish)*

Supporter #14: *"From here, I formally request, under the protection granted by the Law of Historical Memory, that Camp Nou be demolished for being a monument built by Franco." (Originally in Spanish)*

In a manner evocative of the offensive chants exchanged between rival football supporters during live matches at Santiago Bernabéu or Camp Nou stadium, FCB fans, including many who are not Catalans or even Spaniards, have fostered an online environment to fervently uphold the honor, image, and reputation of their globally popular club, much like Laporta did during his press conference. FCB supporters' comments on RM's institutional video (YouTube, 2023b) and Marca's (YouTube, 2023c) YouTube channel triggered two different ways of comprehending and responding to RM's counterattack, thus constituting the next two themes of this study.

Fear, Repression, and Persecution: Explaining FCB's Compliance with Franco's Regime

While Benoit's (2015) theoretical and practical study on image repair strategies, when individuals or organizations face persuasive attacks that damage one's reputation, focuses predominantly on how justifications, excuses, and/or apologies are given by attacked individuals or organizations themselves, in our case, as football fans who consider themselves as *symbolic owners* of their teams (see Belk, 1988), they might feel compelled to provide such replies. According to Benoit (2015), the response can either reject or reduce one's responsibility, reduce the offensiveness of the blame, or finally accept the accusation and apologize from any wrongdoing. Amongst the available *reducing offensiveness* strategies there are six different variants, being them: (i) bolstering; (ii) minimization; (iii) differentiation; (iv) transcendence; (v) attacking one's accuser; and (vi) compensation (Benoit, 2015). Important to our discourse analysis three of those variants are apparent in both theme 3 (Fear, Repression, and Persecution – minimization and transcendence) and theme 4 (whitewashing RM's past – attacking one's accuser).

In terms of minimizing importance, Benoit (2015) argues that a successful repair strategy involves showing how an attitude or behavior is not as bad as it first appeared. In terms of our discourse analysis, that appeared when FCB fans uttered that the actions taken by the club during the Franco regime were based on fear, repression, and persecution if the club did not comply with the regime's desires. Moreover, as the Franco regime is brought into discussion in those utterances, those fans seek to use a form of transcendence to demonstrate that those actions were born out of the historical context in Spain and, consequently, would have been different in another scenario. While not challenging the accuracy of the information presented in RM's video, supporters of FCB put into doubt its real legitimacy, questioning whether the club's leadership at the time willingly complied with Franco's regime, considering the oppressive nature of Franco's dictatorship, which curtailed individual and collective rights, including freedom of speech. Employing a similar tactic of mockery toward their main rivals while maintaining their historically defended position of RM as being the club of the regime, they engage in discussions about how FCB, driven by fear of reprisals and the need for survival, had no choice but to comply with Franco's alleged demands, such as paying respects to him before matches and awarding him medals. While one supporter reminded the death of Josep Sunyol, former President of FCB, in 1936, one international fan from India drew parallels with his oppressed compatriots when India was under British rule.

Supporter #15: *"Now it turns out that Franco was a Barça fan, haha, what nonsense. Everything is invalidated because there are no freedoms in a dictatorship. Can you imagine if they didn't invite the oppressive government to the Camp Nou inauguration? Either you invited them, or the reprisals could be tremendous. I can't imagine the inauguration being done by Lluis Companys (basically because Franco had him executed)." (Originally in Spanish)*

Supporter #16: *"Educate yourselves on the topic. Barça was forced to honor Franco, or else they would be executed. They killed a president of Barça. Get informed." (Originally in Spanish)*

Supporter #17: *"He literally used to call Real Madrid the symbol of his regime and Spain. Barça did whatever they did to survive. You must do that when you are subjugated. Real Madrid was always the favorite; it's a proven fact that you will ignore because of your bias..." (Originally in Spanish)*

Supporter #18: *"Do you really think that what Barcelona did (salute Franco, gave him a medal, etc.) was out of love for him? They had to do it for survival. I'm from India, and even we did the same thing for the British for our survival."*

The comments consistently echoed the well-established historiography of Catalonia referenced in the literature review, reinforcing the argument that Franco held disdain for FCB due to its symbolic association with Catalan culture, which was seen as contrary to his vision of a centralized Spanish nation, including within the realm of Spanish football. The comments also highlighted Franco's authority to appoint the board of FCB during the entire dictatorship, underscoring his complete control over the club and emphasizing the perceived need to regulate FCB, which was and continues to be a symbol of Catalan identity (Usall, 2021).

Supporter #19: *"Franco installed his own people in charge of Barcelona – the president, board members, all were supporters of Franco. He banned Catalan, changed the club's name, even changed the crest. Barcelona did what it had to do to survive. Comparing an enslaved Barça and its enslaved board members and president to Franco's favoritism? Yeah, right..." (Originally in Spanish)*

Supporter #20: *"This video is shameful. I'm not Catalan, but I do know history. It is known that Franco forced the Barcelona directors to award him those medals. Catalonia was one of the regions that suffered the most because it not only experienced the dictatorship that was present throughout Spain but also faced attempts to annihilate Catalan culture. They even forbade Catalans from speaking their own language. I think it's disgraceful to compare and present a video like this, knowing that everything Franco did with Barcelona was to make the people of Catalonia believe that Barca was a friend of Franco. Even a fool who isn't from Spain knows that." (Originally in Spanish)*

While the previous excerpts shed light on the nuanced dynamics between FCB and Franco's regime, acknowledging the alleged coercive control exerted by Franco and recognizing the survival instincts of the club and its supporters, a significant number of supporters took a different stance, challenging the historical accuracy of RM's video despite the evidence presented through videos, photos, and documents. This group of supporters positioned themselves at the other extreme of the rivalry spectrum between FCB and RM, including in relation to other FCB supporters who attributed the club's awards to Franco to the undemocratic circumstances of the dictatorship period. They argued that RM's video itself is a conspiracy, entirely diverging from the widely accepted narrative, evidencing the existence of differing interpretations and perspectives among supporters, and highlighting the complex nature of historical analysis and the influence of individual biases and football allegiances.

"White Washing" the History: Real Madrid's Propaganda and Manipulation

As aforementioned, another of Benoit's (2015) reducing offensiveness strategy involves attacking one's accuser that entails reducing the damage of accusations by challenging the credibility of the source. In some instances, this strategy works by highlighting that the accuser could also be a *victim* of what it has been accusing others, as in our case this appears when FCB fans discursively remind us that RM has profited from Franco's regime. Therefore, what underlines this strategy employed by FCB fans is making visible a whitewashing practice by RM in its video. In our context, whitewashing refers to RM's strategic maneuver to counteract its negative historical association as "the club of the regime." When RM counters its rival, it intends to transfer its negative image created by what they considered "Catalan Narratives," linked to the Franco regime, onto FCB. This strategic shift primarily serves to cleanse RM's image from its ties to Franco, and, in a less favorable case scenario, at least distributes the burden of association with the dictatorship between itself and its main rival. FCB supporters harshly criticize the video's portrayal of the relationship between their club and the regime, claiming the manipulation of history and the dissemination of misleading information, and consequently accusing RM of propagating propaganda and whitewashing their history with General Francisco Franco.

Supporter #21: *"What a joke, hahahaha! How you distort history. Real Madrid is the greatest team in history, that's why it's normal for them to receive favors unintentionally. Saying that Barcelona is the team of the regime makes no sense." (Originally in Spanish)*

Supporter #22: *"Hahaha, what a big manipulation. Franco was never an honorary member of Barcelona, that's a lie." (Originally in Spanish)*

Supporter #23: *"Pure propaganda whitewashing yourselves with Papa Franco." (Originally in Spanish)*

While reinforcing the narrative of manipulation consistent across several supporters' comments and replies, other FCB fans extended the comprehension of manipulation to the intentional omission of historical facts that harmed FCB and benefited RM throughout the Spanish Civil War and Franco's dictatorship. These supporters denounced that the persecution suffered by FCB under Franco's regime, including the murder of former President Josep Sunyol and the imposition of regime-backed presidents at the club for many years, was not acknowledged. They also criticized the lack of acknowledgment of Franco's influence on RM's sporting success and their numerous titles, which was allegedly possible by the facilitation of foreign players' nationalizations, deliberate efforts to facilitate to RM the signing of striker Alfredo Di Stefano, and not opposing to the presence of RM associates exerting influence on the Technical Committee of Referees of the Spanish Football Federation.

Supporter #24: *"The part where at that time Barça had a republican president murdered by Franco and that Franco himself imposed one of his men as president of Barça is conveniently omitted, isn't it? It's a key part of history that you don't mention. It's a shame that a team like Madrid manipulates in this way." (Originally in Spanish)*

Supporter #25: *"Showing videos without explaining the context of that era is very dishonest and easy... Why would you manipulate history so much by showing videos without explaining the context??? If FC Barcelona was truly the club of the regime, why did FIFA press for Di Stefano to be signed by*

Madrid??? If FC Barcelona was truly the club of the regime, why were the presidents of the Technical Committee members and associates of Real Madrid? ... The lie visibly never ends with Real Madrid..." (Originally in Spanish)

Supporter #26: "And let's see how many European cups, Spanish nationalized players to help Madrid, how many leagues they won during Franco's era, and how many suspicious plays occurred. Are they going to tell me that Franco was pro-Catalan to help Barcelona? What a joke! What a way to manipulate history. But of course, Hala Madrid and nothing else, right? Exactly." (Originally in Spanish)

The criticism regarding the selective and intentionally incomplete presentation of historical events during Franco's regime was evident. Few supporters have particularly used extreme comparisons to make their points heard. While supporter #27 expressed it in strong terms, stating, "*This is extremely shameful already. Denying the favors of Francoism and the regime towards Madrid is like saying that Germany and Italy were never fascist; it is their birthmark*" (*Originally in Spanish),* supporter (#28) stated that if "*Real Madrid was not the club of the regime, then Hitler was Jewish,*" *(Originally in Spanish).* Moreover, supporter (#29) ironically said, "*I get it now, Franco was a Barcelona supporter and independentist. What a team of the regime*" *(Originally in Spanish).* Importantly, as viewed, while these supporters argue that the success of RM during Franco's regime should be attributed to the support of the ruling powers, they simultaneously deny the possibility of FCB being considered "the club of the regime." In this exchange of canceling and conflicting narratives, FCB supporters reject the new notions of truth and falsehood promoted by RM's video, backed up effusively by *Madridistas* in the comments sections of the videos analyzed. In an apparent reaction to preserve their emotional attachments to the club and reinforce their collective identity and narrative as FCB supporters, they continue to uphold their belief that FCB could never be even considered the club of the regime but only a symbol of resistance to Franco's dictatorship.

Discussion and Conclusion

The growing number of cancel culture incidents related to sports on Western social media platforms, including YouTube – the digital media platform examined in this chapter – has surprisingly not been covered at a similar pace within the academic field of sports management. This chapter contributes to advancing the sport management literature by illuminating a unique case of institutional canceling involving RM and FCB. Our initial aim was to identify and discuss the impacts of the online confrontations on supporters' reactions to the allegations linking their clubs with Franco's regime. We also seek to understand the motivations behind FCB and RM engaging in the culture of social media canceling and comprehend their official institutional positions in managing the ensuing repercussions and the practical consequences from economic and brand/image perspectives.

While Benoit's (2015) work on image repair theory about the stance of individuals and organizations under persuasive image and reputational attacks has been keen to understand the ownership feelings by FCB supporters and their consequent exploration of three strategies – minimization, transcendence, and attacking the accuser – to reduce offensiveness and the potential damage to their club's history, image, and values inflicted by RM's video, such psychological reactions could likely be comprehended through the lenses of "cognitive dissonance theory" (Festinger, 1957). Cognitive dissonance, a form of psychological discomfort, is aroused when people encounter information that contradicts their beliefs (Harmon-Jones & Mills, 2019). Under this circumstance, individuals or groups intend to alleviate the discomfort by rejecting or refuting the information responsible for establishing dissonance or attempting other individuals or groups to accept the challenged belief by introducing (new) information consonant with those beliefs – an approach known as the "belief-disconfirmation paradigm" (Harmon-Jones & Mills, 2019).

Applying such theory to the case of FCB supporters' comments illustrated on themes #3 and #4 and the fact that historical evidence shows legal and financial benefits given by Franco's regime to FCB, we can understand supporters' resistance as a form of cognitive dissonance, which goes beyond minimization, transcendence, and singular attacks to the accuser (Benoit, 2015). The video released by RM, which presented tangible and intangible benefits and awards exchanged between FCB and Franco's regime, created significant cognitive dissonance among FCB supporters. This dissonance challenged their deeply and collectively ingrained belief that their club, particularly during Franco's regime, was a beacon of freedom, integrity, and opposition to Spanish authoritarian regimes. The intentional reinforcement of the belief that RM's video was a work of manipulation of history evident in FCB supporters' comments and replies (see comments by supporters #21, 22, and 23), along with the defense for the perspective of FCB as a victim in an attempt to dissociate the club from Franco's regime favors (see comments by supporters #15, 16, 17, 18, 19 and 24), apparently served as a mechanism to reduce cognitive dissonance among them. By denying the historical facts presented in RM's video – a counterattack to the historically powerful and dominant "Catalan Narratives" (Vogel, 2017) that portrayed RM as the regime's club – FCB supporters were able to realign their beliefs and maintain their emotional attachment to their club.

These acts of reducing or eliminating cognitive dissonance prompted by FCB supporters entailed activating a "confirmation bias" psychological mechanism, an unconscious tendency that activates distinctive cognition (Peters, 2022). Also called "myside bias" (Mercier & Sperber, 2017), it is, in other words, the tendency of individuals to search for information to support their beliefs and ignore or distort data contradicting them. Highly prevalent in cases of "fake news" (Stibel, 2018), when identified in cases where a group's ideological preconceptions are challenged (Norman, 2016), such as in the case of FCB supporters in light of the discoveries related to Franco's regime, confirmation bias is prompt to create or foster group polarization making extremely hard any alignment with groups who holds dissonant beliefs (Peters, 2022), as is the case of RM supporters. Considering the comments of both RM and FCB supporters, it seems plausible to advocate for the idea that cognitive dissonance and confirmation bias strengthened their respective fan bases' collective identities and "team identification" (Chun & Sagas, 2022).

The concept of "identity work," which underscores the process of shaping, restoring, maintaining, strengthening, or modifying one's self-meanings (Alvesson & Willmott, 2002), is influenced by interpersonal relationships and social factors and contexts (Chun & Sagas, 2022). It seems reasonable to suggest that FCB supporters employed coping strategies to safeguard their collective identity as fans of a club that, in their view, has always defended democracy, freedom, and pro-Catalonia independence sentiments. This defensive mechanism prevented the evidence of Franco's regime's benefits to the club from being considered valid or legitimate, primarily because it would directly impact their collective and, by extension, personal identities as FCB supporters. Conversely, it also seems legitimate to affirm that RM's video represented a new public identity for their supporters, i.e., allowing them to finally detach their selves from the (exclusive) label of supporters of "the regime's club." This sentiment brought an online exclusion act of "othering" from RM supporters that displayed mockery behavior toward FCB supporters, as illustrated in themes #1 and #2, which strengthened their personal and collective identities by defining themselves in relation to what they do not identify with – "supporters of the regime's club."

By looking at the rear mirror of FCB's history, notably the revoking of all awards given to Franco during the 20th century in 2019 based on being given because of the existence of a dictatorship, thus, under apparent obligation, and the following lack of information about these historical facts at its stadium tour and museum (Tobar, 2023), facilitates the comprehension that FCB will not engage in any admission of "wrong-doing" (Burke, 1970) related to its past associated with Franco. FCB's decision to remain silent after the release of RM's video reinforces the club's deliberate effort to reduce the discomfort caused by their main rivals, which promoted dissonance by offering an alternative reinterpretation of the dominant meanings, symbols, and values associated with Franco's past and the history of FCB. The intentional institutional forgetting promoted by FCB about Franco's benefits in the club's history and heritage ultimately contributes to a better understanding of the strong collective manifestation defense from its fan base of the club's immaculate image. Naturally influenced by polarization effects, FCB's stance – and that of its fans in the observed online eco-chambers who called for the spread of "white-washing," aka "fake news" – suggests that the club believes there is nothing to repair in its institutional image. This perspective gives space to advocate the intentional establishment of a "post-truth" scenario (Gonçalves, 2018), where history is distorted to favor a particular narrative, in this case, the criticized "Catalan Narratives" (Vogel, 2017), where RM is the "real" club of Franco's regime.

This conflictive and polarized scenario that prevents mutual acknowledgment and the establishment of common ground, where RM and FCB admit their political and institutional relationships with Franco's regime, can be attributed to the ongoing struggle within Spanish society to reconcile with the legacy of the Spanish Civil War and Franco's regime (See Tobar, 2023). Following Franco's regime's end in 1975, during the so-called "Spanish Transition," politicians opted for a "pact of oblivion" (Pichel, 2019), negatively impacting discussions about the roles various parties and groups played during the Spanish Civil War and Franco's regime. For example, a 2008 survey from *The Centro de Investigaciones Sociológicas* (Sociological Research Center), an independent entity under the Ministry of the Presidency, revealed that half of Spaniards agreed with nullifying the political trials of the dictatorship, and 55% supported the removal of symbols glorifying or paying tribute to Francoism (Medina, 2018). Spain has yet to establish a national public museum to discuss the Spanish Civil War (Parrón, 2019) or commemorate the atrocities committed under Franco's regime, including torture and murder (Cardona & Rojo-Ariza, 2011). Such a unique sociocultural and political environment demonstrates how the generations of Spaniards post-Spanish Civil War still deal radically differently with official responsibilities and moral acceptance of guilt and how the civil conflict continues to form part of the political identity of the country, which is far from achieving a consensus (Pichel, 2019).

Given the intertwined nature of politics and football identities in Spain, the challenges in assessing with neutrality Franco's regime's impact on RM and FCB – two social institutions carrying distinct political symbolism (Oliveira & Capraro, 2020) – including their respective fan bases are unsurprising. As this case reveals, cancel culture on social media involving sports with higher levels of partisanship, like football, can be driven by tribalism (Knijnik & Newson, 2021) that constantly duel on and off the field from distinct political identity positions and perspectives. Remarkably, while increasing the magnitude of the discussions and activities of canceling and counter-canceling on social media, the identified high sports partisanship paradoxically reduces the impact of practical effects of canceling culture among sporting fan bases. This is again explained by the above-commented psychological mechanisms that tend to reject the "other's version" as a possible or valid "truth." Post-canceling and counter-canceling attack repercussions evidenced that RM and FCB have not lost partnerships or sponsorships, nor their supporters declared – circumscribed to the three videos analyzed – that they would stop supporting and consuming their club's brands because of the institutional conflict between clubs. On the contrary, fanatical support was given to the narratives promoted by these clubs, with supporters not boycotting brands associated with their respective clubs nor canceling sponsors of their main rivals – a very distinctive scenario compared to cases of social media canceling and dropping sponsorship deals discussed in the literature review section.

Final contributions promoted by the study center on offering a new understanding of cancel culture in sports by evidencing mutual cancelation between sports organizations on social media platforms, thus, justifying, especially, the use of the term "counter-canceling" along the chapter. The study also significantly contributes to the advancement of literature by exploring how social media constitutes an extension of the stadium's stands for fans to express their opinions, engage in public discourse, and participate in the viral spread of cancel culture (Lee Ludvigsen & Petersen-Wagner, 2022b). The "glocalized" (see Giulianotti & Robertson, 2004) nature of RM and FCB only potentiated the local conflict involving historical Spanish nationalism and regionalism identities and the subsequent struggles of getting to terms with the Spanish Civil War and Franco's regime to achieve a global reach since international supporters also participated on cancelation practices. The contemporary global and cosmopolitan characteristics of sports (Petersen-Wagner, 2017a, 2017b) suggest that researchers studying social media cancelation should remain open to scenarios that deviate from traditional consequences spread on Western social media canceling (e.g., sponsorship losses, damages to institutional brands and images, and reduction or loss of fan base support), given the intricate interplay of different cultures, sociopolitical contexts, supporters' collective identities, and team identifications inherent in these cases.

References

Alabarces, P. (1998). Lo que el estado no da, el fútbol no lo presta: los discursos nacionalistas deportivos en contextos de exclusión social. Paper presented at the XXI Congreso de la Latin American Studies Association (LASA), Chicago.

Alvesson, M., & Willmott, H. (2002). Identity regulation as organizational control: Producing the appropriate individual. *Journal of Management Studies*, *39*(5), 619–644.

Arias, A. (2018). Cuatro "Momentos Institucionales" Del Presidente Del C. De F. Barcelona, D. Enrique Llaudet Ponsá. *Saltataulells*. https://saltataulells.com/fuentes-secundarias/cuatro-momentos-institucionales-del-presidente-del-barcelona-enrique-llaudet-ponsa/

Arias, A. (2021a). Presidentes Falangistas Del Barcelona. *Saltataulells*. https://saltataulells.com/fuentes-primarias/presidentes-falangistas-del-barcelona/

Arias, A. (2021b). Sobre El Catalán Y El Franquismo. *Saltataulells*. https://saltataulells.com/fuentes-primarias/sobre-el-catalan-y-el-franquismo/

Arias, A. (2023). Toda las veces, que el barcelonismo fue "obligado" a realizar acciones franquistas que no estaban en su espíritu, catalán, republicano y democrático. *Saltataulells*.https://saltataulells.com/fuentes-primarias/toda-las-veces-que-el-barcelonismo-fue-obligado-a-realizar-acciones-franquistas-que-no-estaban-en-su-espiritu-catalan-republicano-y-democratico/

Belk, R. W. (1988). Possessions and the extended self. *Journal of Consumer Research*, *15*(2), 139–168.

Benoit, W. (2015). *Accounts, Excuses, and Apologies: Image Repair Theory and Research* (2nd ed.). State University of New York Press.

Best YouTube Channels by Football Clubs. (n.d.). Retrieved 07/06//2023 from https://www.tubics.com/industries/football-clubs

Braun, V., & Clarke, V. (2006). Using thematic analysis in psychology. *Qualitative Research in Psychology*, *3*(2), 77–101.

Burke, K. (1970). *Rhetoric of Religion*. University of California Press.

Burns, J. (1999). *Barça: la pasión de un pueblo*. Anagrama.

Cardona, F. X. H., & Rojo-Ariza, M. C. (2011). Museïtzació de conflictes contemporanis: El cas de la Guerra Civil espanyola [Musealization of contemporary conflicts: The case of the Spanish Civil War]. *Ebre 38: Revista Internacional de La Guerra Civil (1936–1939)*, 6, 131–157.

Castells, M. (2015). *Networks of Outrage and Hope: Social Movements in the Internet Age* (2nd ed.). Polity Press.

Choe, B. (2020). Colin Kaepernick Rejects Independence Day Celebration in Tweet. *Deadline*. https://deadline.com/2020/07/colin-kaepernick-rejects-independence-day-celebration-in-tweet-1202977633/

Chun, Y., & Sagas, M. (2022). Integrated fan identity: Theoretical framework and conceptualization. *Sports Innovation Journal*, *3*, 45–60.

CIES Football Observatory. (2023). *Social Media: Real ahead of Barcelona*. https://football-observatory.com/WeeklyPost426

Cleland, J., Doidge, M., Millward, P., & Widdop, P. (2017). *Collective Action and Football Fandom: A Relational Sociological Approach* (1st ed.). Palgrave.

Conversi, D. (1997). *The Basques, the Catalans and Spain*. Hurst.

Deuze, M. (2006). Participation, remediation, bricolage: Considering principal components of a digital culture. *The Information Society: An International Journal*, *22*(2), 63–75.

Díaz, J. M. (2016). Ochenta aniversario inicio Guerra Civil que casi destruye al Barça. *Sport*. https://www.sport.es/es/noticias/barca/ochenta-aniversario-inicio-guerra-civil-que-casi-destruye-barca-5274664

Dun, S., Rachdi, H., Memon, S. A., Pillai, R. K., Mejova, Y., & Weber, I. (2022). Perceptions of FIFA men's world cup 2022 host nation Qatar in the twittersphere. *International Journal of Sport Communication*, *15*(3), 197–206.

Duncan, S. (2023). No vax, no entry: Understanding Australia's rejection of Novak Djokovic. *Sport, Ethics and Philosophy*, *17*(2), 143–161.

Edouard, W. (2021). The Houston Astros' cheating scandal: A case study on crisis communication in sports. In *BSU Honors Program Theses and Projects*. Item 469. Available at: https://vc.bridgew.edu/honors_proj/469

Escobar, C. J. (2021). The billion-dollar tweet: Assessing the impact of the fallout between the NBA and China. *Sports Lawyers Journal*, *28*, 1.

Espinosa, J. S. (2014). El legado histórico franquista y el mercado de trabajo en España. *Revista Española de Sociología*, *21*, 99–128.

Expósito, J. F. N. (2020). *El presidente del Real Madrid más ignorado y desconocido: Juan José Vallejo González (1912–1978)*. https://www.cihefe.es/cuadernosdefutbol/2020/04/el-presidente-del-real-madrid-mas-ignorado-y-desconocido-juan-jose-vallejo-gonzalez-1912-1978/

Fairclough, N. (2010). *Critical Discourse Analysis: The Critical Study of Language* (2nd ed.). Longman.

Farràs, J. P. (2021). Catalonia in the face of the USSR: Soviet intervention in the Spanish civil war, 1936–9. *Journal of Contemporary History*, *56*(4), 1061–1083.

Festinger, L. (1957). *A Theory of Cognitive Dissonance*. Stanford University Press.

Fitzpatrick, D., & Hoey, P. (2022). From fanzines to foodbanks: Football fan activism in the age of anti-politics. *International Review for the Sociology of Sport*, *57*(8), 1234–1252.

Fitzpatrick, R. (2012). *El Clasico: Barcelona V Real Madrid: Football's Greatest Rivalry*. Bloomsbury Publishing.

García-Soler, J. (2019). *La Memoria Histórica, el Barça y el monasterio de Montserrat*. El Plural. https://www.elplural.com/autonomias/barca-medallas-francisco-franco-memoria-historica-jordi-garcia-soler_225392102

García, A. A. (2022). *Turón, ¿campo de concentración republicano de trabajo o de exterminio?* El Debate. https://www.eldebate.com/historia/20220529/turon-campo-concentracion-republicano-trabajo-exterminio.html

Gifford, C. (2023). *Real Madrid*. https://www.britannica.com/topic/Real-Madrid

Giulianotti, R., & Armstrong, G. (2001). Afterword: Constructing social identities; Exploring the structured relations of football rivalries. In G. Armstrong & R. Giulianotti (Eds.), *Fear and Loathing in World Football*. Berg.

Giulianotti, R., & Robertson, R. (2004). The globalization of football: A study in the glocalization of 'serious life'. *The British Journal of Sociology*, *55*(4), 545–568.

Gonçalves, J. (2018). Composed and decomposed pasts: Cultural heritage on memory and no-memory times. *Revista Sillogés*, *1*(1), 61–74.

González Calleja, E. (2014). El Real Madrid, ¿"equipo de España"? Fútbol e identidades durante el franquismo. *Política y Sociedad*, *51*(2), 275–296.

Grez, M. (2023). *Real Madrid and Barcelona in War of Words over Spain's Fascist Past*. https://www.cnn.com/2023/04/19/football/real-madrid-barcelona-referee-scandal-franco-regime-spt-intl/index.html

Gunther, R., Sani, G., & Shabad, G. (1986). *Spain after Franco*. University of California Press.

Harmon-Jones, E., & Mills, J. (2019). An introduction to cognitive dissonance theory and an overview of current perspectives on the theory. In E. Harmon-Jones (Ed.), *Cognitive Dissonance: Reexamining a Pivotal Theory in Psychology* (2nd ed., pp. 3–24). American Psychological Association. https://doi.org/10.1037/0000135-001

Hartzell, K. (2023). Sportswashing and the liv golf tour. In N. Brown-Devlin, J. McClearen, & M. Butterworth (Eds.), *Second Annual Politics in Sports Media Report | Moody College of Communication*. Texas University. Retrieved 07/07/2023 from https://moody.utexas.edu/centers/sports-communication-media/second-annual-politics-sports-media-report

Honneth, A. (1996). *The Struggle for Recognition: The Moral Grammar of Social Conflicts* (J. Anderson, Trans., 1st ed.). Polity Press.

Jackson, S. J., Bailey M., & Welles, B. F. (2020). *#HashtagActivism: Networks of Race and Gender Justice*. The MIT Press.

Jenkins, H. (2006). *Convergence Culture: Where Old and New Media Collide* (1st ed.). New York University Press.

Kassing, J. W. (2019). "Mes Que un Club" and an empty camp Nou: A case study of strategic ambiguity and Catalan nationalism at football club Barcelona. *International Journal of Sport Communication*, *12*(2), 260–274. https://doi.org/10.1123/ijsc.2018-0097

Keeley, G. (2023). *How Mass Graves like Pico Reja Haunt Present-Day Spain*. Euronews. https://www.euronews.com/my-europe/2023/02/07/inside-a-real-life-chamber-of-horrors-how-mass-graves-like-pico-reja-haunt-present-day-spa

Knijnik, J., & Newson, M. (2021). 'Tribalism,' identity fusion and football fandom in Australia: The case of Western Sydney. *Soccer & Society*, *22*(3), 248–265.

Leal, J. M. (2014). *De las urnas a las armas: El Frente Popular y los orígenes de la Guerra Civil en la provincia de Alicante*. Instituto Alicantino de Cultura.

Lee Ludvigsen, J. A. (2019). Transnational fan reactions to transnational trends: Norwegian Liverpool supporters, 'authenticity' and 'filthy-rich' club owners. *Soccer & Society*, *20*(6), 872–890.

Lee Ludvigsen, J. A. (2023). Football fans' contestations over security: between offline and online fan spaces and channels. *Sport in Society*, *OnlineFirst*, 1–15.

Lee Ludvigsen, J. A., & Petersen-Wagner, R. (2022a). From television to YouTube: Digitalised sport mega-events in the platform society *Leisure Studies*, 42(4), 615–632.

Lee Ludvigsen, J. A., & Petersen-Wagner, R. (2022b). *The UEFA European Football Championships: Politics, Media Spectacle, and Social Change*. Routledge.

Lewis, R., & Christin, A. (2022). Platform drama: "Cancel culture," celebrity, and the struggle for accountability on YouTube. *New Media & Society*, *24*(7), 1632–1656.

Mañas Viniegra, L. (2018). La aportación internacional de la marca Real Madrid a la ciudad de Madrid (España) como destino turístico de eventos deportivos. *Turismo y Sociedad*, *24*, 129–148. https://doi.org/10.18601/01207555.n24.06

Marca. (n.d.). *Values*. Retrieved from https://www.marca.com/en/values.html

Marres, N. (2017). *Digital Sociology: The Reinvention of Social Research*. Polity.

Martialay, F. (2017). *El fútbol en la Guerra. Tomo V: Federación Regional Castellana*. CIHEFE.

Martin, F., & Southby, B. (2023). *Real Madrid's Social Media Post Explained as La Liga Champions Continue Bitter Feud with Barcelona - Inside Europe*. https://www.eurosport.com/football/liga/2022-2023/real-madrids-social-media-post-explained-as-la-liga-champions-continue-bitter-feud-with-barcelona-in_sto9566460/story.shtml

Masià, V. (2014). *La españolización del fútbol en 1940.: La Futbolteca. Enciclopedia del Fútbol Español*. http://lafutbolteca.com/la-espanolizacion-del-futbol-en-1940/

McCarthy, B. (2021). Reinvention through CrossFit: Branded transformation documentaries. *Communication & Sport*, *9*(1), 150–165.

McCarthy, B. (2022). 'Who unlocked the kitchen?': Online misogyny, YouTube comments and women's professional street skateboarding. *International Review for the Sociology of Sport*, *57*(3), 362–380.

McLuhan, M. (1964). *Understanding Media: The Extensions of Man*. Routledge.

McClearen, J. (2023). Introducing the critical case studies. In Brown-Devlin, N., McClearen, J., & Butterworth, M. (Eds.). (2022). *Second Annual Politics in Sports Media Report | Moody College of Communication*. Texas University. Retrieved 07/07/2023 from https://moody.utexas.edu/centers/sports-communication-media/second-annual-politics-sports-media-report

Medina, A. (2018). *¿Importa la Guerra Civil? El Museo de la Batalla del Ebro recibe mil visitas al año. La Información*. https://www.lainformacion.com/economia-negocios-y-finanzas/importa-la-guerra-civil-el-museo-de-la-batalla-del-ebro-recibe-mil-visitas-al-ano/6398420/

Mercier, H., & Sperber, D. (2017). *The enigma of reason*. Harvard University Press.

Mesler, R. M., Howie, K., Vredenburg, J., & Chernishenko, J. (2022). Athlete–brand relationships in the era of "cancel culture": Insights, analyses, and strategic development. In *Sport Marketing in a Global Environment* (pp. 219–243). Routledge.

Norman, A. (2016). Why we reason: Intention–alignment and the genesis of human rationality. *Biology and Philosophy*, *31*, 685–704.

Núñez Seixas, X. M. (2009). El nacionalismo español regionalizado y la reinvención de identidades territoriales, 1960–1977. *Historia del Presente*, *13*, 55–70.

Oliveira, J. R. de, & Capraro, A. M. (2020). Independência catalã, identidade e globalização no Fútbol Club Barcelona. *Motrivivência*, *32*(61), 01–21. https://doi.org/10.5007/2175-8042.2020e64993

Parrón, I. (2019). El primer museo de España dedicado a la Guerra Civil. *Cadena SER*. https://cadenaser.com/programa/2019/04/01/la_ventana/1554130373_237764.html

Peters, U. (2022). What is the function of confirmation bias? *Erkenntnis*, *87*(3), 1351–1376. https://doi.org/10.1007/s10670-020-00252-1

Petersen-Wagner, R. (2017a). The football supporter in a Cosmopolitan epoch. *Journal of Sport & Social Issues*, *41*(2), 133–150.

Petersen-Wagner, R. (2017b). Cultural consumption through the Epistemologies of the South: 'Humanization' in transnational football fan solidarities. *Current Sociology*, *65*(7), 953–970.

Petersen-Wagner, R., & Lee Ludvigsen, J. A. (2022a). Digital transformations in a platform society: A comparative analysis of European football leagues as YouTube complementators. *Convergence*, 29(5), 1330–1351. https://doi.org/10.1177/13548565221132705

Petersen-Wagner, R., & Lee Ludvigsen, J. (2022b). The video assistant referee (VAR) as neo-coloniality of power? Fan negative reactions to VAR in the 2018 FIFA men's world cup. *Sport in Society*, 1–15.

Petersen-Wagner, R., & Lee Ludvigsen, J. A. (2023). The Paralympics on YouTube: Alternative content creation and the digital consumption of the Paralympics. *International Review for the Sociology of Sport*, *OnlineFirst*, 1–24.

Pichel, M. (2019). Guerra Civil de España: Cómo sigue presente 80 años después de haber terminado. *BBC News Mundo*. https://www.bbc.com/mundo/noticias-internacional-47749895

Poell, T., Nieborg, D., & Duffy, B. E. (2022). *Platforms and Cultural Production*. Polity Press.

Porat, A. B. (2010). Football fandom: A bounded identification. *Soccer & Society*, *11*(3), 277–290.

Quiroga, A. (2015). Spanish fury: Football and national identities under Franco. *European History Quarterly*, *45*(3), 506–529. https://doi.org/10.1177/0265691415587686

Quiroga, A. (2020). Football and nation. F. C. Barcelona and Athletic de Bilbao during the Franco dictatorship (1937–1977). *Journal of Iberian and Latin American Studies*, *26*(1), 65–82. https://doi.org/10.1080/14701847.2020.1726102

Rademeyer, C. (2000). "No normal sport in an abnormal society"-sports isolation and the struggle against apartheid in South African sport, 1980–1992. *Southern Journal for Contemporary History*, *25*(1), 17–41.

Real Madrid C.F. (2002a). *Libro Oficial Del Centenario – Tomo I – Historia del Real Madrid, 1902–2002: La Entidad, Los Socios, El Madridismo*. Everest.

Real Madrid C.F. (2022b). *Libro Oficial Del Centenario – Tomo II – Historia del Real Madrid, 1902–2002: La Entidad, Los Socios, El Madridismo*. Everest.

Richards, M. (2013). *After the Civil War: Making Memory and Re-making Spain since 1936*. Cambridge University Press.

Rieck, J. (2021). Real Madrid: "Franco's Club" or "Ambassador of Spain"? *STADION*, *45*(1), 6–31. https://doi.org/10.5771/0172-4029-2021-1-6

Rieder, B. (2015). *YouTube Data Tools*. In Version 1.22. https://tools.digitalmethods.net/netvizz/youtube/

Sailofsky, D. (2022). Masculinity, cancel culture and woke capitalism: Exploring Twitter response to Brendan Leipsic's leaked conversation. *International Review for the Sociology of Sport*, *57*(5), 734–757.

Shobe, H. (2008). Place, identity, and football: Catalonia, *Catalanisme* and Football Club Barcelona, 1899–1975. *National Identities*, *10*(3), 329–343. https://doi.org/10.1080/14608940802249965

Solé, J. M. (1986). *La repressió franqusita a Catalunya, 1938–1953*. Edicions 62.

Stibel, J. (2018). Fake News: How Our Brains Lead Us into Echo Chambers that Promote Racism and Sexism. *USA Today*. https://eu.usatoday.com/story/money/columnist/2018/05/15/fake-news-social-media-confirmation-bias-echo-chambers/533857002/

Tobar, F. B. (2023). Exploring the interpretation of difficult heritage at football grounds in Spain, Portugal, and Germany. [Dissertation thesis, Clemson University]. Retrieved from https://tigerprints.clemson.edu/all_dissertations/3343

Tomàs, M. (2023). *75 años de la reapertura del campo de Les Corts después de la Guerra Civil*. https://www.fcbarcelona.es/es/club/noticias/1123620/75-anos-de-la-reapertura-del-campo-de-les-corts-despues-de-la-guerra-civil

Turner, M. (2022). The safe standing movement in English football: Mobilizing across the political and discursive fields of contention. *Current Sociology*, *70*(7), 1048–1065.

Usall, R. (2021). *Futbolitica*. Altamarea.

van Dijck, J., Poell, T., & de Waal, M. (2018). *The Platform Society: Public Values in a Connective World*. Oxford University Press.

Vogel, A. (2017). *Bikinis, fútbol y rock & roll: Crónica pop bajo el franquismo sociológico (1950–1977)*. Foca.

Whealey, R. H. (2004). *Hitler and Spain: The Nazi Role in the Spanish Civil War, 1936–1939*. University Press of Kentucky.

Williams, M. (1990). *The Story of Spain: The Bold and Dramatic History of Europe's Most Fascinating Country*. Lookout publications.

Woods, J., & Lee Ludvigsen, J. (2022). The changing faces of fandom? Exploring emerging 'online' and 'offline' fandom spaces in the English Premier League. *Sport in Society*, *25*(11), 2234–2249.

YouTube. (2023a). *Data API*. Retrieved 09/06/2023 from https://developers.google.com/youtube/v3

YouTube. (2023b). *Livestream: Joan Laporta's Press Conference*. Retrieved 09/06/2023 from https://www.youtube.com/watch?v=1dLh9676-pg

YouTube. (2023c). *¿Cuál es el equipo del régimen?* Retrieved 09/06/2023 from https://www.youtube.com/watch?v=Wt8ozBQPTaw

YouTube. (2023d). *El Real Madrid contesta a Laporta: "¿Cuál es el equipo del régimen?" I MARCA*. Retrieved 09/06/2023 from https://www.youtube.com/watch?v=LoxYQlKa0ZM

YouTube. (2023e). *Barça: La comparecencia completa de Joan Laporta sobre el 'Caso Negreira'*. Retrieved 09/06/2023 from https://www.youtube.com/watch?v=TN9Q0ZAZWBY

YouTube. (2023f). *Barça: El escudo no se mancha*. Retrieved 09/06/2023 from https://www.youtube.com/watch?v=xBFFS_4q-dQ_

PART II

Misinformation and Social Media

How Coordinated Influence Operations Use Social Media to Spread Threats and Fear with Misinformation

Angeline Close Scheinbaum

Now that we have focused on companies and brands, we turn to a more global, and potentially scarier context of the dark side of social media – geopolitics. Part II, called, *Misinformation and Social Media: How Coordinated Influence Operations Use Social Media to Spread Threats and Fear with Misinformation*, gets more into the government, propaganda, and politics across the world. While Part I really focused on corporate cancel culture, the next set of chapters takes a deep dive into some dark topics about coordinated influence operations and misinformation in the political context. With some examples from China and Russia, Darren Linvill and Patrick Warren (who are known as experts across the globe on the topic of misinformation) contribute some models to help explain and or predict aspects of coordinated influence operations. Their groundbreaking chapter is called "Paths to Influence: How Coordinated Influence Operations Affect the Prominence of Ideas."

Linvill and Warren's chapter is very complementary to the next chapter, which also covers the dark topic of misinformation at a global level as propagated by social media. The author, Hyeong-Gyu Choi, writes an important chapter entitled, "The Spread of Misinformation and Its Potential Threats: A Motivational Theory Approach."

DOI: 10.4324/9781032670546-5

4

PATHS TO INFLUENCE

How Coordinated Influence Operations Affect the Prominence of Ideas

Darren Linvill and Patrick Warren

Introduction

Malicious, inauthentic digital content has, in recent years, become an issue of increased concern. The online ecosystem is used by foreign provocateurs to influence elections (Linvill & Warren, 2020), by autocrats to control domestic discourse (Martin et al., 2019), and by fraudsters who are making off with more of their victims' money with each passing year (Lyngaas & Rabinowitz, 2023). The ways in which bad actors work to engage with their audiences, however, can too often be narrowly conceived. Troll farms are not all run the same way, and their tactics and strategies are shaped in important ways by their goals and by their capabilities.

Even if we take what is perhaps the most famous social media coordinated influence operation (CIO) to date, the Russian Internet Research Agency's (IRA) efforts to influence the 2016 U.S. election, we can see multiple approaches. While the IRA did employ accounts which purported to be genuine Americans of various political beliefs, what may now be considered the prototypical troll accounts, they conducted more specialized activity as well.

Among these were at least 55 newsfeed accounts identified by Linvill and Warren (2020). These accounts each purported to be news aggregators, most from a specific U.S. city. They appeared professional with well-designed profiles giving the appearance of credibility. These "Newsfeeds" almost exclusively posted real news they gathered from genuine local sources. Their efforts were not altruistic in nature, however. Ehrett et al. (2022) found that these accounts were attempting to serve an agenda-setting function. They shared stories which portrayed the world as a dangerous place, especially for vulnerable minority groups, at rates far greater than did the outlets from which they pulled their

DOI: 10.4324/9781032670546-6

stories. The stories were real, but their prominence was not, and in this way, they fanned the flames of disillusionment and discontent prior to the election.

But online fraud and disinformation are not always farms of trolls diligently pretending to be your neighbor or local news outlet. The work of the IRA in 2016 and after can be juxtaposed to ongoing efforts affiliated with the People's Republic of China (PRC). In October 2019, Daryl Morey, then general manager of the National Basketball Association's Houston Rockets tweeted an image saying "Fight for Freedom. Stand with Hong Kong." The Wall Street Journal (Cohen et al., 2019) reported that in the week following Morey's tweet, he was flooded with replies from thousands of PRC-affiliated troll accounts. These accounts not only attacked Morey personally but also pushed narratives about Chinese sovereignty and American hypocrisy. In the wake of these attacks, Morey apologized for his tweet.

In these two cases, the goals of Russian- and Chinese-affiliated accounts were opposite. The IRA worked to highlight narratives they preferred. China worked to suppress narratives they did not. These examples, pulled from genuine Russian and Chinese influence operations, illustrate the breadth of tactics bad actors may employ through social media to influence people for nefarious ends. Tactics vary depending on the goals and constraints of the actor. The objective of this chapter is to build a model capturing how inauthentic influence operations are conducted and why they target specific conversations using the tactics they do. First, however, we will illustrate the set of tactics operations have to choose from through specific, real-world examples.

Many Paths to Influence

Social media influence operations may have a variety of specific goals. They can, for instance, attempt to espouse a particular narrative or worldview, engage in reputational management, motivate group action, persuade users of a particular argument, or sow chaos and division. To simplify the list of potential goals, we will start with the generalization that social media influence operations work to affect the prominence of ideas. There are, however, myriad tactics one might employ to engage in such influence, and the ideal choice of tactic depends on a variety of factors. As we discussed in the introduction, depending on both context and goals, two social media influence operations may appear staggeringly different from one another and yet each be utilizing the best tactics available given the actors' constraints.

Influence-operation tactics all fall into one of four relatively broad categories dependent on two simple factors. Actors choose which category of tactics they employ, but constraints may limit reasonable options and push an operation into employing a particular tactic set. The first factor is the actor's goal; is an operation working to either promote or demote a focal idea relative to the organic prominence it would have absent the work of

	Direct Mechanism	Indirect Mechanism
Goal: Promote Focal Idea	Promote Focal Idea by Strengthening Focal Idea	Promote Focal Idea by Weakening Alternative Idea(s)
Goal: Demote Focal Idea	Demote Focal Idea by Weakening Focal Idea	Demote Focal Idea by Strengthening Alternative Ideas(s)

FIGURE 4.1 Influence Operation Tactics Matrix

the operation. An actor may desire an idea be more salient (promote) or less salient (demote) in the minds of the public. The second factor addresses the mechanism by which the goal is targeted. What ideas are best exploited in order to influence the salience of the focal idea will vary but there are two basic choices, one can employ a direct mechanism and exploit the focal idea itself or one can employ an indirect mechanism and exploit one or more ideas that are not the focal idea. Depending on the goal (promote or demote) and the mechanism (direct or indirect), any operation may be placed in at least one of four blocks in a matrix (see Figure 4.1). We will explain each of these tactical categories below, by example.

Example Tactic #1: Directly Promote Focal Idea

The IRA Troll farm first rose to prominence following a 2015 New York Times report about their activity (Chen, 2015). They became infamous, however, due to their attempts to influence the 2016 U.S. Presidential election. But before they were active in U.S. politics, they operated in Russian – targeting a domestic audience and Russian speakers in neighboring Ukraine. Though the organizational structure of this persistent operator is murky and appears to have changed over time, the IRA or a successor organization has continued to operate up to, at least, the summer of 2023 and may continue today.

Throughout its operation, the IRA has used myriad strategies and methods of influence. But the method they are best known for is the creation and cultivation of deep and complex identities, both individual and organizational, with the goal of promoting particular ideas. In the context of the infamous campaign targeting the US in 2016, these identities fell into one of several specific types (Linvill & Warren, 2020), including the newsfeed accounts previously discussed but also accounts that purported to be individuals with identities and messaging focused on either specifically right leaning or left-leaning ideologies. These included numerous prominent accounts with tens and even hundreds of thousands of followers. Some of these persona were deep, with accounts on multiple platforms and quotes attributed to them across mainstream media (Xia et al., 2019).

But despite a degree of bespoke heterogeneity, accounts shared several common characteristics. IRA persona engaged in messaging consistent with extreme, partisan versions of these ideological groups and attacked moderate perspectives. The IRA operation attacked centrist and institutionalist world views from both the left and the right simultaneously. They questioned democratic processes, scientific consensus, and America's place on the global stage. The IRA worked to promote an extreme view of the world, one which they evidently hoped would spread disillusionment and discontent among those that engaged with the messaging and accrue indirect benefit to the Kremlin.

The divisive ideas IRA trolls worked to promote are clear in the content they shared (Linvill & Warren, 2020). One of the most used hashtags from their right-leaning X/Twitter persona included #IslamKills and they targeted right leaning users with messages such as "#ThanksObama We're FINALLY evicting Obama. Now Donald Trump will bring back jobs for the lazy ass Obamacare recipients." Similarly, a top hashtag from left-leaning IRA X/Twitter persona was #PoliceBrutality and they targeted left-leaning users with messages such as "NO LIVES MATTER TO HILLARY CLINTON. ONLY VOTES MATTER TO HILLARY CLINTON." These ideas were already circulating throughout the social media ecosystem; it was a tactical choice for the IRA to raise the prominence of these ideas through direct promotion. There were no constraints posed by the ideas themselves beyond the ability of Russian operators to convincingly engage with American users, and these difficulties were overcome by a well-resourced operation.

Example Tactic #2: Indirectly Promote Focal Idea

In March, 2022, Russia's full-scale invasion of Ukraine was faltering and so was their related propaganda war. Footage of Russian losses (e.g., Sabbagh, 2022) was damaging perceptions of Russian military superiority and calling into question Russian leadership. The Russian disinformation and propaganda machine needed some positive messaging to bolster the homefront and ensure support for the Kremlin. For Russia, however, there was very little good news coming out of the conflict in those early weeks. An expected easy victory had not transpired, Kyiv had not fallen, and losses were mounting. Something had to be done.

Without good news to promote the war and Russian dominance, the Kremlin turned instead to attacking information about Ukrainian successes. This mostly involved undermining Western media and Ukrainian claims of battlefield success. One form these efforts took was in posts from inauthentic social media accounts believed to be affiliated with the Russian IRA (Silverman & Kao, 2022a). These accounts, engaging in Russian, shared cartoons and other satirical messages lampooning Western narratives about the course of the invasion. They also shared stories that were clearly fake. One video shared by these accounts claimed to show a German broadcast of a journalist standing in front of what was purported to be dozens of civilian

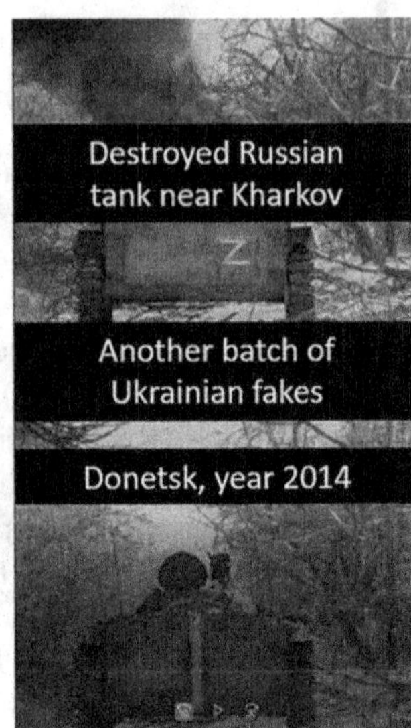

FIGURE 4.2 Example Screenshot of Russian Fake Fact Check Video (Left), with English Translation (Right)

body bags in Kyiv. In the middle of the broadcast one of the "bodies" sits up. The troll accounts claimed the video proved the West was spreading fake news about casualties when, in fact, the video was from a protest in Austria against global climate change and the body bags contained live protestors.

Perhaps yet more malicious, these and other Russian-affiliated accounts also shared fake fact checks of Ukrainian claims (Silverman & Kao, 2022b). These posts shared juxtaposed images. One image would show an "original," easily found from an internet search. These included images of Russian vehicles or Ukrainian cities. The other would show a Ukrainian "fake," an altered version of the first image to show the Russian vehicle burning or the Ukrainian city being shelled (see Figure 4.2). These fact checks would suggest that Ukraine was responsible for the altered images and that the Ukrainians were spreading disinformation. Analysis of image metadata, however, showed these fake fact checks were created at the same moment by the same person as the alleged "Ukrainian fake," which never previously existed and did not spread independently.

Russian attempts to undermine Western and Ukrainian narratives about the war employed a common disinformation tactic – the Firehose of Falsehood – using vast quantities of false or ambiguous claims to undermine users' beliefs in any objective truth (Paul & Matthews, 2016). Russian influence operations may not have been able to convince their audience that the war was going well, but it was perhaps sufficient to level the propaganda playing field and persuade their audience to believe nothing. By diminishing other narratives, they raised at least the relative prominence of their target ideas.

Example Tactic #3: Directly Demote Focal Idea

China hosted the Beijing Winter Olympics in February 2022. As with any host nation, China used the games as a promotional opportunity. Some human rights activists, however, saw the games as a moment to raise awareness of Chinese atrocities, especially those committed against China's Uyghur Muslim minority.

Human rights organizations have accused China of crimes against humanity targeting the Uyghur, a Muslim minority from north-western China's Xinjiang region. Evidence exists of crimes including forced sterilization, forced labor, and forced detention of Uyghur Muslims (Maizland, 2022). Prior to the 2022 Beijing Olympics, activists began using #GenocideGames to organize conversations on social media. The hashtag was intended to directly link conversations about the Olympics with conversations about atrocities committed against the Uyghur.

A report from the *Wall Street Journal* found PRC-affiliated X/Twitter accounts flooded the platform with tens of thousands of posts using #GenocideGames prior to the Beijing games (Wells & Lin, 2022). Counterintuitively, it was claimed Chinese-affiliated accounts were using the hashtag in an attempt to weaken the usefulness of the hashtag and silence their critics. By using the hashtag on messages that were entirely unrelated to discussions of Uyghur atrocities, China made it incrementally less likely for authentic users wanting to engage in those conversations to find what they were looking for. In using clearly inauthentic accounts, China may have also been working to influence X/Twitter's algorithm into suppressing these same conversations.

China faced a variety of constraints in deciding how to address human rights related attacks while keeping the focus on a successful Olympic Games. It was difficult to engage directly with accusations regarding the Uyghur, there was ample evidence of China's abuses and engaging with the conversations directly could serve to simply spotlight them. Without the option to change hearts and minds, flooding the hashtag and diluting the discourse was a logical tactic.

Example Tactic #4: Indirectly Demote Focal Idea

In September, 2021, Chinese virologist Li-Meng Yan published a report alleging the Covid-19 virus was artificially created in a Chinese laboratory (Timberg, 2021). Though the report was discredited at the time by prominent researchers, this narrative remained a clear threat to China. It was well established that Covid-19 originated in Wuhan, China, but prior to Li-Meng Yan's report, little evidence had been presented which pointed blame at the Chinese government for its creation.

Impacting conversations about Covid-19, however, would have been extremely difficult. In September 2021 social media was awash with users discussing the virus, the pandemic remained the biggest news item of the year.[1] Attempts to discredit Li-meng Yan's story about Covid-19's origins

FIGURE 4.3 Memes Shared by Chinese Disinformation Campaign Attacking Li-Meng Yan

Source Credit: Created by Chinese propaganda campaign and posted by fake accounts on social media.

would need to focus on discrediting her and not on influencing wider conversations about the pandemic.

A report from the Australian Strategic Policy Institute (ASPI) found tens of thousands of tweets posted between April and June, 2021, which they linked to a Chinese state operation (Zhang, 2021). The messages attacked the credibility of Yan, as well as the Chinese dissident billionaire Guo Wengui and the Republican strategist Steve Bannon, both of whom worked to promote Yan's work. Importantly, all of the tweets identified in the report used the hashtags #StopAsianHate along with #LiMengYan. The posts employed the same memes and messaging which suggested Yan's report blaming China for the virus was anti-Asian discrimination.

Conversation online about racism targeting Asians were particularly prominent in this period of the pandemic and employing #StopAsianHate was an attempt to co-opt these discussions and link them to Yan. The ASPI report found content from this campaign (see Figure 4.3) across thousands of accounts and multiple online platforms. Co-opting existing narratives to discredit Yan and her report as a form of racism was a reasonable tactic given the constraints any operations would have faced trying to steer the much larger discourse which existed around the origins of Covid-19.

An Economic Model of CIO Behavior

We present, in this section, an economic model of the productive decisions of a CIO. In it, the CIO decides what ideas to target for strengthening or weakening, and how much of what inputs to use to exert that influence. This model borrows much from the standard economic model of profit maximization by a multiple-product monopolist who produces a variety of related products (Forbes, 1988).

The input side is straightforward, where for whatever output profile the producer chooses he will choose the input mix that minimizes his costs of producing that output. Those inputs could come in a variety of forms: paid staff, computing power, AI-generated posts, bots for hire, advertisements, media, and a huge variety of other sources of influence. Holding output fixed, the mix of inputs will depend on their relative prices and productivities. Differences in circumstance that shift the level or mix of outputs will only affect input mixes to the extent that they might affect those relative productivities. For example, if one of the inputs (what you might call the high-quality input) is relatively advantageous when producing high levels of influence, we would predict to see that input used more intensely when the producer has particularly strong incentives to influence a narrative. Thus, we might expect mostly low-quality inputs (cheap and simple bots, substantial reuse of content) when the desired level of influence is low but substantial use of high-quality inputs (human-curated content, cyber-enabled influence, original media) when the desired level is high.

Optimal influence output choices for each idea will depend on these costs of production, but also on the value to the producer of a marginal shift in the prominence of that idea and the patterns of substitution amongst alternative ideas. All else equal, we'd expect more influence to be exerted when the prominence of an idea is more important, when influence efforts have a bigger impact on prominence, and when influence is inexpensive to produce.

This model provides some clear predictions for when we should expect CIOs to appear in each sector of our 2 × 2 schema of promotion/demotion and strengthening/weakening, mostly depending on their goals and the relative impact of influence. At one extreme, when the CIO has one or a handful of ideas in the topic that he is particularly interested in making prominent, we should typically see intense strengthening of those ideas, using high-quality inputs. The exception occurs when that idea is particularly difficult to successfully influence, relative to alternatives. In that case, the CIO might adopt a strategy of weakening all the alternatives, using low-quality inputs. At the opposite extreme, when the CIO has one or handful of narratives in the topic that he is particularly interested in making less prominent, the optimal strategy is more typically a mix of weakening the focal idea and strengthening alternatives, depending on the effectiveness of strengthening versus weakening.

Formalizing the Model

Consider a CIO who wants to influence the beliefs and/or behavior of some collection of consumers/citizens. Suppose, for simplicity, that there is a set of N ideas, indexed by *i*, that are competing for attention and support on some focal topic in an information space. The CIO can take some set of costly actions to influence the prominence of each of these narratives, but the impact of these actions depends on some characteristics of the ideas and of the CIO.

Formally, the operator can choose a three-dimensional vector of investments (x_i, q_i, d_i), where x_i represents the quantity investment in promoting idea *i*, and q_i represents the quality investment in promoting idea *i*, and $d_i \in \{1, -1\}$ represents the direction of influence, where the difference between quality and quantity is how their relative efficiencies in the production of influence change with the scale of influence. These investments come with constant marginal costs $p_x > 0$ and $p_q > 0$, which are independent of idea but might vary across topics or influence actors.

The impact of these investments on the strength of an idea is given by $a_i d(1+\alpha d) f(x,q)$, where the $f(x,q)$ is the **influence effort** and a_i is the **influence factor,** which might vary by idea, and $\alpha \in [0,1]$ represents how differentially difficult it is to *weaken* an idea. If $\alpha = 1$, weakening an idea is impossible, while if $\alpha = 0$ weakening an idea is no more difficult than strengthening it. In principle, $\alpha < 0$ could represent it being relatively easy to weaken idea, although we do not think of that case as common. The functional form of $f(x,q)$ is common across ideas (but might vary across topics or influence actors). It is increasing in both its arguments, but with diminishing marginal products and decreasing returns to scale. Finally, we'll assume that the marginal return to quality decreases more slowly than the return to quantity, such that the expansion path of influence involves increasing use of quality-intensive production as the level of influence increases.

Each idea is endowed with some base strength $0 \leq b_i$, which represents the strength of that idea in the absence of any intervention by the influence actor. Investments in influence increase the **strength** of each idea in the discourse, for investments (x_i, q_i), the strength of idea *i* is given by $s_i = \max\left\{b_i + a_i\left(d + \alpha d^2\right) f\left(x_i, q_i\right), 0\right\}$, and its equilibrium **prominence** (z_i) is given by

$$z_i = \frac{s_i}{s_1 + s_2 + \cdots + s_N}, \tag{4.1}$$

where we chose the typical Tullock/market-share form for this contest function for computational simplicity, although it limits the substitution patterns among the ideas and would probably need to be generalized for empirical estimation (Berry & Haile, 2021).

Finally, the influence actor is endowed with preferences that depend on the equilibrium prominence of each idea and on the total costs of the investments they make. Specifically, assume their preferences are given by

$$u(z,x,q) = \sum_{i=1}^{N} \left[u_i \; z_i \; - \; p_x x_i - p_q q_i \right], \tag{4.2}$$

where $u_i \geq 0$ is the marginal return to the prominence of idea i.

With this setup, the influence actor's optimal behavior is fairly easy to characterize. We begin by characterizing the optimal input choices, conditional on some generic strength profile and only then work back to characterizing the optimal influence profile.

Cost-Minimizing Input Profile

For a targeted strength profile $(s_1, s_2, \ldots, s_N)$, the CIO's cost-minimization problem is to choose the vector of inputs (x,q) that minimizes $p_x \sum_{i=1}^{n} x_i + p_q \sum_{i=1}^{n} q_i$ while still satisfying $f(x_i, q_i) = \frac{s_i - b_i}{a_i\left(d + \alpha d^2\right)}$, for each i.

But given our assumptions about the symmetry and separability of production, this problem can be solved idea by idea, and the solution is symmetric across all ideas. For any strength profile that includes inducing strength of s_i for idea i, the cost-minimizing input mix contributing to that strength, $\left(x^*_i, q^*_i\right)$ can be characterized by two equations:

$$\frac{f_x\left(x^*_i, q^*_i\right)}{f_q\left(x^*_i, q^*_i\right)} = \frac{p_x}{p_q}, \tag{4.3}$$

and

$$b_i + \; a_i\left(d + \alpha d^2\right) f\left(x^*_i, q^*_i\right) = s_i. \tag{4.4}$$

The first equation says that the relative marginal productivities of the quality and quantity have to be equal to their relative prices. Otherwise, the input mix should be shifted to the more cost-efficient means. The second equation says that sufficient inputs need to be used to attain the desired strength.

These conditions have several immediate implications about how a CIO will produce its desired profile of idea strengths. First, if two ideas require the same level of influence effort, that effort will be produced in the same way.

This is true even if (for instance) they have very different influence factors, base prominence rates, or direction of influence. Second, for given prices, the cost of producing a given level of strength is given by an increasing, convex function $c(\cdot)$, which takes as an argument the required level of influence effort, $\dfrac{s_i - b_i}{\alpha_i d_i (1+\alpha_i d_i)}$.

Optimal Narrative Strengths

With these cost-functions in hand, we can now back up to the optimal decision about idea strength. We can now rewrite the CIO's problem as

$$\max_{s:s_i \geq 0}(u_1 s_1 + u_2 s_2 + \cdots + u_N s_N) / \sum_{i=1}^{N} s_i - \sum_{i=1}^{n} c\left(\frac{s_i - b_i}{a_i d_i (1+\alpha d_i)}\right) \tag{4.5}$$

The solution to this problem breaks into two cases, where it is useful to define $S = \sum_{i=1}^{n} s_i$ and $U = \sum_{i=1}^{n} s_i u_i$, where U/S represents the overall prominence-weighted average payoff from the entire topic.

- If $u_i - \dfrac{U}{S} > 0$, so the CIO would like to increase the prominence of idea i,
    - $s_i^* = b_i$ for all i such that $u_i - \dfrac{U}{S} < \dfrac{S}{a_i(1+\alpha)} c'(0)$, and
    - s_i^* satisfying $u_i - \dfrac{U}{S} = \dfrac{S}{a_i(1+\alpha)} c'\left(\dfrac{s_i^* - b_i}{a_i(1+\alpha)}\right)$, for all others.
- While if $u_i - \dfrac{U}{S} < 0$, so the CIO would like the decrease the prominence of idea i,
    - $s_i^* = b_i$ for all i such that $\dfrac{U}{S} - u_i < \dfrac{S}{a_i(1-\alpha)} c'(0)$,
    - $s_i^* = 0$ for all i such that $\dfrac{U}{S} - u_i > \dfrac{S}{a_i(1-\alpha)} c'\left(\dfrac{b_i}{a_i(1-\alpha)}\right)$, and
    - s_i^* satisfying $\dfrac{U}{S} - u_i = \dfrac{S}{a_i(1-\alpha)} c'\left(\dfrac{b_i - s_i^*}{a_i(1-\alpha)}\right)$, for all others.

The left-hand side of these conditions represents the degree to which the CIO prefers idea i to be prominent, relative to the prominence-weighted average idea. The right-hand side represents how difficult it is to make idea i more prominent, which increases as the overall strength of ideas in this topic (S) increases or as the cost of exerting influence ($c'()$) increases but decreases as the strength of the particular idea is more amenable to influence (a_i) or when the goal is weakening versus strengthening (α).

In one natural case where the cost of the first unit of influence is very small ($c'(0) = 0$), these conditions say that the CIO will invest in *strengthening* all ideas that yield a higher marginal utility than the weighted average received in equilibrium from all ideas and in *weakening* all ideas that yield worse marginal utility than the average. If the cost of the first unit of influence is substantial ($c'(0) > 0$), the CIO will influence only those ideas that give a utility that is *sufficiently* different from the average, and the degree it is different from the average needs to be larger if the idea is harder to influence (larger S / a_i).

For those ideas that the CIO decides to influence, it will exert greater influence when it cares more about the idea's prominence, relative to the average narrative (higher $| u_i - U / S |$), when the idea is easier to influence (larger a_i), when the cost of exerting more influence is smaller (smaller $c'(\cdot)$ and $c''(\cdot)$, perhaps from lower input prices) and when the overall strength of the topic is lower (smaller S), either because of lower base strengths ($b_i's$) or because of all-else-equal smaller investments in other ideas by the CIO. As long as $\alpha > 0$, so strengthening is easier than weakening, the CIO will be more likely to exert influence and will exert more effort to strengthen ideas that they prefer, rather than to directly weaken the idea that they do not.

Finally, anything that leads to greater investments in influence will induce the CIO to use more quality-intense influence production methods.

Putting the Model to Work

Consider two simplified polar strategic situations in which a CIO might find itself. One, which we refer to as a pure promotion goal, is a strategic situation in which the CIO has one particular idea that it is especially interested in making more prominent. One, which we refer to as pure demotion goal, is a situation in which the CIO has one particular idea that it is especially interested in making less prominent.

Pure Promotion Goal

Assume $u_1 = 1$ for the focal idea and $u_i = 0$ for the ($N - 1 > 1$) alternatives. The focal idea has influence coefficient a_1, and all the alternatives share $a_i = a$. All ideas begin as equally prominent, with $b_i = 1$.

Under these conditions, if the CIO influences the focal idea, it will do so to increase its strength to $s_{f,\text{pro}} \geq 1$. The CIO will use the direct mechanism of strengthening the focal idea whenever

$$\frac{(N-1)s_{a,\text{pro}}}{(1+(N-1)s_{a,\text{pro}})^2} a_1(1+\alpha) > c'(0), \tag{4.6}$$

where $s_{a,\text{pro}}$ represents the strength of the alternative ideas. If the CIO does choose to influence the focal idea, it will choose a level of influence such that the equilibrium strength of the focal idea satisfies

$$\frac{(N-1)s_{a,\text{pro}}}{(s_{f,\text{pro}}+(N-1)s_{a,\text{pro}})^2} a_1(1+\alpha) = c'\left(\frac{s_{f,\text{pro}}-1}{a_1(1+\alpha)}\right). \tag{4.7}$$

If the CIO influences the alternative ideas, it will only ever *lower* their strength to $s_{a,\text{pro}} \leq 1$. As all the alternative ideas are symmetric, the CIO will either lower them all or none of them. It will use this alternative mechanism of weakening alternatives if

$$\frac{s_{f,\text{pro}}}{(s_{f,\text{pro}}+(N-1)s_{a,\text{pro}})^2} a(1-\alpha) > c'(0), \tag{4.8}$$

where $s_{f,pro}$ represents the strength of the focal idea. If the CIO does choose to influence the alternative ideas, it will induce equilibrium strength $s_{a,\text{pro}}$ satisfying

$$\frac{s_{f,\text{pro}}}{(s_{f,\text{pro}}+(N-1)s_{a,\text{pro}})^2} a(1-\alpha) = c'\left(\frac{1-s_{a,\text{pro}}}{a(1-\alpha)}\right).^2 \tag{4.9}$$

All else equal, more influence is exerted on strengthening the focal idea than on weakening the alternative ideas. This pattern occurs for two reasons. First, the gap between the payoff from the focal idea and the average idea is larger than the gap between the alternative ideas and the average, because the average is mostly made up from the alternative ideas. That large gap is what makes the focal idea special. Second, more influence is used on the focal idea because strengthening ideas is easier than weakening them, and the CIO is interested in strengthening the focal idea but weakening the alternatives.

Despite all those factors, if influence is sufficiently inexpensive and effective, both strategies will be used simultaneously. If both strategies are used, we would expect more quality-intense efforts to be used in strengthening the focal idea than in weakening the alternatives. This general pattern can be upset if the focal idea is particularly hard to influence, relative to the alternatives ($a_1 << a$). This might be the case if the focal idea is particularly implausible or boring or complex.

Increasing the number of alternative ideas has offsetting effects for the investment in the focal idea. On the one hand, it increases the gap between payoff from the focal idea and that of the average idea– making investment more attractive. On the other hand, more ideas refer to a stronger topic, overall, reducing the impact of strength on idea prominence – making investment less attractive. But more alternatives make investing in weakening alternatives less attractive. We would, therefore, expect lower investment in each alternative and lower quality investment in the alternative ideas as they are more numerous.

To sum up, when facing a situation in which there is one idea that the CIO would like to make more prominent, it will almost always use the direct mechanism of investing in strengthening that idea but will sometimes simultaneously engage in the mechanism of weakening alternatives – if there aren't too many of them and weakening is sufficiently effective. Only in the rare extreme case where the focal idea is very difficult to strengthen might, we see the CIO exclusively using the alternative mechanism.

This case covers the first two motivational examples, the Russian promotion of certain ideas about the US by strengthening those narratives and their promotion of certain ideas about Russian successes in Ukraine by the weakening of alternative ideas. According to the model, the choice between those two paths to influence is driven, primarily, by the difficulty of strengthening the two sorts of narratives. Usually, the more direct path of targeting the focal narrative is the more efficient approach, but when that idea is implausible, boring, or very unpopular, or when the alternatives are plausible, interesting, or attractive, the indirect path may dominate.

Here, the ideas pushed by the IRA in America were very easy to strengthen – they had natural audiences and fit with important organic conversations around race and culture that were already growing in prominence. In contrast, the idea that Russia was doing well in Ukraine was very difficult to push. There were no punchy stories of quick victories – in contrast to initial expectations, the invasion was clearly bogging down. Also, the story of a large country defeating its smaller neighbor is just not interesting relative to the David versus Goliath story Ukraine could tell. The alternative underdog story is much more likely to go viral. But, refocusing influence efforts to undermine alternative narratives could, and likely did, prove appealing. Fact checks of videos of Ukrainian successes are interesting because Ukraine and its allies creating fake videos would be big news and fit with broader narratives regarding the ubiquity of disinformation on social media (a narrative made famous by Russia itself). Outside the mainstream media, these fact checks would be very attractive to the conspiratorially minded and debunks of these fake fact checks would be unlikely to convince them. Furthermore, those sort of meta-debunks might just confuse people. When you are behind on the facts, muddying the waters might be the only plausible strategy.

Pure Demotion Goal

Assume $u_1 = 0$ for the focal idea and $u_i = 1$ for the ($N - 1 > 1$) alternatives. The focal idea has influence coefficient a_1, and all the alternatives share $a_i = a$. All ideas begin equally prominent with $b_i = 1$. Under these conditions, the CIO will use the direct mechanism and exert influence to weaken the focal idea if

$$\frac{(N-1)s_{a,\text{dem}}}{(1+(N-1)s_{a,\text{dem}})^2} a_1(1-\alpha) > c'(0). \tag{4.10}$$

If it does exert influence to weaken this focal idea, the equilibrium strength, $s_{f,\text{dem}}$, will be chosen to satisfy

$$\frac{(N-1)s_{a,\text{dem}}}{(s_{f,\text{dem}}+(N-1)s_{a,\text{dem}})^2} a_1(1-\alpha) = c'\left(\frac{1-s_{f,\text{dem}}}{a_1(1-\alpha)}\right).^3 \tag{4.11}$$

The CIO may also use the indirect mechanism and exert influence on strengthening the alternative ideas, by symmetrically choosing $s_{a,\text{dem}} \geq 1$. It will do so whenever

$$\frac{s_{f,\text{dem}}}{(s_{f,\text{dem}}+(N-1))^2} a(1+\alpha) > c'(0), \tag{4.12}$$

where $s_{f,\text{dem}}$ is the strength of the focal idea, and if the CIO does exert influence in this way, $s_{a,\text{dem}}$ will be chosen to satisfy

$$\frac{s_{f,\text{dem}}}{(s_{f,\text{dem}}+(N-1)s_{a,\text{dem}})^2} a(1+\alpha)c'\left(\frac{s_{a,\text{dem}}-1}{a(1+\alpha)}\right). \tag{4.13}$$

In contrast with the promotion case, we cannot decisively say which mechanism the CIO will use first, even if all ideas are equally easy to influence ($a_1 = a$). With a pure demotion goal, each mechanism has an advantage: focusing on weakening the focal idea is attractive because its payoff diverges more from the average; but focusing on strengthening alternative ideas is also attractive, because strengthening ideas is easier than weakening them. Either can dominate, depending on their relative scales. If weakening ideas is very difficult ($\alpha \approx 1$), the indirect mechanism will dominate. But if, for instance, weakening is no more difficult than strengthening ($\alpha \approx 0$), the direct mechanism will dominate. The direct mechanism becomes more attractive as the focal idea becomes relatively easy to influence (a_1 increases, relative to a). As before, increasing the number of alternative ideas has an ambiguous impact on investments in the focal idea, but unambiguously decreases investments in influencing the alternative ideas.

This case covers the second two motivational examples, the Chinese demotion of the specific idea of labeling the Beijing Olympics as the #GenocideGames through weakening that idea by flooding it with junk content and of their demotion of the idea of an insider (virologist Li-Meng Yan) revealing that COVID originated in a lab by strengthening alternative narratives about her motivations. As in the promotion case, the decision between these paths is mostly about the difficulty of influence. As the #GenocideGames idea was quite narrow, a specific hashtag on a specific platform, it was relatively easy to affect its strength directly – flooding with bots would likely be enough to muddy the waters and reduce its prominence. However, Li-Meng Yan's claim about the COVID lab origination had already been covered on Fox News and in the New York Times. Directly weakening that idea would be costly and difficult. Instead, strengthening titillating alternatives involving bribes and anti-Asian racism proved a more efficient route.

Contrasting Promotion and Demotion

In addition to comparative-static style analyses within each of the examples, we can also usefully compare the conditions in the two examples above to learn something about how CIO behavior when the goal is primarily promotion compares and contrasts with that when the goal is primarily demotion. All-else-equal, the highest level of influence effort is applied in the case strengthening the focal idea in promotion, and the lowest level of influence goes to weakening the alternative ideas in promotion. The two demotion cases fall between them, and either one can receive more effort than the other. This ranking also implies that we expect to see the highest quality of influence effort used in attempts to promote important ideas, with lower quality inputs applied to the other tasks, including the lowest quality in weakening alternative ideas in the promotion case.

If we stretch our examples a little to allow for the alternative ideas to be heterogeneous with respect to their influence coefficients, then the CIO will "start" with the alternatives that are easier to affect, it will invest more in influencing those alternatives, and will use higher-quality inputs in conducting that influence. Furthermore, the contrast among those alternative investments will be stronger in the demotion case, where the actor is strengthening the alternatives than it will be in the demotion case.

Generalizing the Paths to Influence

Beyond Our Three Examples – The Preliminaries of Quantification

The examples that motivated the analysis in this chapter were chosen to represent a variety of paths of influence, to draw the reader's attention to the heterogeneity of CIO behavior. The role of the model, in this exercise, is to formalize an intuitive account of why that heterogeneity might arise and what it might imply about how CIOs operate. To play this role, the model does not have to be taken very literally – as long as it captures the key features of the strategic situation it does not matter much if the details are rough or wrong, as these simplifications can ease exposition and highlight core intuitions.

Yet, if we are willing to take the details of the strategic situation more seriously, at the cost of complexity, a model such as we present could take up a different role, as the backbone of an empirical estimation exercise. The payoff of that approach would be substantial. It could reveal details of the productive possibilities of various influence actors which could inform countermeasures. It could be used to estimate actual influence by simulating counterfactual prominence distributions in the absence of the CIO interference. It could even be used to infer CIO priorities – how much a given CIO values prominence of various ideas in the narrative and how those values shifted over time.

Methods for this sort of structural estimation in other economic settings are well developed but face substantial hurdles in this context (Gandhi & Nevo, 2021). The key hurdles relate to the availability of representative data, on both the supply and demand side. First, on the supply side, we lack a full picture of CIO output choices. Datasets are mostly limited to those provided by the social media companies themselves, which comes with a medley of selection issues. For one, the companies have complicated incentives around disclosing troll behavior.

Disclosures highlight vulnerabilities to users, advertisers, and shareholders alike. Any datasets created by the platforms are inherently restricted to the trolls and CIO actors that they successfully catch – potentially biasing the samples to less sophisticated CIO tactics. Third, disclosing CIOs can become implicit feedback to future CIO actors regarding how to create more resilient and survivable accounts in the future. Fourth, not all platforms devote the same resources to detection or follow the same disclosure practices. To the extent that campaigns or sub-campaigns flow across platforms (or, perhaps more importantly, differ in that choice), analyses that depend on platform disclosures might miss important outputs on non-reporting platforms.

The data shortfall is also quite severe on the demand side. Estimating the demand side of models requires, at least, the market share attained by each idea. For broadcast or print media, subscription or viewership numbers are available. Put together with transcripts, and a methodology for categorizing text into ideas, one could feasibly estimate idea shares.[4] But using this approach on social media has several complexities. First, most social media data that are available at sufficient resolution to recognize specific ideas are on output – message counts, re-shares, reactions, and the like. But the prominence of an idea is not only (or even primarily) represented by these output numbers but, rather, by the share of the messages viewed by the relevant people which represent that idea. But social media viewership data is rarely available at sufficient resolution to make that determination, especially over time. Second, even when viewership is available, it is almost never possible to link those data to individual viewers, or even groups of viewers. Thus, identifying viewership among the relevant population (as determined by the CIO's preferences) is particularly difficult.

Despite the difficulties in acquiring data on both sides of the market, none of these hurdles seems completely insurmountable. On the supply side, we could begin by reasonably limiting our attention to CIOs that focus on one or two platforms, where their activities have been well documented or to CIOs with insider leaks that have revealed the full scope of their activities. But, eventually, our field needs to eventually move beyond our full dependence on platform-specific CIO identification and releases. Cross-platform methodologies for detection and measurement must be developed. Preliminary progress on the demand side of the problem might be made in similar ways. Some platforms (e.g., YouTube) publish views data, which could be gathered over time. Others (X/Twitter) have recently implemented it. There is also Neilson-style tracking data on views for small panels of users. Taken together, these two sorts of data could be used to build models to predict actual view rates, as a function of more observable features (like likes and shares). Yet, again, cross-platform methodologies are going to be required to do this right.

Beyond International Politics

All of our examples of CIO behavior, so far, have been drawn from the context of international politics, but this phenomenon, and our analysis of it, is not limited to that context. On the contrary, commercial applications of CIOs are common. To wrap up this essay, we will briefly discuss how our results can inform our understanding of three of them: financial scams, fake reviews, and reputation management.

Financial scams use CIOs to make financial assets seem more or less popular, valuable, or legitimate than they actually are. This inauthentic popularity can be used for a variety of final purposes, including simple astroturfing, pump-and-dump fraud, making balance sheets look better than they really are, or establishing individual advisors' reputations for achieving supernormal returns (Xu & Livshits, 2019; Li, Shin, & Wang, 2021). As most of these schemes have the goal of inflating valuations, our promotion example from earlier in the chapter is a good starting point. According to this model, we should expect focused attention on a single asset, using relatively high-quality inputs.

The strength of the investment will be bigger in smaller asset markets (where the overall strength of the topic is smaller), and in situations where influence is more impactful (when astroturfing detection technologies are weaker). We should see the targeting of alternative assets for demotion only rarely (unless shorting is feasible, which turns this more into the demotion case), when the set of alternatives is quite small and demotion is quite easy. Xu and Livshits (2019) find, for instance, that pump-and-dump influencers target crypto exchanges with relatively low volumes and which have weak influence-detection techniques.

A second sort of commercial behavior that could be well captured by our model of CIO behavior is the production of fake product and service reviews. There is a large literature on the detection of fake reviews, and a smaller literature on their economic impacts, but relatively little is known of the determinants of investment in those reviews (Mayzlin, Dover, & Chevalier, 2014; Luca & Zervas, 2016). Again, these schemes often have the goal of making a small set of products appear to be more popular or high quality than they really are, so the promotion example from earlier is probably the best fit. According to this model, we should expect focused attention on a single asset, using relatively high-quality inputs. The strength of the investment will be bigger for markets with fewer substitute products, where the initial product strength is low, as with new products, in situations where influence is more impactful (e.g., when demand for the product is more elastic to influence, as may be the case with less differentiated/more competitive products).

We should see the targeting of substitutes for weakening only rarely, when the set of alternatives is quite small and weakening is quite easy – again, pointing to situations where the products are close substitutes. Luca and Zervas (2016) find patterns in Yelp restaurant ratings that fit this prediction. There are twice as many presumably fraudulent 5-star reviews as 1-star reviews, all driven by independent (non-chain) restaurants. Restaurants with more reviews are less likely to have fraudulent 5-star reviews. Restaurants that face many chain competitors are less likely to create fake reviews, but those with close substitutes (i.e., other independents of the same food time) are more likely to do so.

A final example of commercial behavior that could be captured by our model is reputation management. Here, we might interpret the topic as the set of discourses or narratives in some population about some individual or organization. The individual might like some of those, as they burnish its reputation, but might be embarrassed or threatened by others. The motivated entity could hire a reputation management service to engage in influence activities to shift the prominence of this set of ideas. This application could easily be mostly promotion or mostly demotion, depending on the context, but perhaps the most interesting case is when the entity has one particular story or idea about them that they are particularly interested in hiding – often an embarrassing or revealing incident from their past.

In this case, the demotion model is probably the best fit. That model predicts that the strategy of the reputation management firm will turn crucially on how easy weakening is, relative to strengthening. If, for instance, weakening an idea is easy – as it might be in a regime with easy filing of takedown requests or little protection against costly libel litigation – the firm will focus on that approach. But if weakening is difficult, we should expect a promotion strategy, with significant investments in the strengthening of alternative ideas to crowd out the disfavored idea. Again, these investments will be larger if the pre-intervention ideas about the topic/person were pretty weak, and if the conditions of influence make efforts more impactful (as if, for example, bad search algorithms make results easy to game). Unlike the two cases above, there is very limited empirical evidence about the use of reputation management services, like these, but our model could very easily structure such an investigation.

Conclusion

This chapter investigated the many paths by which a coordinated actor might affect the prominence of the alternative narratives and what might drive the choice amongst those paths. We built a formal economic model of that decision and used it to explain the observed choices in four case studies. We sketched out how you might use this model to perform a more quantitative estimation of its key parameters and how those parameters might inform both our scientific understanding of these markets and help in designing policies to govern them. Finally, we extended beyond the domain of politics to show that this model can also be useful in the analysis of commercial influence.

Notes

1 There is some evidence that China attempted to create a narrative that Covid-19 originated from frozen Maine lobster which were shipped to Wuhan, but this attempt was not significant or successful (Solon et al., 2021).
2 The influence could potentially reduce the strength of these alternative ideas down to zero, but we ignore that boundary case, here.
3 Again, we ignore the boundary case weakening the narrative to zero strength.
4 See, for example, Ash, Gauthier, and Widmer (2023) on the detection of economic narratives in Congressional speeches and other texts.

References

Ash, E., Gauthier, G., & Widmer, P. (2023). Text aemantics capture political and economic narratives. *Political Analysis*, 1–18. https://doi.org/10.1017/pan.2023.8

Berry, S., & Haile, P. (2021). The foundations of demand estimation. *NBER Working Paper #29305*. https://doi.org/10.3386/w29305

Chen, A. (2015, June 2). The agency. *The New York Times*. https://www.nytimes.com/2015/06/07/magazine/the-agency.html

Cohen, B., Wells, G., & McGinty, T. (2019, October 16). How one tweet turned pro-China trolls against the NBA. *The Wall Street Journal*. https://www.wsj.com/articles/how-one-tweet-turned-pro-china-trolls-against-the-nba-11571238943

Forbes, K. (1988). Pricing of related products by a multiproduct monopolist. *Review of Industrial Organization*, *3*(3), 55–73. https://doi.org/10.1007/BF02229566

Ehrett, C., Linvill, D. L., Smith, H., Warren, P., Bellamy, L., Moawad, M., Moran, O., & Moody, M. (2022). Inauthentic newsfeeds and agenda setting in a coordinated inauthentic information operation. *Social Science Computer Review*, *40*(6), 1595–1613. https://doi.org/10.1177/08944393211019951

Gandhi, A., & Nevo, A. (2021). Empirical models of demand and supply in differentiated products industries. InHo, K., Hortaçsu, A. & Lizzeri, A. (Eds.), *Handbook of Industrial Organization* (vol. 4, issue 1, pp. 63–139). Elsevier. https://doi.org/10.1016/bs.hesind.2021.11.002

Li, T., Shin, D., & Wang, B., (2021). *Cryptocurrency Pump-and-Dump Schemes*. Available at SSRN: https://ssrn.com/abstract=3267041 or https://doi.org/10.2139/ssrn.3267041

Linvill, D. L., & Warren, P. L. (2020). Troll factories: Manufacturing specialized disinformation on Twitter. *Political Communication*, *37*, 447–467. https://doi.org/10.1080/10584609.2020.1718257

Luca, M., & Zervas, G. (2016). Fake it till you make it: Reputation, competition, and yelp review fraud. *Management Science*, *62*(12):3412–3427. https://doi.org/10.1287/mnsc.2015.2304

Lyngaas, S., & Rabinowitz, H. (2023, March 13). FBI says $10 billion lost to online fraud in 2022 as crypto investment scams surged. *CNN*. https://www.cnn.com/2023/03/13/politics/fbi-online-fraud-report/index.html

Martin, D. A., Shapiro, J. N., & Nedashkovskaya, M. (2019). Recent trends in online foreign influence efforts. *Journal of Information Warfare*, *18*(3), 15–48. https://www.jstor.org/stable/26894680

Maizland, L. (2022, September 22). China's repression of Uyghurs in Xinjiang. *Council on Foreign Relations*. https://www.cfr.org/backgrounder/china-xinjiang-uyghurs-muslims-repression-genocide-human-rights

Mayzlin, D., Dover, Y., & Chevalier, J. (2014). Promotional reviews: An empirical investigation of online review manipulation. *American Economic Review*, *104*(8): 2421–2455. https://doi.org/10.1257/aer.104.8.2421

Paul, C., & Matthews, M. (2016). *The Russian `Firehose of Falsehood' Propaganda Model: Why It Might Work and Options to Counter It*. RAND Corporation. https://www.rand.org/pubs/perspectives/PE198.html and https://doi.org/10.7249/PE198

Sabbagh, D. (2022, March 10). Drone footage shows Ukrainian ambush on Russian tanks. *The Guardian*. https://www.theguardian.com/world/2022/mar/10/drone-footage-russia-tanks-ambushed-ukraine-forces-kyiv-war

Silverman, J., & Kao, J. (2022a, March 8). In the Ukraine conflict, fake fact checks are being used to spread disinformation. *ProPublica*. https://www.propublica.org/article/in-the-ukraine-conflict-fake-fact-checks-are-being-used-to-spread-disinformation

Silverman, J., & Kao, J. (2022b, March 11). Infamous Russian troll farm appears to be source of anti-Ukraine propaganda. *ProPublica*. https://www.propublica.org/article/infamous-russian-troll-farm-appears-to-be-source-of-anti-ukraine-propaganda

Solon, O., Simmons, K., & Perrette, A. (2021, October 21). China linked disinformation campaign blames Covid on Maine lobsters. *NBC News*. https://www.nbcnews.com/news/china-linked-disinformation-campaign-blames-covid-maine-lobsters-rcna3236

Timberg, C. (2021, February 12). Virus claim spread faster than scientists could keep up. *The Washington Post*. https://www.washingtonpost.com/technology/2021/02/12/china-covid-misinformation-li-meng-yan/

Wells, G., & Lin, L. (2022, February 8). Pro-China Twitter accounts flood hashtag critical of Beijing Winter Olympics. *The Wall Street Journal*. https://www.wsj.com/articles/pro-china-twitter-accounts-flood-hashtag-critical-of-beijing-winter-olympics-11644343870

Xia, Y., Lukito, J., Zhang, Y., Wells, C., Kim, S. J., & Tong, C. (2019). Disinformation, performed: Self-presentation of a Russian IRA account on Twitter. *Information, Communication, & Society*, *22*(11), 1646–1664. https://doi.org/10.1080/1369118X.2019.1621921

Xu, J., & Livshits, B. (2019) The anatomy of a cryptocurrency pump-and-dump scheme. *Proceedings of the 28th USENIX Security Symposium* USENIX Association, 1609–1625. https://doi.org/10.48550/arXiv.1811.10109

Zhang, A. (2021, July 1). #StopAsianHate: Chinese diaspora targeted by CCP disinformation campaign. *The Strategist*. https://www.aspistrategist.org.au/stopasianhate-chinese-diaspora-targeted-by-ccp-disinformation-campaign/

5

THE SPREAD OF MISINFORMATION AND ITS POTENTIAL THREATS

A Motivational Theory Approach

Hyeong-Gyu Choi

Your close friend confides in you, expressing feelings of drowning despite knowing how to swim. They feel helpless, trapped, and overwhelmed by anger. In response, you attempt to console them by suggesting it might just be a bad day. Additionally, you share a method you heard about – intermittent fasting that heals anxiety and improves mood by skipping meals. You also express your willingness to listen to their concerns. While you may have thought you were being a good friend with good intentions, and that this exchange was harmless, the truth is that this encounter was far from a supportive one as your approach falls short of providing the support your friend needs. Your friend is likely undergoing severe depression, and your diagnosis and suggestion of intermittent fasting, which only temporarily manipulates bodily sensation, could further endanger their mental health. In fact, fasting has been linked with detrimental effects on mental well-being, especially with regard to disordered eating attitudes and behaviors. Moreover, asking about their trauma without sensitivity may have triggered emotions they were not yet ready to confront, possibly re-traumatizing them by making them relive horrific events (Amatenstein, 2022; Russell, 2021, Yurkevich, 2023). Would you want to put your friend through such a situation? Unfortunately, lightly dramatized scenarios like this happen every day.

Over 20% of American adults are affected by a mental health condition, and the same is true for youth aged 12–18 years, with either current or past experiences of gravely debilitating mental illness during their lives. Approximately, 1 in 25 US adults struggle daily with serious conditions like schizophrenia, bipolar disorder, or major depression (Center for Disease Control and Prevention, 2023). Alarmingly, a survey found that 30% of Gen Z participants searched for health information on TikTok, a short-form

DOI: 10.4324/9781032670546-7

video hosting service, while 44% searched on YouTube, a popular online video-sharing platform, before consulting medical professionals or seeking treatment for their health conditions. Surprisingly, some participants reported trusting social media network (SNS) health influencers more than medical professionals due to factors like accessibility (37%), affordability (33%), and approachability (23%) (Gordon, 2022).

In a Pew Research study, Shearer (2021) finds that eight-in-ten Americans get their news from digital devices. This can include news that is also fake news or misinformation for one's health or mental health. Meanwhile, the trend of seeking free medical advice, particularly related to mental health topics, has grown significantly, increased by over 80% during the pandemic; past works indicate that 83.7% of mental health advice on TikTok is inaccurate, while approximately 14.2% of videos include content that could be harmful (PlushCare, 2022). Even more concerning is the fact that 91% of reviewed videos with mental health-related content are created by individuals who are neither licensed nor qualified (Dreibelbis, 2022). Unfortunately, misinformation, which refers to false assertions made without any deliberate intention to deceive (Garrett, 2020; Legido-Quigley et al., 2020; Mian & Khan, 2020; Pennycook et al., 2020), is something people are generally prone to. It has been in human history as far back as the development of written record.

History, Human, and Misinformation

The second president of the United States, John Adams (1735–1826) expressed his skepticism about the press in a note, scoffing at the idea that a free press would lead to the advancement of knowledge and better public information. He believed that in the last ten years leading up to 1798, more new erroneous news had been spread by the press than in the previous hundred years (Mansky, 2018). Justifying Adam's negative sentiment, his time was indeed marked by the era of "yellow journalism," where newspapers attracted audiences through sensationalism and reported rumor as if they were factual. One notable example was the New York Sun, which published a sensational but a false claim in 1835, stating that there was an alien civilization on the moon, complete with a graphical depiction of the Great Moon (Young, 2017). Even the Catholic Church promoted the false explanation of the 1755 Lisbon Earthquake, claiming that the tragedy was prompted by Voltaire, a French Enlightenment writer, philosopher, and historian (1694–1778), who spoke against religious dominance (Soll, 2016).

The history of misinformation continues to persist. The scope of misinformation is vast in the modern day, encompassing gravely misleading mental health tips, political rhetoric both on an international and domestic level, climate change denial, and even everyday casual daily conversation. For instance, during the 2016 presidential election, misinformation played a significant role, spreading fabricated stories about President Barack Obama and Presidential Candidate Hillary Clinton. One such false claim involved Pope Francis endorsing Donald Trump for President, crafted to generate advertisement revenues. These pieces of misinformation confused voters and convoluted civic discord.

Misinformation widely circulated throughout the 2016 presidential election often took the form of "fake news" – fabricated information resembling news media materials in form but without organizational process or intent, published by platforms that lack news media's editorial standards and protocols for verifying the accuracy and credibility of information (Lazer et al., 2018). These stories were mostly traced back to a small city in Macedonia, where teenagers churned out sensational stories to earn money from advertisements by exploiting internet traffic. According to one of the teenagers interviewed, "The Americans loved our stories, and we make money from them. Who cares if they are true or false?" (Kirby, 2016).

The emergence of personal technology, such as smartphones, laptops, and tablets, has not only revolutionized contemporary society but also transformed the methods by which we acquire information. Powered by such technologies and the Internet, our modern lives, often referred to as "hyperconnected lives," allow us to tap into the collective digitized knowledge of crowds through web search engines. Additionally, we can communicate with others through a diverse range of mediums, including texting, email, Facebook, Instagram, Snapchat, and the recently rebranded X (previously known as Twitter) (Schneider, 2018). Being powered, especially by SNS platforms, we can connect with people with personal ties and similar interests, and access and exchange information and news (Cheung et al., 2022).

As our access to information and personal reach expand exponentially, it also facilitates the rise of misinformation – defined as false assertions that are made without any deliberate intention to deceive. The motives of the misinformation communicators may appear innocent, but a highly memorable story can be easily propagated, as it is enriched with affect, compatible schema, and relative ease of storytelling. On the other hand, disinformation is designed to accomplish a malicious purpose by deliberately spreading falsehoods (Garrett, 2020; Legido-Quigley et al., 2020; Mian & Khan, 2020; Pennycook et al., 2020). To counter the harmful effects of misinformation, an ecosystem that captures, verifies, and counters misinformation, if necessary, is needed.

Social media platforms have become integral components of our modern ecosystem, with a growing number of internet users relying on them as their primary sources of information, even though these platforms are known to harbor misinformation and facilitate its dissemination among individuals. Although social media has democratized us from the constraints of conventional media, it has become a fertile ground for the dissemination of disinformation and accelerated the speed with which it disseminates (Greenspan & Loftus, 2021), as an increasing number of people rely on social media for their sources of news: half of US adults at least sometimes use social media as their news sources, while approximately a third of US adults regularly acquire news from social media, such as Facebook. A quarter of US adults regularly use YouTube as their news source (Matsa, 2023). Despite bringing forth the democratization of information and creating a rich environment for the dissemination of disinformation, the dominance of social media would likely persist, as it will evolve continuously and tap into the inherent nature of human beings, longing for human connection (Kerpen, 2021).

Nevertheless, it highlighted the erosion of information literacy in the internet age, and it can gravely undermine the fundamental definition of truth, as repeated exposure to misinformation can lead to illusory truth effect – referred to the tendency of individuals to develop a belief in a statement or idea due to repeated exposure (Brown & Nix, 1996a, 1996b) for both true and false statements (Fazio et al., 2015). Succinctly put, repeated exposure to misinformation can affect beliefs about truth, as the tendency of people to perceive claims as true increases with rise in the number of repetitions (Hassan & Barber, 2021). As the rate of information exponentially increases and the conduit for the ever-accelerating spread of information, namely social media, will likely persist, an in-depth understanding of the motivations of modern-day netizens, who voluntarily or involuntarily assume the role of carriers of misinformation, is warranted.

Misinformation Defined: What It Is and What It Is Not

Decades of research pertinent to misinformation on human memory suggests that we are all highly susceptible to misinformation (Greenspan & Loftus, 2020), as post-event information can distort the individuals' memory of the original event (Frenda et al., 2011). Debunking and mitigating the detrimental effect of misinformation, such as ever-polarized debates on global warming (Zhou & Shen, 2022) and the relation between MMR vaccine and autism (Greenspan & Loftus, 2020), still remain difficult. Misinformation bears stark resemblances to rumors, which are defined as unverified and instrumentally relevant pieces of information that circulate in contexts of ambiguity, peril, or a potential threat based on people's attempts to comprehend and mitigate risk (Bordia & DiFonzo, 2017).

Misinformation encompasses both intended and unintended spread of unverified information (Garrett, 2020; Greenspan & Loftus, 2021; Legido-Quigley et al., 2020; Mian & Khan, 2020; Pennycook et al., 2020), while disinformation refers to unverified and false information that is devised to deceive and mislead the audience (Baines & Elliott, 2020). In the same vein, fake news could be regarded as disinformation that was disguised in the form of news media (Domenico & Visentin, 2020; Zimdars & McLeod, 2020), sharing the similarity that both forms intend to mislead the audience. In addition, both forms share another resemblance: they utilize human beings as the carrier of the spread and amplify their effect based on human motivations, namely fact-finding motivation, and self-enhancement motivation.

In a social context, sociometer theory suggests that individuals are driven to monitor their social interactions with others by measuring their social belonging and the quality of interpersonal relationships. The perceived measurements of the social standing of individuals influence their self-esteem (Leary & Downs, 1995; Leary et al., 1995), motivate them to seek accurate information, and evaluate such information by comparing it with knowledge that they already know. Simply put, an individual motivation for fact-finding leads them to respond and cope with the physical and social environment that must be attuned to the information, supporting their preexisting information and confirmation biases – defined as the inclination to search for, interpret, favor, and remember information that validates or aligns with one's preexisting beliefs or values (Nickerson, 1998; Zhou & Shen, 2022).

Consequently, when accurate information is not readily available to individuals, they become susceptible to misinformation. They often attempt to compensate for their uncertainty – a psychological state of doubt with regard to the meaning or likely future of current events (Bordia & DiFonzo, 2017) – depending on their anxiety level. Besides, they often turn to unverified information that mitigates the information void. Individuals could more likely gravitate toward misinformation to reduce uncertainty and make sense of unfamiliar and uncommon situations.

For a brand-based example, in 2019, a video of a Tesla's "self-driving vehicle" colliding with a prototype robot at CES, an influential consumer electronics show, went viral with numerous media sources publishing headlines stating, "Self-driving Tesla car kills robot." For already skeptical Americans who expressed their concerns for the safety of self-driving cars (Eisenstein, 2019), the news worsened the prevailing negative perception. Nonetheless, the footage was entirely fabricated as Tesla did not possess a self-driving model at that particular period. Some experts within the disinformation field suspected that the video was a calculated assault on the US stock market orchestrated by "foreign actors" (Atkinson, 2019; Marshall, 2019). While various news outlets published the misinformation, and the YouTube footage was viewed more than 1 million times in 2022, this incident of misinformation spread can be explained by the individuals' motivation for fact-finding given the scarce information, as the case was primarily based on a single YouTube footage, and the individuals' self-enhancement motivation that others found the misinformation worthy to share due to its novelty, not to mention, the Tesla owners' anxiety, which might have also aided the spread of the misinformation.

A consumer's self-enhancement motivation can facilitate the spread of misinformation. As individuals are motivated to feel positive about themselves, they actively uphold a favorable self-perception and engage in behaviors that boost self-worth (Bordia & DiFonzo, 2017; Kunda, 1999). In other words, sharing behavior is more self-centered to satiate one's internal needs rather than altruistic sharing. While individuals may engage in various behaviors, such as defensive reasoning – where failures are attributed to external causes while successes are attributed to one's own qualities (Argyris, 1999) – and downward comparisons – individuals compare themselves to others with misfortunes (Boecker et al., 2022), people often engage in self-sharing, telling others their thoughts, opinions, achievements, and experiences to boost their own self-worth. Self-sharing, which is an inherent human tendency, is increasingly driven by the proliferation of online SNSs and platforms that provide intrinsic rewards for self-disclosing information about one's self (Berger, 2013; Pemment, 2020).

Thus, social media users may share misinformation due to its novelty, confirmation with existing worldviews, and downward comparisons. The misinformation may be on purpose as a mechanism to deceive or persuade (e.g., propaganda), or they may be ignorant of the fact that the information is wrong. For instance, in 2016, approximately 1 million messages were exchanged utilizing the phrase "PizzaGate." Prior to the 2016 presidential election, an online conspiracy theory had emerged, alleging that Hillary Clinton and Democratic elites were operating a child sex trafficking operation from the basement of a Washington pizzeria, Comet Ping Pong. This baseless notion originated on the online message board, 4chan, then spread across the internet, fueled by far-right media influencers like Alex Jones – a radio show host and conspiracy theorist, Jerome Corsi – a conspiracy theorist and author, and Michale Flynn Jr. – son of disgraced General Flynn, and social networking sites like Facebook, X, and YouTube also played a significant role in spreading the conspiracy theory (Bloom & Moskalenko, 2021; Kang & Frenkel, 2020; Lopez, 2016). In reality, the conspiracy theory had even darker and deeper roots. Followers of QAnon, a conspiracy-theory group, believed in the existence of a secret cabal of devil-worshipping Democrats who fed off the blood of children. They believe that elite democrats are not human but instead reptilian creatures living on Earth in human form. While not everyone embraced this wild notion, some individuals joined the QAnon movement, and some individuals found the story disturbing, particularly concerning the fate of the presumed imprisoned children and victims of sex-trafficking in the basement of Comet Ping Pong Pizzeria in Washington.

One man, Edgar Welch, became so consumed by the conspiracy theory that he decided to take matters into his own hands, embarking on a search and rescue mission. Welch drove 350 miles armed with a loaded rifle, intent on uncovering what he believed to be a satanic dungeon. When he arrived at Comet Ping Pong and realized there was no basement, he fired his rifle at a closet he couldn't access. Eventually, realizing the closet contained only computers and not what the conspiracy theory described, he put down his weapons and surrendered to the police. Welch, who lost his 16-year-old brother when he was 8 and was a father of two daughters, received a four-year prison sentence for his actions. This incident demonstrates how misinformation can have a strong impact on certain vulnerable individuals, even leading them to violence. Despite his crime and mistaken belief, Welch's intention albeit misguided was to save the supposed child victims. He even recorded a video for his daughters on his way to Comet Ping Pong (Lopez, 2016; Miller, 2021; Ortiz, 2017; Wendling, 2016), saying:

> I can't let you grow up in a world that's so corrupt by evil without at least standing up for you and for other children just like you.
>
> *Edgar Welch*

Discussion

Digitized information is increasingly becoming an essential element for modern day, as it touches all areas of society, business world, and daily lives. As much as it fuels the world economy and influences our lives, it also gave us information epidemic in the era of COVID-19, and instability in financial markets where more than 50% increases of abnormal stock trading activity and approximately 40% of price volatility were induced by fake news (Petratos, 2021). We have reached a crucial juncture in history where the production of misinformation has surpassed human intervention capabilities. With the advent of generative AI (artificial intelligence) in tools such as ChatGPT and Google Bard, narratives can now be produced at a speed that humans cannot match. AI can generate scripts in minutes, a task that would take human writers weeks or months to accomplish.

Nonetheless, these AI tools generate content without regard for accuracy or quality. AI can generate misinformation, which has serious consequences for businesses and society. Attempted by news outlets like CNET to use AI for generating stories resulted in articles full of errors, requiring significant editorial corrections (Silberling, 2023; Thorbecke, 2023). NewsGuard, an organization dedicated to tracking misinformation, identified 49 websites that solely rely on AI software to produce their content. These sites churn out hundreds of articles daily, some of which contain false information alongside numerous advertisements. The primary goal is to generate programmatic or algorithmically driven ads revenue. Some of the content, often labeled as "breaking news," raises questions about its authenticity, like the announcement of the passing of Mr. Biden and the promotion to presidential post of Vice President Harris (Matthew, 2023; Sadeghi & Arvanitis, 2023). Besides, the rise of AI-powered deep fakes, which are manipulated videos or audios created by AI to portray events or statements that never actually occurred, adds to the proliferation of misinformation (Johnson & Johnson, 2023). The very definition of truth could be hindered, as the expression of "seeing is believing" is becoming irrelevant.

In addition to their perceived lack of credibility and believability, the spread of such misinformation remains a major concern. For example, when examining X pertinent to the 2016 US presidential election, research found that a mere 0.1% of over 16,000 users were responsible for disseminating over 80% of the fake news, and 80% of that fake news appeared in the feeds of just 1.1% of X users (Grinberg et al., 2019). However, more than 90% of X post impressions were created within the first three hours (Key, 2023), regardless of the seemingly wild and unfounded nature of the content. False stories, such as "Pope Francis shocks the world, endorses Donald Trump for president," spread rapidly and widely. Another concerning example is Alex Jones, the head of the fake news infoWars, claimed on his show that President Barack Obama and Presidential Candidate Hillary Clinton were demons and accused Hillary Clinton of personally murdering children. The video was viewed over 420,000 times before being taken down (Lopez, 2016).

In September 2017, a shocking picture circulated on Facebook, depicting former Seattle Seahawks defensive lineman Michael Bennet waving a burning America flag in the team's locker room while surrounded by cheering teammates and coaching staff. The image was first posted on the Facebook page of an organization called "Vets for Trump," known for promoting an extreme expression of Trump's narrative. This posting coincided with a time when San Francisco quarterback Colin Kaepernick and other players were kneeling during the national anthem as a form of protest against police brutality – Kaepernick's actions were criticized as unpatriotic, antimilitary, and un-American. Upon closer examination, the picture's low-quality image manipulations were evident, but many people were so overwhelmed by anger and disgust that they failed to critically assess its authenticity. In fact, the original picture was taken two years earlier, when the Seahawks were celebrating a significant victory against their rival, the Arizona Cardinals. Despite warning signs, such as the low-quality image manipulation, the sole source being the organization "Vets for Trump," and no confirmation by other media outlets, people continued to share this misinformation. Within a single day, this particular misinformation garnered over 10,000 shares within one day (Jenkins, 2017; Mallonee, 2017).

Any misinformation can have significant and far-reaching negative consequences, especially when amplified through SNSs. An illustrative example of its impact occurred during the 2012 South Korean presidential election, which became known as the "SNS election." Political parties and the government allegedly manipulated public opinions through various online platforms, with a particular focus on X. They employed tactics like tweet bots, programmed to retweet political messages, and macro program systems that automatically disseminated political content to sway public opinion. Shockingly, even the National Intelligence Service (NIS), which is the spy agency of South Korea, was found to have operated as many as 30 teams dedicated to this purpose, starting two years prior to the election. These teams disguised pro-government comments as public opinions on SNS and news sites (Stent, 2018).

While exposure to misinformation might not appear damaging on an individual level, decades of research on the mere exposure effect suggest that repetitive exposures to stimuli can result in favorable preferences toward those stimuli, even without conscious recall or recognition of previous exposure. People often develop preferences for things that they perceive as familiar (Bornstein, 1989; Janiszewski, 1993; Zajonc, 1980). Once familiarity is established, it can create perceived truth as repeated exposures of stimuli, such as declarative statements, garner higher truth rating than newly presented ones. This phenomenon is commonly referred to as the illusion of truth (Henkel & Mattson, 2011; Parks & Toth, 2006).

Trillions of digital social signals are generated daily, ranging from news updates and SNS status updates to advertisements, notifications, and communications from peers. The Internet and SNS play a significant role in this digital information explosion, leading to the hyper-socialization of our society and the creation of mass persuasions and trends (Aral, 2021). As humans, we are naturally inclined to seek affirmation from others, especially when we feel alone or uncertain. In today's digitally connected world, we find ourselves incessantly exposed to a massive barrage of amplified noise, misinformation, and disinformation, which shape our perceptions and influence our behaviors. These digital trends and mass persuasions have become an integral part of our lives as we find ourselves immersed in the vast ocean of digital information surrounding us. Regardless of whether the misinformation is a product of accidental coincidence or an intentional deception, it often has detrimental effects on its recipients that force them to become victims of baseless fear and contribute to the polarization of our society, wherein unification and altruism are needed more than ever.

References

Amatenstein, S. (2022, June 28). Quotes about Depression & What it Feels Like to Sufferers. https://www.psycom.net/depression/what-does-depression-feel-like

Aral, S. (2021). *The hype machine: How social media disrupts our elections, our economy, and our health--and how we must adapt.* Currency.

Argyris, C. (1999). The next challenge for TQM--Taking the offensive on defensive reasoning. *The Journal for Quality and Participation*, *22*(6), 41.

Atkinson, C. (2019, April 25). *Fake news can cause irreversible damage to companies and sink their stock price*. NBC News. https://www.nbcnews.com/business/business-news/fake-news-can-cause-irreversible-damage-companies-sink-their-stock-n995436

Baines, D., & Elliott, R. J. (2020). Defining misinformation, disinformation and malinformation: An urgent need for clarity during the COVID-19 infodemic. *Discussion Papers*, 20(06), 20–06. Department of Economics, University of Birmingham.

Berger, J. (2013). *Contagious: Why things catch on*. Simon and Schuster.

Bloom, M., & Moskalenko, S. (2021). *Pastels and pedophiles: Inside the mind of QAnon*. Stanford University Press.

Boecker, L., Loschelder, D. D., & Topolinski, S. (2022). How individuals react emotionally to others'(mis) fortunes: A social comparison framework. *Journal of Personality and Social Psychology*, *123*(1), 55.

Bordia, P., & DiFonzo, N. (2017). *Psychological motivations in rumor spread*. Routledge.

Bornstein, R. F. (1989). Exposure and affect: Overview and meta-analysis of research, 1968–1987. *Psychological Bulletin*, *106*(2), 265.

Brown, A. S., & Nix, L. A. (1996a). Age-related changes in the tip-of-the-tongue experience. *The American Journal of Psychology*, *109*(1), 79–91.

Brown, A. S., & Nix, L. A. (1996b). Turning lies into truths: Referential validation of falsehoods. *Journal of Experimental Psychology: Learning, Memory, and Cognition*, *22*(5), 1088.

Center for Disease Control and Prevention (2023, April 25). *About mental health*. CDC. https://www.cdc.gov/mentalhealth/learn/index.htm

Cheung, M. L., Leung, W. K., Yang, M. X., Koay, K. Y., & Chang, M. K. (2022). Exploring the nexus of social media influencers and consumer brand engagement. *Asia Pacific Journal of Marketing and Logistics*, *34*(10), 2370–2385.

Domenico, D. G., & Visentin, M. (2020). Fake news or true lies? Reflections about problematic contents in marketing. *International Journal of Market Research*, *62*(4), 409–417.

Dreibelbis, E. (2022, December 9). *Doctors: TikTok mental health advice video are a cesspool of misinformation*. PC Magazine. https://www.pcmag.com/news/doctors-tiktok-mental-health-advice-videos-are-a-cesspool-of-misinformation

Eisenstein, P. (2019, March 14). *Three-quarters of Americans afraid of fully autonomous vehicles*. NBC NEWS. https://www.nbcnews.com/business/autos/three-quarters-americans-afraid-fully-autonomous-vehicles-n983091

Fazio, L. K., Brashier, N. M., Payne, B. K., & Marsh, E. J. (2015). Knowledge does not protect against illusory truth. *Journal of Experimental Psychology: General*, *144*(5), 993.

Frenda, S. J., Nichols, R. M., & Loftus, E. F. (2011). Current issues and advances in misinformation research. *Current Directions in Psychological Science*, *20*(1), 20–23.

Garrett, L. (2020). COVID-19: The medium is the message. *The Lancet*, *395*(10228), 942–943.

Greenspan, R. L., & Loftus, E. F. (2020). Eyewitness confidence malleability: Misinformation as post-identification feedback. *Law and Human Behavior*, *44*(3), 194.

Greenspan, R. L., & Loftus, E. F. (2021). Pandemics and infodemics: Research on the effects of misinformation on memory. *Human Behavior and Emerging Technologies*, *3*(1), 8–12.

Grinberg, N., Joseph, K., Friedland, L., Swire-Thompson, B., & Lazer, D. (2019). Fake news on Twitter during the 2016 US presidential election. *Science, 363*(6425), 374–378.

Hassan, A., & Barber, S. J. (2021). The effects of repetition frequency on the illusory truth effect. *Cognitive Research: Principles and Implications*, 6(1), 1–12.

Henkel, L. A., & Mattson, M. E. (2011). Reading is believing: The truth effect and source credibility. *Consciousness and Cognition, 20*(4), 1705–1721.

Janiszewski, C. (1993). Preattentive mere exposure effects. *Journal of Consumer Research, 20*(3), 376–392.

Jenkins, A. (2017, September 29). *An image of an NFL player burning the U.S. flag is circulating on social media—It's fake.* Time. https://time.com/4963312/seattle-seahawks-michael-bennett-burning-american-flag-fake/

Johnson, D. & Johnson, A. (2023, Jun 15). *What are deepfakes? How fake AI-powered audio and video warps our perception of reality.* Business Insider. https://www.businessinsider.com/guides/tech/what-is-deepfake

Kang, C. & Frenkel, S. (2020, December 8). *'PizzaGate' conspiracy theory thrives anew in the TikTok era.* The New York Times. https://www.vox.com/policy-and-politics/2016/12/5/13842258/pizzagate-comet-ping-pong-fake-news

Kerpen, C. (2021 January 26). *Social media is dead, right? Well....* Forbes. https://www.forbes.com/sites/carriekerpen/2021/01/26/social-media-is-dead-right-well/?sh=1b7cf5df2736

Key, K. (2023, April 26). *Why disinformation and misinformation are more dangerous than malware.* PC Magazine. https://www.pcmag.com/news/why-disinformation-and-misinformation-are-more-dangerous-than-malware

Kirby, E. J. (2016, December 5). *The city getting rich from fake news.* BBC News.

Kunda, Z. (1999). *Social cognition: Making sense of people.* MIT press. https://www.bbc.com/news/magazine-38168281

Lazer, D. M., Baum, M. A., Benkler, Y., Berinsky, A. J., Greenhill, K. M., Menczer, F., ... & Zittrain, J. L. (2018). The science of fake news. *Science, 359*(6380), 1094–1096.

Leary, M. R., & Downs, D. L. (1995). Interpersonal functions of the self-esteem motive: The self-esteem system as a sociometer. In M. H. Kernis (Ed.), *Efficacy, agency, and self-esteem.* Plenum Press.

Leary, M. R., Tambor, E. S., Terdal, S. K., & Downs, D. L. (1995). Self-esteem as an interpersonal monitor: The sociometer hypothesis. *Journal of Personality & Social Psychology, 68*(3), 518–530.

Legido-Quigley, H., Asgari, N., Teo, Y. Y., Leung, G. M., Oshitani, H., Fukuda, K., ... & Heymann, D. (2020). Are high-performing health systems resilient against the COVID-19 epidemic? *The Lancet, 395*(10227), 848–850.

Lopez, G. (2016, December 6). *Pizzagate, the fake news conspiracy theory that led a gunman to DC's Comet Ping Pong, explained.* Vox. https://www.vox.com/policy-and-politics/2016/12/5/13842258/pizzagate-comet-ping-pong-fake-news

Mallonee, L. (2017, October 4). *That flag-burning NFK photo isn't fake news. It's meme.* Wired. https://www.wired.com/story/that-flag-burning-nfl-photo-isnt-fake-news-its-a-meme/

Mansky, J. (2018, May 7*) The age-old problem of "Fake News"*. Smithsonian Magazine. https://www.smithsonianmag.com/history/age-old-problem-fake-news-180968945/

Marshall, A. (2019, January 8). *A Tesla-Robot Crash stunt shows we need robocar schooling.* Wired. https://www.wired.com/story/tesla-promobot-pave-self-driving-education/

Matsa, K. E. (2023, November 15). *Social media and news fact sheet.* Pew Research. https://www.pewresearch.org/journalism/fact-sheet/social-media-and-news-fact-sheet/

Matthew, C. (2023, May 8). *Nearly 50 news websites are 'AI-generated', a study say. Would I be able to tell?* The Guardian. https://www.theguardian.com/technology/2023/may/08/ai-generated-news-websites-study

Mian, A., & Khan, S. (2020). Coronavirus: The spread of misinformation. *BMC Medicine*, *18*(1), 1–2.

Miller, M. E. (2021 February 16). *Pizzagate's violent legacy*. The Washington Post. https://www.washingtonpost.com/dc-md-va/2021/02/16/pizzagate-qanon-capitol-attack/

Nickerson, R. S. (1998). Confirmation bias: A ubiquitous phenomenon in many guises. *Review of General Psychology*, *2*(2), 175–220.

'Ortiz, E. (2017, June 22). *'Pizzagate's Gunman Edgar Maddison Welch sentenced to four years in Prison*. NBC News. https://www.nbcnews.com/news/us-news/pizzagate-gunman-edgar-maddison-welch-sentenced-four-years-prison-n775621

Parks, C. M., & Toth, J. P. (2006). Fluency, familiarity, aging, and the illusion of truth. Aging, *Neuropsychology, and Cognition*, *13*(2), 225–253.

Pemment, J. (2020, October 15). *Sharing yourself: reflections on social media use*. Psychology Today. https://www.psychologytoday.com/us/blog/blame-the-amygdala/202010/sharing-yourself

Pennycook, G., McPhetres, J., Zhang, Y., & Rand, D. (2020). Fighting COVID-19 misinformation on social media: Experimental evidence for a scalable accuracy nudge intervention. *Psychological Science*, *31*(7), 770–780.

Petratos, P. N. (2021). Misinformation, disinformation, and fake news: Cyber risks to business. *Business Horizons*, *64*(6), 763–774.

PlushCare (2022, November 18). *How accurate is mental health advice on TikTok?* Plush Care. https://plushcare.com/blog/tiktok-mental-health/

Russell, T. (2021, March 11). *Real Philly therapists on the worst mental health advice and trends they've seen on TikTok*. Philly Magazine. https://www.phillymag.com/be-well-philly/2021/03/11/tiktok-mental-health-advice-trends/

Sadeghi, M., & Arvanitis, L. (2023, May 1). *Rise of the Newsbots: AI-generated news websites proliferating online*. NewsGuard. https://www.newsguardtech.com/special-reports/newsbots-ai-generated-news-websites-proliferating/

Schneider, D. E. (2018). Unstructured personal technology use in the classroom and college student learning: A literature review. *Community College Enterprise*.

Shearer, E. (2021, January 12). *More than eight-in-ten Americans get news from digital devices*. Pew Research Center. https://www.pewresearch.org/short-reads/2021/01/12/more-than-eight-in-ten-americans-get-news-from-digital-devices/

Silberling, A. (2023, May 3). *AI can't replace human writers. As TV writers strike, networks refuse to budge on demands not to use AI*. Tech Crunch. https://techcrunch.com/2023/05/03/ai-replace-tv-writers-strike/

Soll, J. (2016, December 18). *The long and brutal history of fake news*. Politico. https://www.politico.com/magazine/story/2016/12/fake-news-history-long-violent-214535/

Stent, D. (2018, August 31). *Social media manipulation of public opinion in Korean elections*. The Diplomat. https://thediplomat.com/2018/09/social-media-manipulation-of-public-opinion-in-korean-elections/

Thorbecke, C. (2023, January 26). *Plagued with errors: A news outlet's decision to write stories with AL backfires*. CNN Business. https://www.cnn.com/2023/01/25/tech/cnet-ai-tool-news-stories/index.html

Wendling, M. (2016, December 2). *The sage of 'Pizzagate': The fake story that shows how conspiracy theories spread*. BBC News. https://www.bbc.com/news/blogs-trending-38156985

Young, K. (2017, October 21). *Moon shot: Race, a hoax, and the birth of fake news*. The New Yorker. https://www.newyorker.com/books/page-turner/moon-shot-race-a-hoax-and-the-birth-of-fake-news

Yurkevich, V. (2023). *Why experts worry TikTok could add to mental health crisis among US teens*. CNN Business. https://www.cnn.com/2023/01/11/tech/tiktok-teen-mental-health/index.html

Zajonc, R. B. (1980). Feeling and thinking: Preferences need no inferences. *American Psychologist*, *35*(2), 151.

Zhou, Y., & Shen, L. (2022). Confirmation bias and the persistence of misinformation on climate change. *Communication Research*, *49*(4), 500–523.

Zimdars, M., & McLeod, K. (Eds.). (2020). *Fake news: Understanding media and misinformation in the digital age*. MIT Press.

PART III

Influencers and Memes

How Even the Fun Aspect of Social Media has Downsides for Brands and Societal-Well Being

Angeline Close Scheinbaum

To wrap up this book on corporate cancel culture, we now focus on some of the usually fun aspects of social media in the entertainment sector. Even these sectors have some downsides to business and society from a well-being lens. As we mentioned in Part I, even sports have been dragged into the whole cancel culture world, when two of the most famous soccer (football) teams have received criticism for political affiliations and social media activity (Tobar et al., Chapter 3). Part III begins with Sayan Gupta and Medha Reddy Edunuri, who are one of the first set of authors to really investigate social media influencers and the brands they endorse from a purely critical lens. As they mention in their groundbreaking chapter, "The Dark Side of Social Media Influencers for Brands," most of the scholarship in influencer marketing has really focused on marketing-oriented topics such as how to enhance ROI, how to have the best influencer-brand fit, differences in influencer types (e.g., micro-influencers vs. macro-influencers), and characteristics of influencers for sales-related outcomes. In a new lens, Gupta and Edunuri (Chapter 5) examine many cases of when influencer marketing has gone wrong. They have shown that in many of these cases, companies can learn lessons and avoid pitfalls associated with influencer marketing.

Their work flows well into the next chapter (Chapter 6), that also studies social media influencers. In Chapter 6, scholars Jingyun Hu and Kevin Flynn take a multi-disciplinary (economics and marketing) approach to focusing on the livestream aspect to social media. Namely, many social media sites incorporate e-commerce or shopping, and they use live influencers during live "sales casts" (called livestreams) to help sell products via e-commerce/ social media. Livestreams on social media represent a hot topic; there are

DOI: 10.4324/9781032670546-8

more papers coming out on this topic just in the last year or so, as it is a newer sales or marketing approach. While it has been popular in some Asian countries, other countries such as the US are seeing livestreams more in their e-commerce or social media screens. Hu and Flynn make a very timely and rigorous contribution with the chapter "The Dark Side of Social Media Livestream for Brands and Profits." Some may equate the notion of livestreams with the traditional "Home Shopping Network," or even infomercials as they equate a bit of entertainment with information and the ability to "call now" to order or to place a sale. In today's modern era, social media is a place where the influencers on livestreams can entertain and inform. But there is a dark side to this, as consumers can become addicted, buy too much, or have other mental health impacts. From a sales lens, the companies can have issues with the influencers and their personal transgressions can negatively transfer to the platform or the brand/product being sold via livestream.

While usually shopping online and via social media is fun, there is the dark side to influencer marketing. This brings us to the final chapter to conclude this book on the dark side of social media and corporate cancel culture. The authors from the esteemed Moody College of Communications at The University of Texas at Austin, Kat Williams and Scott R. Stroud, investigate the usually bright side topic of Memes. Their timely and novel chapter, "The Dark Side of Memes for Brands and Society," looks at usually fun memes involving politicians, cats, and other societal spoofs. Many of these are attempted forms of spreading fun and humor on the Internet, namely social media (especially YouTube).

But what happens when these memes go too far? They can hurt people, harm their name/image/likeness, and harm their human brand or personal reputation. Imagine googling yourself and the first thing that pops up is a meme, or a spoof of a picture of you. It has happened to many businesses, politicians, and celebrities. In fact, I even have a student who has become a meme, as her reaction to Clemson losing a sport game to our rival summed up the fan attitude perfectly. Her name/image/likeness with a stunned face was put on the jumbotron and subsequently captured on social media (without her name). While she took this in good light and shared this with our class in a bought of humor, for many, the "memefication" of society has gone too far. Williams and Stroud illuminate this concept, and they even turn to Kant for the moral philosophy to explain how memes can go wrong, and what brand and societal impacts can result from the modern meme culture.

6

THE DARKER SIDE OF SOCIAL MEDIA INFLUENCER MARKETING FOR BRANDS AND THEIR ECOSYSTEM

Sayan Gupta and Medha Reddy Edunuri

Introduction

The Rise and Rise of Social Media Influencer (SMI) Marketing

As we start writing this chapter, one of the biggest business-related news stories in the US is the downfall of America's (no-longer) biggest beer brand, Bud Light. The reason – their decision to celebrate Dylan Mulvaney's gender transition anniversary on social media platforms which sparked an enormous backlash from conservative-leaning netizens. Unless one has been living under the rock (or away from social media networks), they would know that Mulvaney is a TikTok star influencer known for detailing her gender transition in daily videos since early 2022. This story has potential for several takeaways about societal issues plaguing the country today. However, as marketers and business professionals, we can't help but reflect on the impact social media influencers (SMIs) have had and continue to have on consumers and brands.

Social media and user-generated content from the ever-increasing numbers of its users have become primary sources of information for consumers (Burtch et al., 2022; Lou & Yuan, 2019; Shiau et al., 2018). The 3.6 billion social media users in 2020 are expected to continue their exponential population growth and reach a massive 4.4 billion landmark in 2025 (Statista, 2021), thus making social media the go-to strategy for brands to engage their consumers (Osei-Frimpong & McLean, 2018; Shahbaznezhad et al., 2021).

SMI marketing is already brands' most sought-after promotional tool (Digital Marketing Institute, 2021) and has become an integral part of the business ecosystem – conservative estimates suggest its economic value to be pegged at $13.8 billion in 2021 (Kozinets et al., 2023; Statista, 2021).

DOI: 10.4324/9781032670546-9

E-Marketer (2023) suggests 86% of marketers will employ SMIs for their campaigns by 2025 while the vast majority of brands believe in their effectiveness. Influencer marketing optimally combines the four types of a brand's social media presence – paid (e.g., pay-per-post influencer campaigns), earned (e.g., unprompted positive word-of-mouth from influencers, traditional media coverage of the influencer campaigns), shared (engagement from the influencer's followers and virality), and owned (brands buying or repurposing existing influencer content), thus making it a lot more persuasive for consumers than other traditional means of advertising in breaking through the information clutter on the internet (Campbell & Farrell, 2020). It is therefore no wonder that brands proactively seek this appeal of influencer campaigns to enhance their brand equity through awareness and relevance.[1]

Aim and Objectives of the Chapter

The growing domination of SMIs as content generators for consumers and a promotional tool for brands and their products has received due attention from academics, as evidenced from several conceptual, empirical, and review papers detailing various aspects of influencer marketing as well as calls for more academic research in several special issues (Appel et al., 2020; Taylor, 2020; Voorveld, 2019). In this chapter, we use existing frameworks and contexts, relevant theories, constructs, and concepts in SMI marketing to examine the current state of the literature and highlight avenues for future empirical research that explores the darker side of this ecosystem (i.e., the consumer-SMI-brand relationship triad).

For doing so, we use a systematic review approach (Hulland & Houston, 2020; Swaminathan et al., 2022) to first consolidate influencer marketing-related themes and theories from multiple journals in marketing, public relations, management, and consumer research. We then use these findings to accomplish the primary objective of this chapter, which is to shed some much-needed light on the potential negative impacts of these highly influential collaborations and some directions in which researchers need to prioritize explorations. We then use a case study approach (Ravenswood, 2011; Eisenhardt, 1989) to suggest possible future research directions – i.e., we present multiple case studies from recent interactions of influencers with businesses and consumers that most closely hint at the overarching malaise of these new-age practices. Finally, we provide some thoughts on ethical, policy, and consumer guidelines that may help avoid these pitfalls, as well as complications in their implementation. In doing so, this chapter hopes to streamline the process of producing academic research that contributes to the protection of key stakeholders involved (Wellman et al., 2020), especially the vulnerable ones.

Themes and Theories in Influencer Marketing Literature

Literature Review Methodology

We performed a systematic literature review to synthesize SMI literature into an integrative framework (Wang & Chugh, 2014, Mihalache & Mihalache, 2016) and identify opportunities for future research pertaining to their negative impacts (Hao et al., 2021; Mishra et al., 2021; Paul & Rosado-Serrano, 2019). The focus of this review was on papers published in peer-reviewed journals documenting SMI-brand and SMI-consumer interactions without any restrictions on the methodology used – so, we included papers with qualitative, conceptual, empirical, experimental, and meta-analytic approaches under its purview.

We took the following steps to choose articles for our review: (1) we used Google Scholar and databases such as EBSCO to identify articles that contained the keywords "social media influencer" or "digital influencer" in their title or abstract; (2) we further screened for marketing and consumer-focused business journals listed on the ABDC ranking that have published research on this topic (for journals such as *Management Science* and *Journal of Business Research*, we included "marketing" and "consumer" as requisite keywords within the article abstract); and (3) we included other articles that were part of previous systematic reviews on this topic, leaving us with 84 articles. We then used the content of each article to code it on the basis of the primary themes and theories observed. We consolidate them in the following sections.

Defining Characteristics of SMIs

Social media empowered numerous regular non-celebrity individuals to create and share unique content pertaining to their lives – in the process, gaining extraordinary "reach" (Hudders et al., 2021) through their legion of direct and indirect followers (Nascimento et al., 2020) and "impact" through their strength of persuasion over their audience (Nyangwe & Buhalis, 2018). As ubiquitous as influencer marketing is, SMI research has had to wrestle with defining influencers as it can often depend on who you ask – marketing scholars, legal practitioners or the influencers themselves (who, often prefer being called a content creator instead). We tend to agree with Kozinets et al. (2023)'s characterization which suggests that SMIs build "meaningful relationships with an audience through consistently providing social media content, featuring authentic performances and a distinctive voice and image, all reflecting and contributing to their personal brand" – in the process, playing multiple roles of a micro-celebrity, an opinion leader, a brand ambassador, a digital marketer, and a content creator all at once.

Classifications can be done based on (1) the industry where an SMI has the strongest sphere of influence, (2) source of popularity (primary careers, social media platform of choice, etc.), (3) influence analytics or breadth of influence (nano- vs micro- vs mega- vs celebrity influencers), and (4) legal status (depending on whether they are consumers or contractual freelancers or brands themselves; Goanta & Ranchordás, 2020). In addition to "expertise" and "authenticity," Hudders et al. (2021) identify "intimacy" as a third crucial ingredient for success – i.e., SMIs' ability to appeal to consumers' quest for similarity, familiarity, and likeability (Ohanian, 1991) of a close peer in addition to, and oftentimes despite, the star-struck feeling they get from associating with a distant celebrity. Next, we note the drivers of these key SMI characteristics – reach, impact, expertise, authenticity, and intimacy.

Psychological and Sociological Foundations of Social Media Influence

Fowler and Thomas (2023) provide an exhaustive list of theories that have been used in understanding the SMI phenomenon especially as it applies to their success in achieving the extent of persuasiveness and engagement from social media users. The Social Learning (Maisto et al., 1999), Identity (Moscovici, 1963), Comparison (Gerber et al., 2018), and Exchange (Cropanzano et al., 2017) (henceforward referred to as SLICE) theories have been predominantly used in explaining the "reach" aspect of influencers. These theories attribute the expansion of SMIs' sphere of influence to their position of importance within the social networks, conferring them social powers through a culmination of six main sources of influence – reward powers, coercive powers, legitimate powers, referent powers, expertise powers, and informational powers (French et al.,1959; Kozinets et al., 2023).

The Persuasion Knowledge Model (Friestad & Wright, 1994) enjoys prominence in explaining the "impact" aspect of influencers, observing that the persuasiveness of SMIs is a direct consequence of the distrust and resistance among consumers against traditional advertising. The inherent willingness to trust SMIs comes about from the appeal of listening to and learning from peers and "real people" as a relief from untrusted salespersons and high-value celebrity endorsements. This theory also highlights the importance of the perceived authenticity of SMIs in the minds of their followers, as does the Source Credibility Model (Hovland & Weiss, 1951; Ohanian, 1991).

The Two-Step Flow of Communication Theory (Katz et al., 2017) explains their "expertise" dimension, as consumers prefer opinion leaders that can assimilate and interpret complex messages from the original source (i.e., the brands) in a linguistic style (Wang et al., 2019) that is more palatable to them. The Elaboration Likelihood Model (Petty & Briñol, 2011) backs this up, especially when expertise is the source of SMI followership, by suggesting that consumers process information from influencers more centrally than in the case of other promotional tools, thus making SMI campaigns stickier.

The intimacy (Feng et al., 2021) dimension comes from consumers' affinity for parasocial interactions (Horton & Wohl, 1956) that existed with celebrities in the past, but technological and social affordances of social media (Bucher & Helmond, 2018) enable the establishment of stronger and more personal bonds between SMIs and audiences who are therefore a lot more prone to invest their emotional energies into these relationships (Munnukka et al., 2019; Kowalczyk & Pounders, 2016). In addition to Ohanian (1991)'s source credibility theory, criteria for SMI success are laid out by Attribution Theory (Oliver, 1993; Weiner, 1985; suggesting that positive attribution of communication improves persuasiveness) and the Match-Up Hypothesis (Kamins, 1990; suggesting higher SMI-brand and SMI-consumer fit improves persuasiveness).

Hence, SMIs attach great importance to intimacy as the mechanism to creating strong parasocial connection and persuasive appeal (Sokolova & Kefi, 2020). The importance of these characteristics is expected to evolve as nano-SMIs gradually transition from relatable associative-group peers to aspirational revered and admired celebrity SMIs (although no robust empirical studies document these mechanisms). Authenticity is also important, and it can be primed on social media (Luoma-aho et al., 2019).

The other set of important theories that pertain to SMI culture comes from sociological foundations which establish influencer economics in the context of the resource-dependency theory (Pfeffer & Salancik, 2015). This observes the influence that the social media platforms exert over the behavioral patterns of SMIs owing to the affordances they provide (Bucher & Helmond, 2018). These platforms clearly provide SMIs with the means to connect with their audiences and therefore, the means to all the social capital they possess in the influencer ecosystem, which in turn gives them financial power when monetized.

This power imbalance is significant – one that these platforms exercise using two key tools – algorithms and data. Kozinets et al. (2023) call this the SMI superstructure, the power of which can be estimated by the tremors running across the $100 billion-plus creator economy in the US after Congress discussed a TikTok ban.[2] Concerns were expressed by none other than second-term presidential hopeful Donald Trump who backtracked on his previously held disdain for Chinese social media companies' data privacy policies in favor of the will of "young people" who would "go crazy" without it.[3]

Managerial Research on Influencer Marketing

Research on Consumer Engagement in Response to Influencer-Brand Collaboration. As mentioned in the preceding section, source credibility is key to consumer engagement (Djafarova & Trofimenko, 2019; Sundermann & Raabe, 2019) and persuasion (Artz & Tybout, 1999; Smith et al., 2013). The perceived attractiveness, expertise, and trustworthiness (Ohanian, 1991) of SMIs make consumers more likely to internalize the brand message. The importance of these credibility factors and their subdimensions depends on SMI classifiers – industry, social media platform, size of followership (Pradhan et al., 2016; Pradhan et al., 2023; among others). For instance, congruity, similarity, and the consequent strength of parasocial relationship (Hu et al., 2021; Shan et al., 2020) may be a strong indicator of early SMI success on Instagram while the perceived expertise dimension would dominate in the case of a YouTube reviewer of automobiles.

Tracking sources of SMI engagement is critical for consumer insights (AlFarraj et al., 2021; Argyris et al., 2020; Giakoumaki & Krepapa, 2020; Jiménez-Castillo & Sánchez-Fernández, 2019; Kostygina et al., 2020; Woodcock & Johnson, 2021). Literature unanimously reports higher impacts on brand attitudes from SMI campaigns than celebrity endorsements (Delbaere et al., 2021; Djafarova & Rushworth, 2017; Jin et al., 2019; Schouten et al., 2021), and attributes this to source credibility dimensions (Lou & Yuan, 2019; Breves et al., 2021; Cooley & Parks-Yancy, 2019; Kay et al., 2020; Sokolova & Kefi, 2020; Trivedi & Sama, 2020). The mechanism is called "networked affect" according to Hillis et al. (2015).

Some key generalizations that marketing literature has been able to draw out about the success of influencer-brand collaborations include the moderating (or rather, the enhancing) effect of endorser-brand-product congruence (Kapitan & Silvera, 2016; Silva et al., 2020; Torres et al., 2019), originality and uniqueness (Casaló et al., 2020), individuality of SMIs in the co-creation process (vs commercial orientation of the post) (Martínez-López et al., 2020; Borchers & Enke, 2021), content hedonicity (Hughes et al., 2019), and brand awareness (Lu et al., 2014). Hudders and De Jans (2022) and Vrontis et al. (2021) provide an exhaustive review of the mediators and moderators impacting the link between influencer marketing and brand consequences and find agreement with Leung et al. (2022)'s empirical findings.

Research on Goldilocks Influencers. This multidimensionality of SMI-brand success and the availability of so many options in the SMI space make it critical for firms to develop their internal standard operating procedures for finding their goldilocks influencers – i.e., the SMIs which would be the optimal fit for the brand campaign and incur the best Return on Investment for the firm. Influencer activity, follower–brand fit, and post positivity have all been shown to exert inverted U-shaped moderating effects on SMI marketing effectiveness, suggesting the need for a balanced approach (Leung et al., 2022). For instance, studies initially identified in-degree centrality of SMIs with respect to other nodes in social networks as a major predictor of success (Bokunewicz & Shulman, 2017; del Fresno García et al.,

2016) which forced advertisers to spend millions recruiting and seeding more popular and centrally located influencers for faster diffusion of information (Goldenberg et al., 2009; Libai et al., 2013; Yoganarasimhan, 2012). However, these weaker ties with celebrity SMIs (Granovetter, 1973) often miss the mark when users actually seek interactive communal relationships (De Veirman et al., 2017).

Subsequent studies that considered both reach and strength of influence are ambivalent with regard to optimal seeding strategies (Hinz et al., 2011; Libai et al., 2013; Chen et al., 2017; Haenlein & Libai, 2013; Barratt, 2021). Two campaign properties – content customization from SMIs and brand familiarity (Purohit & Srivastava, 2001) – are necessary in engaging users who dislike high follower numbers of SMIs. This is still an evolving area of research in influencer marketing and is expected to produce generalizable findings in times to come.

Influencer Sponsorship Disclosures. A major ethical and legal concern with influencer marketing (Goanta & Ranchordás, 2020) has been the lack of transparency and disclosure of sponsored content. Influencers' hesitation in disclosing their sponsored content stems from their followers' expectation of "authenticity" and source credibility (Karagür et al., 2022; De Veirman & Hudders, 2020). Advertising recognition from consumers (Boerman, 2020; De Jans & Hudders, 2020) reduces their efficacy on brand attitudes and purchase intentions, sometimes even harming them (De Veirman & Hudders, 2020) – as would be predicted by persuasion knowledge theories. While most studies support this view, some studies that observed positive effects include Boerman (2020) (on brand recall and post-engagement), (De Jans et al., 2020) (on brand liking) and Kay et al. 2020 (purchase likelihood). Other literature (Sah et al., 2018; Stubb & Colliander, 2019; De Jans & Hudders, 2020) document contingencies for these disparate outcomes.

Naderer et al. (2021), for instance, find a silver lining in that a clear and honest disclosure may increase influencer trustworthiness, so SMIs need to walk the tightrope balancing sponsored and non-sponsored content (Van Dam & Van Reijmersdal, 2019). It is also important to note and recall that even with the obvious downside of sponsorship disclosure, studies consistently find that influencer endorsements are more effective than celebrity endorsements (Schouten et al., 2021; Jin & Muqaddam, 2019).

Need for Research on the Darker Side of SMI Marketing

The popularity of influencers for both content creation and brand promotions has translated into voluminous academic research on influencers (Appel et al., 2020; Taylor, 2020; Voorveld, 2019). Our afore-mentioned analysis conforms with previously conducted systematic and scoping reviews of SMI marketing (Ye et al., 2021, among several others). We find that these

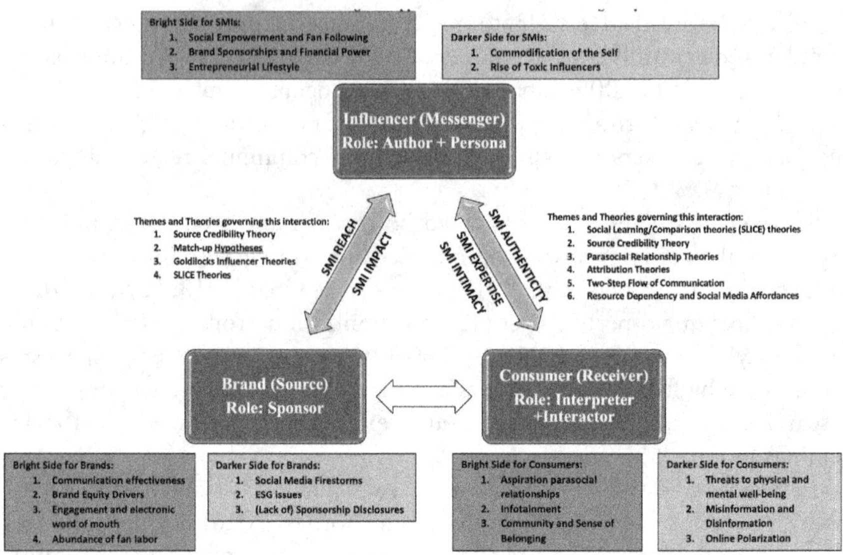

FIGURE 6.1 The Revised Communication Model for Advertising as It Applies to the Current SMI Marketing Ecosystem

publications revolved around a few prevalent themes as laid out in the previous sections – persuasiveness of influencer marketing; analysis of positive impact on stakeholders (primarily, consumers and brands); identification, selection, and activation of influencers to maximize these positive impacts; and the moderating influence of sponsorship disclosures on these positive impacts. Evidently, the focus of extant studies in influencer marketing has been to unravel SMI success mechanisms while explaining their effectiveness (Hudders et al., 2021). Negative aspects of SMI marketing in academic literature have largely been limited to themes surrounding the lack of transparency in advertising disclosures (Karagür et al., 2022).

The ever-growing success of SMIs in these contexts makes this an opportune time to take a step back from expounding on their bright sides and theorize on the dark sides of these brand-SMI-consumer interactions. This study fills this gap by highlighting these dark sides as they affect the three primary stakeholders in influencer marketing – the brands, the consumers, and the SMIs themselves. In doing so, we shed light on several aspects of influencer culture that show the need for the field to develop ethical guidelines and professional best practices so that the risks to these stakeholders are minimized, especially the most vulnerable ones.

We use a three-sided framework (Figure 6.1) based on the Revised Communication Model for Advertising (Stern, 1994) – treating brand communications as messages sent from a source (brands) to a receiver (social media users) mediated through a communication channel (SMIs, in this case), often including complex interactions between these three agents. Hudders et al. (2021) suggest that influencers are increasingly empowered to move away from being passive spokespersons and take up the role of the creator instead, thus encumbering them with higher creative and even legal responsibility for the advertising messages. In addition, the consumer in the social media context acts not just as an active listener to the communication, but also as a participant providing feedback to the source and messenger and in turn, constantly influencing the behavioral tendencies of the other agents in the communication process. In the following sections, we use this framework to extend the theories and themes from the previous sections to postulate the flipsides of SMI marketing to these three key stakeholders in the communication process.

Darker Side of SMI Marketing for Consumers

Consumer Mental and Physical Well-being

CASE 6.1 THE VIRAL MUKBANG TREND AND THE DESIRE TO OVERCONSUME.

The Mukbang phenomenon is a prime example of how the social media ecosystem can exploit basic human desires (the pleasure of eating vicariously, in this case) and amplify them into a negative spiral of consumer brand desire. Mukbang, literally translated to "eating broadcast," is an online audiovisual livestream in which "Mukbangers" devour a large meal portion and record themselves eating enthusiastically while engaging with food lovers who tune in for an interactive experience. Even though the feast for the eyes is calorie-free, it is certainly not inconsequential to people making and watching these videos. Mukbang emerged in prominence in South Korea in 2009 when TV and movie scenes of actors and actresses eating and whetting others' appetites gained popularity (Kim, 2021) – this caught on in the US in 2015 when a bunch of YouTubers reacted to a mukbang video. At the time, people reacting to the video did not realize just how big of a trend this was going to become.

There is, however, a vast majority of the population on the internet who are perplexed by the very nature of these videos and absolutely cannot fathom their popularity. They do not get the appeal of watching individuals eat a meal that is meant for a family of ten in a single sitting. While some people take issue with the chewing, gulping, and swallowing food effects, others can't stand the mere mess and the way the food is eaten. For some others, the whole practice just screams gluttony and wastefulness. But Mukbangers do not care. They continue to reach more people, get more likes, increase the shock value of their content, and grab more attention.

Why do people watch mukbangs? Kim (2021) puts it down to the inherent natural drive for "carnal" experiences (i.e., experiences and expressions appealing to consumers' "sentient, sensual and sensible ensemble of materialized capabilities and agency"), no more different than the human indulgence for porn or even foodporn, where people show off their food on social media The familiarity and relatability aspects of the source attractiveness model dictate that these videos don't struggle to find their audience. However, the uniqueness requirements of source attractiveness make it imperative for SMIs to produce over-the-top content in order to stand out in the vast majority of food content creators – so, the aesthetics of mukbang videos have gradually devolved into being vulgar, multi-sensual, and excessive. Regardless of whether these videos elicit relaxation or disgust, they "engage." Kim (2021) further notes that "eventually, the articulation of [SMIs'] desire and will to consume food and achieve fame and money, along with fans' desires to [reciprocate], realize the logic of the 'attention economy'" (Goldhaber, 1997; Andrejevic, 2004; Dahl et al., 2015; van Dijck et al., 2018). The number of other agents invested in this activity (restaurant owners, corporates, social media platforms) only aids in fueling this fire and creates a "social network market" (Banks & Humphreys, 2008).

Where this turns problematic is the normalization of consuming unhealthy, strange, and dangerously large portions of food in a society that is already plagued by physical health and obesity issues – not to mention the lack of sensitivity toward the underfed populations of the world. The SLICE theories predict that such videos can lead to craving, hunger, and even overeating in consumers – particularly people who suffer from food-reward sensitivity (Maxwell et al., 2020). The absence of mechanisms to protect vulnerable audiences who have a complicated relationship with food makes it a dangerous and dark side-effect of the SMI phenomenon. Mukbangs are only one of the many byproducts of the social media superstructures fueling consumers' unhealthy doomscrolling addiction.

CASE 6.2 PHOTOSHOP, PHOTO-FILTERS, AND BODY DYSMORPHIA.

The old, the young, the bold, the beautiful, the fast, the furious – everyone's chasing after unrealistic beauty standards upheld by social media.

For centuries, it has been common for humans, especially women, to conform to societal norms and transform into different shapes and forms. But social media comes with its unique challenges in this regard. The need for social attractiveness, especially among beauty influencers, makes it imperative for them to invest their financial, emotional, and temporal resources to shapeshift at the whim of a new beauty trend. Although these standards are impossible to live up to, SLICE mechanisms make them impossible to ignore for the large following they have been able to cultivate. Lo and Behold: Social Media filters – Now, people have the chance to look like their popular parasocial friend, albeit only for a snap. Now, they can project a face that looks like a better version of their true self.

Now, their heavily edited photograph receives more likes than an unedited one. Now, they can (un)safely internalize the message that all they need to look good enough is to make their noses a bit smaller, lips a bit fuller, teeth straighter, jawlines more sculpted. Now, they can give off the perfect illusion of youth by using the new TikTok age filter, which according to Dr. Dominic Castellano, "gives an idealized artificial appearance of youth, applying a one size fits all template." As ephemeral as these filters and social media posts are, the permanent damage to the well-being of vulnerable (read, young and impressionable) social media users can range from mental (body dysmorphia) to physical (going under the knife in search of the filter-look) to anything in between. While it is hard to blame SMIs for what is clearly a social media tool and an undeniable economic nexus with the billion-dollar beauty industry, it is important to note their hypocrisy in spreading the message of being "comfortable in your own skin."

How truly impactful was Kim Kardashian in the rise of Botox, facial fillers, and butt-lift surgeries (Guardian, 2022)? Is it really a coincidence that the huge increase in SMI expenditure during the COVID-19 pandemic coincided with a significant increase in cosmetic procedures (Aktas et al., 2023)? While literature still looks into these questions, it is well-understood that the more authentic and intimate the perceived relationships in the minds of the SMI followers, the higher their vulnerability to undergo this distress. The above two cases are just a few examples of how SMIs can prove to be disseminators of toxic positivity[4] in a bid to maintain their social attractiveness among their followers. Can SMI marketing even work with realistic influencers when they are recruited to promote positivity and principles of "good vibes only" and "happiness is a choice"? It's hard to imagine, but it would be worth understanding its holistic impacts on consumers and devising policies and best practices accordingly.

Misinformation/Disinformation

CASE 6.3 ALT. HEALTH AND CONSPIRITUALITY INFLUENCERS.

Baker (2022) documents the impact of 4 alt. health SMIs on anti-vaccine misinformation during the COVID-19 pandemic – (1) Pete Evans – a "chef, nutritional and emotional well-being and expanded consciousness influencer," whose claim to fame included a pseudoscientific non-medical Bio-Charger for treating COVID-19 among others, (2) David Avocado Wolfe – an "author, actor, public speaker, entrepreneur, and the rock star and Indiana Jones of superfoods and longevity," who sold coated silver as a COVID immunity booster, (3) Kelly Brogan – drug-free life influencer, and (4) Sacha Stone, sovereign expression influencer and "founder of the World Health Sovereignty Summit." These SMIs used their popularity on social media platforms for socioeconomic and political gains (Baker, 2022) thorough misinformation, conspirituality (Parmigiani, 2021), and political extremism before these platforms removed them. YouTube suspended Sacha Stone and David Avocado Wolfe's accounts while Facebook deactivated Stone and Pete Evans' account. Journalists in mainstream media have written about YouTube radicals (Roose, 2019).

Why do these influencers resort to propaganda? Baker (2022) argues for a three-step transition rooted in the source attractiveness and persuasion knowledge theories. First, their initial micro-celebrity status comes from the great equalizing democratic force of social media (Boyd, 2014) that facilitates participatory culture (Jenkins, 2006) where their accessibility incentivizes them to earn their followers' trust by creating an "authentic, autonomous and credible alternatives to institutional authority" persona (Baker & Rojek, 2020). Second, the desire to preserve this uniqueness among their followers makes them susceptible to the persecuted-hero rabbit-hole where their symbolic anti-establishment positioning gives way to conspiracy theories and political extremism.

Finally, they take advantage of the intimacy and participatory affordances of social media to encourage followers to invest emotionally in the issues and individuals they are exposed to online (e.g., lifestyle and wellness influencers calling on their followers to participate in a "journey of self-discovery, self-transformation and spiritual awakening"). These examples highlight the need for marketing research to examine the negative impacts of misinformation from SMIs who clearly excel at personal branding and influence consumers independently or in collaboration with brands. Other forms of misinformation that need investigation from the consumers' point-of-view include a wide range of influencer activities – clickbait, deceptive advertising, self-victimizations for political marketing, and influence farming, to name a few.

Online Polarization

CASE 6.4 AMBER HEARD VS JOHNNY DEPP.

Johnny Depp the star vs Johnny Depp the real person, Johnny Depp the abuser vs Johnny Depp the abused, online petitions to put Depp back in the Pirates franchise vs feminists demanding justice for the victimized Amber Heard, Johnny Depp using his clout against his estranged ex-wife vs calls for canceling Amber Heard, the Gone-Girl style manipulator. These were just a few ways SMIs framed the televised and highly publicized courtroom trial between the celebrity couple. Regardless of how the court ruled, there is no doubt who the real winners were – content creators, their followers, and the social media platforms enabling them – completely desensitized to the line between entertainment and real legal proceedings. For information on polarization, Iyengar et al. (2019) notes how this can be problematic

It was the microcosmic embodiment of influencer culture – the social power of stardom, parasocial relationships that blur our judgment, attempts to enhance one's own likeability often by downplaying someone else's, pumping up the under-dog, the Hollywood royal rumble – and both parties had PR teams incessantly working behind the scenes to sway public opinion in their favor using the unmatched reach and persuasiveness of SMIs. Actor Johnny Depp sued his ex-wife and actor Amber Heard for $50 million over a 2018 op-ed she wrote for The Washington Post, which chronicled her experiences as a domestic abuse survivor. While Depp was never mentioned by name, his lawyers contend that it was obvious who Heard referred to in the piece, and that the article damaged Depp's career and reputation.[5]

The he-said, she-said drama was closely followed on social media with a variety of trending polarized hashtags including #JusticeForJohnny, #AmberHeardIsAPsycopath, #AmberHeardIsInnocent, and #IStandWithAmberHeard. The jury delivered a verdict that, though mixed, strongly favored the plaintiff Depp. Since the case was contested as much on social media as it was inside the Virginia courtroom, the SMIs supporting the Pirates of the Caribbean star rejoiced while Team Amber cried foul play.

Could one even argue that the social media chatter plays no role in influencing jury decisions? How does such polarized SMI chatter influence complicated judicial proceedings? These are all questions academic research needs to find answers to. As for the reason one should expect influencer opinion to be polarized – there is voluminous literature in marketing and economics expounding on subscription revenue models and the dangerous bias it induces in media channels' content (Mullainathan & Shleifer, 2005). We see it play out in traditional news media outlets broadcasting news with a political "spin" that keeps their subscribers satisfied and loyal. This involves sensationalization of mundane stories, pitching stories in the form of arguments, and otherizing opinions from the opposite end of the aisle. SMIs are driven by the same economic incentives. Kozinets et al. (2023) note three enabling forces for the current influencer culture – namely, dramatization, intensification, and commodification.

Dramatization involves producing a narrative in which influencers incorporate themselves into an ongoing story (Hearn, 2008), and intensification entails deliberate attention-grabbing efforts to insert strong, vivid, evocative, or emotional content into lifestyle stories (Just, 2019). A currently popular way to ensure these two effects is by co-opting a larger social purpose and making it a cornerstone of content creation – it could be climate change, LGBTQIA+ issues, or, as in the case of the above example, feminism and women's rights (for Team Amber) and men's rights (for Team Depp). On several occasions, such a single-minded focus on purpose forces the extremization of SMIs where they develop provocative, controversial, strong, and polarizing beliefs and opinions so that the social media algorithms can grab them more eyeballs which only serves to positively reinforce this polarization (which is especially harmful in politics according to Layman et al., 2006). It is no wonder that we are seeing a rapidly growing population of influencer activists that fit the spectrum from veganism lifestyle gurus to "gunfluencers." Whether influencer activism and polarization are good or bad, remains to be seen, but such conversations can be hotbeds for misinformation and rumors (Shore et al., 2018), lead to strong negativity spirals (Dhaoui & Webster, 2021), and turn into a dark sidecycle of strengthening echo-chambers.).

This is not limited to the political arena, as a majority of social media discourse devolves into polarized communities and hateful counterarguments – be it brand communities, celebrity fandoms, or comic book and movie lovers. Echo chambers are further accentuated through algorithmic biases and personalization of content, and the centrifugal forces of echo-chambers are most pronounced in influencer-follower relationships as audiences self-select into trusting every word that comes out of their favorite opinion leader's mouths. Research on the negative impacts on consumers from being in these closed loops would lead to fruitful academic contributions.

Mitigating the Dark Side of SMI Marketing for Consumers

It may be interesting to ponder if businesses should be punished for endorsing Mukbangers to promote their food products and beauty influencers to promote their cosmetic products. Similar questions revolve around the role played by social media platforms in SMIs continually succumbing to the temptations of misinformation, polarization, and sensationalization. Even in the presence of policies regulating such behavior, it is debatable how realistically regulators can attribute these impacts on the multiple-faceted SMI ecosystem, let alone enforce these policies. These difficulties make us believe that the solution must come from within, at least in the near term – i.e., through self-regulation within the SMI ecosystem. This is because all three players – brands, SMIs, and their preferred social media platforms – have economic incentives to self-regulate as consumer trust is critical for their success. Khamitov et al. (2024)'s meta-analysis on trust, for instance, highlights the importance of integrity-based trust factors and reliability-based trust factors on consumers' attitudinal and behavioral success indicators – engagement, purchase intention, satisfaction, and loyalty.

The importance of consumer trust in brands and organizations is especially striking in today's business climate, because several notable industry reports underscore its steep decline for decades.Thus, adopting mitigative measures not only provides an additional layer of brand safety (covered in a later section) but also provides them with a competitive advantage in nurturing consumer trust. Some of these measures include hiring people as fact checkers), DEI policies in SMI recruitments (Veresiu & Parmentier, 2021), and algorithmic innovations that prevent brand desire spirals and protect vulnerable consumers (Kozinets et al., 2023).

For instance, some notable fact-checking organizations include FactCheck.org, Snopes, PolitiFact, and FullFact, offer automated fact-checking tools DEI policies within the SMI ecosystem need a focus on influencer pay structure ageism and body positivity (Veresiu & Parmentier, 2021), mental illness advocacy (Griffith & Stein, 2021), and intersectionality (such as the importance of understanding intersections of being queer and a racial minority as an influencer) There are positive signs of consumers welcoming inclusion-based social media platforms such as Neufluence,[6] body-positivity advocates such as Sofia Grahn[7] and mental illness influencers like Chloe Hayden.[8] Such voices are few and far between, but with the right nudges from the superstructures and algorithms of influence management, we may be able to replicate a more "real" virtual world on these platforms. It is thus encouraging to see the success of apps like BeReal[9] that are finding acceptance from consumers who find the filtered updates on other social media apps stressful and fake.

Finally, we should expect a positive impact from platform-initiated interventions that recognize vulnerable consumers from their behavioral characteristics and mitigate their over-exposure to triggering content through algorithmic advisories when deemed necessary. Luo et al. (2024), among other related studies, provide social media use characteristics that boost impulsive buying tendencies among consumers. Since digital marketing has practically nullified all tracking and verification costs (Goldfarb & Tucker, 2019), it behooves the leading organizations in the space to use their competencies to not only react to but also prevent these overindulgences. Several studies in the network sciences domain hail the efficacy of algorithmic interventions in reducing online polarization – for instance, Garimella et al. (2018) find that simple and inexpensive "bridge-building" between polarized communities provides them a way to talk to each other without conversations turning toxic.

In summary, some of the questions that firms and social media platforms need to ask themselves before SMI campaigns are: what vulnerable populations (children, poor, demographic minorities, consumers in ideological echo-chambers) may end up being targeted and harmed in the process? How, if at all, does our campaign reinforce stereotypes or exploit weaknesses among sections of consumers? What information and background check can we acquire about the history of the endorsed SMIs polarizing and misinforming their followers? While still a tall order, these are key requirements in making the social media space safe and healthy for every user.

Dark Side of SMI Marketing for Brands

Social Media Firestorms and Brand Safety

CASE 6.5 DYLAN MULVANEY AND THE DECLINE OF BUD LIGHT.

Dylan Mulvaney is a young American actor, an influencer who identifies as a transgender woman, and a transgender-rights activist. Bud Light partnered with her in March of 2023 for their new marketing campaign and the whole event met with extraordinary backlash on social media. So much so that Bud Light sales have fallen off a cliff,[10] losing its spot as the best-selling beer in America. While influencer marketing can yield significant benefits for brands, it also carries risks. When influencers bring backlash to a brand, it can have far-reaching consequences on its reputation and consumer perception. What began with the influencer celebrating a year of womanhood by posting a short video of herself with Bud Light turned into outraged political conservatives crushing beer cans, shooting beer bottles with bullets and boycotting the brand. Bud Light had a reputation of being a macho or fraternity boy beer brand and choosing Mulvaney as their spokesperson was seen as a social and political statement.

The then-Marketing VP of the brand said in an interview, "this brand is in decline, it has been in decline for a really long time and if we don't attract young drinkers to come and drink this brand there will be no future for Bud Light."[11] While Bud Light may have wanted a campaign that represents light-hearted fun and inclusivity, their handling of the crisis made it a lot worse. Multiple interviews of the brand's spokespersons failed to address the issue or simply didn't make an impactful statement providing clarity on the issue. As Bud Light continues to struggle, influencers opposed to the transgender movement are having their told-you-so moment. Go broke-Go woke slogans and hashtags keep appearing on social media newsfeeds sending a message to corporate executives about the dangers of partnering with controversial SMIs.

The Match-up Hypothesis has endorser-brand congruence as the key performance indicator of brand-SMI collaborations, so things can go awry when the SMI reflects nothing that the brand stands for. Brands have been punished for maintaining relationships with celebrities accused of wrongdoings even before social media kicked into full gear – for instance, Knittel and Stango (2014) analyze the Tiger Woods controversy in 2012 and the abnormal drops in the stock prices of brands he was an ambassador of. While influencer activism is not a transgression per se, it is certainly controversial as it goes against the ideologies and moralities of a significant part of the population.

The Bud Light example represents a perfect storm of when this population forms a majority of the consumer base of the brand – who immediately started questioning the authenticity of the brand's collaboration leading to a boycott and an irreparable damage to the brand's reputation Social power that influencers have garnered in shaping public opinion can easily backfire against the brand and make a three-month news story out of a three-minute TikTok post. Other dangers arise out of brands' collaboration with SMIs because of the level of co-creation involved in the process. The very nature of influencer marketing dictates that SMIs not just be the spokesperson for the brand but actively participate in the communication process. It gives more credibility to the message and builds stronger associations with the brand. This, however, makes the sponsor–persona separability more difficult in the minds of the consumers, and therefore, any missteps committed by either of those parties reflect very strongly on the other – making these collaborations riskier. Finally, the social media affordances empower SMIs to initiate brand-boycotts which is evident in the burgeoning of the "cancel culture" – the successful Bud Light boycott, for instance, was led by mostly conservative-leaning political influencers while Goya faced a backlash from their liberal counterparts in 2020.[12] These characteristics of influencer culture raise pertinent questions about brand safety (Johnson et al., 2023) in the environment they operate in today.

Influencer Marketing and ESG Issues for Brands

CASE 6.6 OVER-CONSUMPTION AND OVER-THE-TOP CONSUMERISM.

Over-consumption in the clothing and fashion sphere has plagued platforms like Instagram, YouTube, and TikTok in recent years, manifest in the increasing popularity of shopping haul videos – i.e., the practice of SMIs buying stuff in bulk and sharing the experiences with followers. SMIs show multiple outfits in one short video and that requires them to shop every other week while they continually stigmatize outfit-repeating by following the tacit social media rule of not donning the same clothes twice. This leads to the vicious cycle of an increase in fast-fashion consumption and a decrease in the span of trend cycles, which in turn incentivizes brands to invest even more in fast fashion.

Research on fast fashion (Niinimäki et al., 2020) suggests it is environmentally damaging, unethical to workers in factories, and prone to counterfeits. While fast fashion makes it convenient and affordable for lower income groups, they do undermine and devalue the hard labor involved in the making of these garments, diminishing the dignity of labor. Fast-fashion brands operate at lightning speeds to bring the cheaper knock-off version of the original high-priced clothes to consumers – it takes as little as three days to design, manufacture, and deliver these clothes.

Using unsustainable materials that take years to decompose, they end up normalizing counterfeiting and the ongoing dangerous environmental impact caused by over-consumption. They pave the way for micro trends in the fashion industry that last for only about a couple of months and are detrimental in the long run to the original designers, factory workers, influencers, fashion industry, consumers and the planet. At times, micro influencers are a better decision (Ching, 2021). So, brands' strategy of giving in to this hustle of fast turnover by shipping SMIs truckloads of clothes to ensure a social media click and to secure an endorsement, reeks of a departure from their ESG goals of sustainable production.

What SMI marketing mechanisms drive brands away from their ESG goals? The hustle culture of the attention and gig economy embedded within the influencer ecosystem turns SMIs into "autopreneurs" (autobiographical entrepreneurs) – where the social media algorithms make them feel the need to document every moment of their life. In order to gain more followers and attract traction, fashion influencers need to post regularly to hold their audience and invite more to join their community. This immediacy gets dire in TikTok more so than the other platforms because of the under-one-minute algorithms. It would be interesting to understand how enabling such over-consumption practices affect brands' ESG scores and their financial performance.

A strict enforcement of fast-fashion related policies within ESG may actually be able to encourage apparel brands to take a stand against the unwarranted overuse of resources that could be better spent toward improving the lives of the less privileged. Instead, brands are constantly being forced to satisfy the hedonic treadmills. Diener et al. (2009) fueled by this over-the-top consumerism. Additionally, Diversity, Equity, and Inclusion (DEI) issues within the SMI community are another area of concern when it comes to brands' ESG goals. Software tools and influencer management platforms tend to favor white (traditionally) beautiful and heterosexual content creators and undermine diversity and inclusion goals (Kozinets et al., 2023). There are structural elements in the influencer ecosystem that lead to unfair pay gaps and inequity. Brands, agencies, platforms, regulators, and SMIs themselves need to fully commit and co-ordinate in order to reverse these trends in reality.

Violation of Sponsorship Disclosures and Ethical Guidelines

CASE 6.7 FYRE FESTIVAL: THE MUCH-NEEDED SMI MARKETING ANTI-CLIMAX.

There is something about the seduction of charm, charisma, and confidence of con-artists that makes the world oblivious to truth and be swooned by their perfect illusion. Anna Delvey, Elizabeth Holmes, the Tinder swindler, and so on, but the infamous, Fyre Festival is the best example that shows the humongous power of influencer marketing as well as its darkest flipside. The Fyre Festival was a highly publicized music festival that was scheduled to take place in the Bahamas over two weekends in April and May of 2017. The event was promoted as a luxury experience featuring renowned musical performances, high-end accommodations, gourmet food, and celebrity endorsements. However, the festival turned out to be a massive failure and gained widespread attention for its disastrous execution – leading to Fyre Media CEO McFarland being sentenced to six years in federal prison in October 2018 and ordered to forfeit $26 million and pay restitution to his victims.[13] The mind-bending horror story that unfolded included delayed flights, chaotic transportation to the festival site, disaster relief tents instead of the luxurious villas and beachside bungalows advertised, poorly constructed tents with no running water or electricity, lack of essential facilities and services, unsanitary toilets, and the list goes on.

What made the event look promising? The lethal combination of the "reach" and "impact" of SMIs – or from the followers' perspective, their desire to associate with a socially attractive individual (albeit in a parasocial relationship) and the incredible trust that comes from their persuasive abilities. Fyre Festival managed to sell out of tickets largely due to their marketing strategy of promoting the festival through roughly 400 SMIs – including celebrity influencers such as Bella Hadid, Hailey Bieber, and Emily Ratajkowski.[14]

They received millions for social media stories promoting the #FyreFestival but failed to disclose any financial relationships and conflicts of interest. So, consumers paid thousands of dollars for the tickets (some tickets were priced at a quarter of a million dollars) as they were consumed by the FOMO (Fear of Missing Out) on this lavish event of a lifetime. While the Fyre Festival owners were (rightly) punished, almost no recruited influencer faced criminal charges (or even apologized). The preponderance of such slap-on-the-wrist response to SMI transgressions makes it critical for brands to tread carefully with their campaigns.

Mitigating the Dark Side of SMI Marketing for Brands

We propose the following solutions to these crippling impacts of SMI actions on brands:

Influencer Vetting and the Role of SMI Recruiting Agencies. The case studies in this section point to the importance of influencer vetting in the development process of SMI marketing campaigns – i.e., the process of investigating, evaluating, and examining the suitability of an SMI as a communication partner, such as considering rating on points of: Relevance, Reach, Resonance, Recognition, and References.). Larger SMI marketing campaigns require collaborations outside of the marketing functions of organizations – such help comes from in-house talent teams, technology companies' and social media platforms' influencer tools, influencer marketing platforms (e.g., Grin and IZEA), or influencer agencies (e.g., Activate and Open Influence). The increasingly volatile impacts of brand-SMI collaborations suggest the need for building more expertise and specialized skill sets in this area. Mechanisms of risk-sharing between brands and SMI-recruiting agencies could make influencer vetting more reliable, efficient, and less error-prone. There are already applications of AI and other emerging technologies (often clubbed together within "MarTech") in influencer identification software, whether they are used on a stand-alone basis, integrated within platforms or accessed by agencies. More quantification for influencers is necessary (Deborah et al., 2019).

Interventions from Influencer Responsibility Governing bodies (such as FTC and ESG). Digital co-creation between consumers and brands is a relatively new phenomenon (Hoyer et al., 2010), and SMI marketing takes this to the extreme, so trust is an imperative ingredient for such collaborations to succeed. This often involves complex contracts involving multiple functions within organizations and those of agencies when they are involved. Policies need to evolve keeping this spirit of collaboration in context so as to examine the culpability of SMIs in precipitating tragedies such as the Fyre Festival.

While FTC endorsement guidelines now fully apply to SMI-sponsored posts, enforcement strategies are complicated and need oversight to protect vulnerable consumers as FTC gradually moves away from their traditionally preferred tactic to target brands instead of influencers. Since influencer reputation and credibility are key to the sustenance of their relationships with their followers, it is reasonable to expect that developing mechanisms to identify and target SMIs for these ethical and moral transgressions would be a fruitful exercise to undertake. It is also important to note here that the growing popularity of non-human influencers (e.g., AI influencer @lilmiquela, deepfakes that look real, animal influencer Mr. Pokee the hedgehog etc.) further complicates the formulation of ethical boundaries and guidelines for brand-SMI interactions.

Similar arguments apply for international agencies such as ESG to carefully monitor brand activities that indirectly contribute to over-consumption and over-the-top consumerism. A lot of ESG policies become actionable based on what organizations intend to do rather than what they actually do (De Freitas et al., 2020). Stricter regulations are required for a greater alignment between brands' actions and their ESG goals. In this regard, it is worth pointing out that one of the blind spots for brands and ESG has been the algorithmic biases embedded within the influencer vetting software solutions that replicate organizations' skewed pre-conceptions in unjustly unselecting non-white and non-heteronormative SMIs. In general, these governmental and non-governmental organizations need to develop multi-pronged policies for every stakeholder in the SMI ecosystem – the brands, the advertising and PR agencies, the influencers, as well as the publishing and media platforms.

Self-regulation using brand syndicates. For better or for worse, a large part of the mitigation strategies from SMI-related crises falls squarely on the shoulders of brands themselves, because the buck almost certainly stops at their doorstep. In addition to questions about what their product is and who it is being marketed to, brands have to constantly scrutinize how their products and services are being marketed – whether their sales tactics are moral and ethical, if false claims are being made across their channels of communication, whether their influencer communications make them look better than they really are, and so on. Kozinets et al. (2023) provide the following sample of rules to be followed by brands in order to avoid such pitfalls: (1)

Always be truthful; (2) Never Make Unverified Claims; (3) Never Exaggerate Product Claims; (4) Never Make any False Comparisons; and (5) Never Stereotype. Brands need to come up with such self-regulatory moral codes of conduct especially when dealing with a social media rife with misinformation, post-truths, non-human influencers, and subjective moralities arising out of all of these complexities.

Dark Side of SMI Marketing on Influencer Community

Commodification of the Self and Toxic Followership

CASE 6.8 TEEN INFLUENCER'S FATHER KILLS STALKER FOLLOWER.

As reported by Cheong (2022), Ava Majury joined TikTok when she was 13 years old. By 2020, she had over a million followers, mostly men. A devoted fan caught her attention by repeatedly attempting to connect via Snapchat, Instagram, and in TikTok comments. Deeming their interactions harmless, Ava's parents allowed her to sell a couple of selfies to this fan for about $300, which is where things went south. Eric began asking for inappropriate sexual photos and threatening to assault her when her family demanded he stop contacting her. Things escalated further when the teenager fan arrived at Ava's family home in Naples, Florida, carrying a shotgun, blew open the front door and fortunately, could not harm her as his weapon jammed.

Later, the online stalker returned to the house. Ava's father told him to drop the shotgun, but he pointed it at him instead. Then, in self-defense, the retired policeman shot the 18-year-old stalker, and the young man later died. What began as an enterprising young woman's influencer account turned into a tragic awakening about how online fame can lead to stalking and real-world violence. While this interaction may seem like a one-off, there is a whole social media platform – Only Fans, dedicated to the service of such creepy followers and stalkers with an eye for kink. It is one of the many specialized paid subscription-based social media platforms that allow audiences the opportunity to consume additional content and influencers the opportunity to earn revenues unavailable on general advertisement-centric social media platforms. OnlyFans comes with the USP that it doesn't censor sexual or adult content which means that it can cater to passionate followers who want more intimate contact with their favorite influencers – at least the ones that are willing to create risqué and tantalizing content. When contemplated alongside the Ava Majury tragedy, it raises questions of regulation as well as the ethicality of providing a marketplace for potentially dangerous consumers.

What are the antecedents and consequences of commodification? Influencers are participants of the affective labor market, where they perform emotional labor to create desire toward their personal brands and creative content. Their commodification of themselves and their relationships often form the basis for their marketization potential. Commodification happens when things that were not previously sold (friendship, sex, etc.) enter a buyer-seller marketplace – OnlyFans obviously being an extreme and literal case. In the influencer context, it refers to monetization of publicly disseminating traditionally private user-generated content to engage the audience in a way that potentially attracts attention and publicity (Raun, 2018). In the case of influencers, they engage in a social performance (Goffman, 1959) of self-presentation and personal branding through stream-of-consciousness and autobiographical storytelling, often involving family members as well – in the process, building parasocial relationships that, by their very essence, are superficial. These commodified relationships constitute triggers for toxic fan followership and harmful consequences for the SMIs.

Rise of Toxic Influencers

CASE 6.9 ELIOT ROGER AND ANDREW TATE.

Safety has always been an issue for women across nations, cultures, and generations – but what's especially scary about the social media is that it allows hateful comments, problematic views, and dangerous opinions on women to be spread through anonymity, enabling misogynists to find a space such as Reddit to validate their misogyny and misanthropy at large. One such community that is increasing in popularity in the "manosphere" is the incel community – the group of "involuntarily celibates" who blame their lack of romantic success on women. They hold hostile views toward women and are consumed by homicidal rage. Eliot Roger is the infamous "incel hero," who gained notoriety for killing six people in 2014 before killing himself but not before publishing an autobiographical document echoing themes of self-loathing, self-harm, and hatred toward women. A more contemporary social media personality in the toxic-masculinity conversation is Andrew Tate who positions himself as an entrepreneur, motivational speaker, and self-proclaimed dating coach. He offers courses and coaching programs that focus on self-improvement, fitness, relationships, and other aspects of life.

In the process, he openly propagates misogynistic views and upholds the appeal of the traditional gender roles that allows aggrieved entitlement in men, conspicuous consumption of material wealth, and the good old ideals of the patriarchy that serves only men of certain social and economic status. Tate's online presence and motivational speaking have an impact on vulnerable individuals seeking guidance and self-improvement. Despite numerous criminal lawsuits against him, his controversial views combined with persuasive communication skills have swayed several individuals toward adopting these harmful beliefs or engaging in problematic behaviors. Dissemination of such regressive opinions is dangerous, especially in a world that is already maligned with harassment of women, death and rape threats, body shaming, character assassination, and unsolicited pictures of genitalia. The enforcement of strict rules on polarizing and extremist content could help regulate some of the toxicity.

What encourages such narcissistic and toxic behavior in SMIs? As powerful as social media can be for a positive change, it can be even more so for negativity. Casale and Banchi (2020) suggest that parasocial relationships provide a fertile breeding ground for narcissism – a personality style characterized by "excessive self-admiration, self-aggrandizement, and a tendency to see others as an extension of oneself" (Gerstner et al., 2013) – and that current generations with access to round-the-clock social media is much more susceptible to it. Healthy narcissism can make one confident and assertive but the preponderance of self-love posts on social media begins to challenge the lines of toxic positivity. Personal branding makes outlandish thoughts sound charismatic especially with a humongous population of vulnerable content-hungry social media users who suddenly find a sense of belonging hearing their own toxic thoughts being vocalized.

Social media thus provides narcissists with the voyeuristic attention they crave and the validation they seek. Oftentimes, the more outrageous the posts are, the more attention they garner – social media is many things but not a sanctum of nuanced thoughts and well-researched opinions, as proven by the increasing dominance of platforms with shorter form content over time. Academic research should delve into the questions regarding the impact of virtual fan-following of toxic influencers on real-life toxicity, as a large amount of anecdotal evidence suggests.

Mitigating the Dark Side of SMI Marketing for Influencers

The primary responsibility for regulating toxic behavior of SMIs needs to be shouldered by the social media platforms that have the greatest power in the ecosystem. This power imbalance helps create a "superstructure" dictated by the rules of an attention economy (that incentivizes SMIs to constantly seek audiences' attention), gig economy (forcing an entrepreneurial lifestyle for SMIs), reputation economy (that makes SMIs' online reputation a key asset), algorithmic culture (that forces SMIs to exercise "algorithmic branding" to stay relevant within the ecosystem), and surveillance capitalism (that potentially weaponizes SMIs' high levels of self-disclosure against themselves) (Kozinets et al., 2023). The constant marketization of influencers' abilities is a primary reason that SMIs fall prey to a toxic hustle culture filled with phatic exchanges (Miller, 2008), narcissistic dramatization, and self-commodification.

The pressure to compete manifests itself in SMIs often pushing themselves beyond their own limits in the disguise of self-improvement, a relentless pursuit of personal branding that blurs the lines between private and public life. With their marketization potential being constantly monitored by their follower counts, engagement rates, click-throughs, etc., their commodification and propensity for toxic self-glorification are well and truly in motion even before they jump into the arena. It would be a disservice to call out only the platforms for fostering this culture since the SMIs obviously self-select into this world, but platforms do have a huge responsibility on their hands, especially when so many American GenZers want to be influencers of some sort on social media. Fixing this broken ecosystem would entail a serious look at the dark side of the incentivization mechanisms and maybe then one could prevent the ongoing commodification of vulnerable child- and teenage-influencers.

Conclusion

This study systematically synthesized past research on influencer marketing to identify themes and theories that explain the success of SMIs and influencer marketing and detected a critical gap in our collective knowledge that could (and should) pave the way for further research on the strategy of influencer marketing – i.e., understanding its harmful impacts on the key stakeholders. We curated a series of case studies to highlight some phenomena that require imminent attention from marketers and academics. While these darker sides of SMI marketing affect our society as a whole, we attempted to classify these cases based on which key stakeholder in the SMI-communication process is the most affected – the brand (source or sponsor), the consumer (the audience), or the medium (the influencers themselves). Table 6.1 provides a summary of these issues.

As expected, the theories that explain the enormous success of SMI marketing also predict these darker flipsides. It is important to note that the darker sides exemplified in this study are hints toward systemic problems in the influencer ecosystem and not influencers themselves, who are of course humans susceptible to errors and themselves vulnerable to the superstructures governing their behaviors. Since the issues lie with the superstructures, they need oversight. The ethics of influencer marketing need to be looked at

TABLE 6.1 Summary of Darker Sides of SMI Marketing, Mechanisms and Potential Solutions

Dark Side of SMIs	*Real Life Examples*	*Mechanisms Proposed*	*Potential Solutions*
Consumers>>			
Impact of Mental and Physical Well-Being	Mukbang phenomenon Body Dysmorphia Doomscrolling	Social Comparison and Learning, Parasocial Relationships, Content-Hungry Algorithms, Toxic Positivity	Content regulation by platforms, Diversity of SMI body types, Brands' DEI Involvement Consumer Education
Misinformation/ Disinformation	Conspiracy Theorists COVID misinformation Clickbait Fake Tourette TikToker FTX scandal and SMIs Paul Brothers and Scams	Abuse of perceived authenticity and source credibility, Anti-establishment positioning and persecuted hero complex, Hustle Culture	Content regulation by platforms and lawmakers, Brand investments in fact-checkers Digital Perspicacity from Consumers
Online Polarization	SMI Political Activism Johnny Depp-Amber Heard Meghan Markle-British Royal Family Negativity in Brand Fan Pages	Social Media Echo-Chambers, Economics of Media Subscription Business Models, Superstructures demanding dramatization and intensification	Alternatives to Follower-Based Influencer Analytics, Brands vetting out polarizing SMIs, Fact checkers and Regulations against untruths, half-truths and post-truths
Brands>>			
Online Firestorms and Brand Safety	Bud Light-Dylan Mulvaney United Airlines-Fight Club Disney Boycott by conservative SMIs Redditors against Wall Street	Lack of Congruence between brand and SMI, Co-creation and perceived strength of brand associations	Brand Due Diligence in Choosing SMIs Strategic Response Planning for Digital Contingencies

(*Continued*)

TABLE 6.1 (Continued)

Dark Side of SMIs	*Real Life Examples*	*Mechanisms Proposed*	*Potential Solutions*
ESG Issues for Brands	Over-consumption OTT Consumerism DEI issues in influencer ecosystem	Hedonic Treadmill, Content Hungry Algorithms, Attention Economy	Incentivization of long-form content consumption. ESG goal alignment between stakeholders Brand self-regulation mechanisms
Violation of Ethical Guidelines and Sponsorship Disclosures	Fyre Festival Kim Kardashian Deepfakes and AI influencers FTX Scandal and SMIs	Lack of engagement on sponsored posts, Source Credibility and Persuasion Knowledge Models	FTC stricter enforcement Establishment of SMI-governing bodies SMI-community self-regulation
SMI Community>>			
Commodification of Self	OnlyFans Autopreneurship Use of relatives (often young children) in SMI stories	Need for Dramatization and Intensification, Parasocial Relations, Attention Economy	Regulation of commodified content by platforms and lawmakers Identification of harmful followers
Toxicity from Influencers	Andrew Tate Eliot Roger Logan and John Paul	Parasocial Relations, Narcissism, Personal Branding, Attention economy rewarding the outrageous	Identification and Regulation of Toxicity in SMI posts and engagement patterns

from a public policy perspective and dedicated governing bodies need to be able to hold transgressors accountable. The fast-evolving nature of technology mandates that these guidelines and regulations need to keep pace with the beast that is influencer marketing.

Fortunately, a lot of changes are on the horizon. Data privacy regulations (with GDPR) are working and updating round the clock to keep consumers safer in a digital environment fraught with danger. Social media platforms are increasingly being held under scrutiny with TikTok being questioned about data exchanges with the Chinese government (and being outright banned in some countries). Scrutiny is also coming from users themselves as they hold platforms responsible for some of the issues this chapter talks about. The incredible fact that Twitter removed the account of the President of the United States shows the power of the platforms as well as public sentiment. All influencer speech is being subjected to more examination as platforms move away from the unconditional free speech principles. Regulatory bodies like the FTC have started coming down a lot more heavily on sponsorship disclosure violators. These are all positive signs in the direction of safety within the SMI marketing ecosystem, and academics have a role to play in shaping these rapidly evolving but necessary regulations.

We conclude with a brief summary of measures that can be taken by the three stakeholders. The brands and platforms need to take up the bulk of the responsibility since they form the most powerful components of the ecosystem. They need to train and monitor influencers they work with, as well as their agencies, even at the cost of curbing down on some of the co-creation and personalization aspects of brand-influencer collaborations that make them successful. They also need to be constantly listening to social media chatter relating to their brand and be ready to take instantaneous actions in the event of negative word-of-mouth, especially those originating from influencers and influential users.

SMIs need to be aware of the forces enabling the marketization of the ecosystem and protect themselves from its ramifications. They need to bring more nuances into their content which, unfortunately, has turned toxic, superficial, and polarized because of the hustle culture promoted by the social media algorithms. They would also need to keep evolving with the regulations and their stricter enforcement and develop ethical and content guidelines together as a community. Finally, consumers find themselves in an environment that demands not just digital savviness but digital perspicacity – they need to find ways to train themselves accordingly.

Most importantly, they need to understand that not everything that glitters is gold. They need to be discerning about the veracity of information coming from influencers, stay aware and away from social media echo-chambers, and ensure mental and physical well-being for themselves and their near and dear ones. The potential societal impacts from incorporating such interventions and correcting mechanisms are enormous given how much of today's culture is dominated by the three stakeholders discussed in the study (consumers, brands and SMIs). Governing mechanisms – legal, financial, or otherwise – need to make sure that the benefits of social media to society outweigh the terrible costs outlined in this study. Social media is no different from other business endeavors where balancing societal and monetary sustainability is a day-to-day tussle, and one can only hope that we, as an integrated global community, will step up and build checks and balances that ensure our holistic well-being. Future research on the dark side of influencers, these cases, the theoretical mechanisms offered in Table 6.1, and potential solutions to the problems in influencer marketing is strongly encouraged for scholars to continue work that has begun in this chapter and in this corresponding book.

Notes

1 https://www.bavgroup.com/about-bav/brandasset-valuatorr
2 https://www.wsj.com/articles/talk-of-a-u-s-tiktok-ban-is-shaking-up-the-creator-economy-ac9cd718
3 https://www.nytimes.com/2024/03/11/us/politics/trump-tiktok-ban-cnbc.html
4 Toxic positivity is an overgeneralization of optimism and being happy, even when in bad situations or in denial.
5 https://www.forbes.com/sites/carlieporterfield/2022/12/19/amber-heard-settles-defamation-case-with-johnny-depp/?sh=1b9904e23488
6 https://neufluence.com/
7 https://www.instagram.com/isofiagrahn/?hl=en
8 https://www.instagram.com/chloeshayden/
9 https://bereal.com/en/
10 https://www.cnn.com/2023/10/31/investing/bud-light-anheuser-busch-earnings/index.html
11 https://www.youtube.com/watch?v=UnsSoS8s6Ok&ab_channel=MakeYourselfatHome
12 https://www.fooddive.com/news/goya-sales-rise-after-boycott-trump/630737/
13 https://www.nytimes.com/2018/10/11/arts/music/fyre-festival-organizer-sentenced-fraud.html
14 https://thetab.com/uk/2019/01/17/fyre-festival-instagram-models-89928

References

Aktas, E. H., Balci, U. D., & Karacaoglu, E. (2023). COVID pandemic aftermath: Changing dynamics on cosmetic and aesthetic surgery demands. *Aesthetic Plastic Surgery*, 47(4), 1658–1665.

AlFarraj, O., Alalwan, A. A., Obeidat, Z. M., Baabdullah, A., Aldmour, R., & Al-Haddad, S. (2021). Examining the impact of influencers' credibility dimensions: Attractiveness, trustworthiness and expertise on the purchase intention in the aesthetic dermatology industry. *Review of International Business and Strategy*, 31(3), 355–374.

Andrejevic, M. (2004). *Reality TV: The work of being watched*. Rowman & Littlefield Publishers.

Appel, G., Grewal, L., Hadi, R., & Stephen, A. T. (2020). The future of social media in marketing. *Journal of the Academy of Marketing Science*, 48(1), 79–95.

Argyris, Y. A., Wang, Z., Kim, Y., & Yin, Z. (2020). The effects of visual congruence on increasing consumers' brand engagement: An empirical investigation of influencer marketing on Instagram using deep-learning algorithms for automatic image classification. *Computers in Human Behavior*, 112, 106443.

Artz, N., & Tybout, A. M. (1999). The moderating impact of quantitative information on the relationship between source credibility and persuasion: A persuasion knowledge model interpretation. *Marketing Letters*, 10, 51–63.

Baker, S. A. (2022). Alt. health influencers: How wellness culture and web culture have been weaponized to promote conspiracy theories and far-right extremism during the COVID-19 pandemic. *European Journal of Cultural Studies*, 25(1), 3–24.

Baker, S. A., & Rojek, C. (2020). The Belle Gibson scandal: The rise of lifestyle gurus as micro-celebrities in low-trust societies. *Journal of Sociology*, 56(3), 388–404.

Banks, J., & Humphreys, S. (2008). The labour of user co-creators: Emergent social network markets? *Convergence*, 14(4), 401–418.

Barratt, L. (2021). The benefits of nano-influencer marketing. Origin (accessed July21,2022),https://www.origingrowth.co.uk/blog/the-benefits-of-nano-influencer-marketing

Boerman, S. C. (2020). The effects of the standardized Instagram disclosure for micro-and meso-influencers. *Computers in Human Behavior*, 103, 199–207.

Bokunewicz, J. F., & Shulman, J. (2017). Influencer identification in Twitter networks of destination marketing organizations. *Journal of Hospitality and Tourism Technology*, 8(2), 205–219.

Borchers, N. S., & Enke, N. (2021). Managing strategic influencer communication: A systematic overview on emerging planning, organization, and controlling routines. *Public Relations Review*, 47(3), 102041.

Boyd, D. (2014). *It's complicated: The social lives of networked teens*. Yale University Press.

Breves, P., Amrehn, J., Heidenreich, A., Liebers, N., & Schramm, H. (2021). Blind trust? The importance and interplay of parasocial relationships and advertising disclosures in explaining influencers' persuasive effects on their followers. *International Journal of Advertising*, 40(7), 1209–1229.

Bucher, T., & Helmond, A. (2018). The affordances of social media platforms. *The SAGE Handbook of Social Media*, 1, 233–253.

Burtch, G., He, Q., Hong, Y., & Lee, D. (2022). How do peer awards motivate creative content? Experimental evidence from Reddit. *Management Science*, 68(5), 3488–3506.

Campbell, C., & Farrell, J. R. (2020). More than meets the eye: The functional components underlying influencer marketing. *Business Horizons*, 63(4), 469–479.

Casale, S., & Banchi, V. (2020). Narcissism and problematic social media use: A systematic literature review. *Addictive Behaviors Reports*, 11, 100252.

Casaló, L. V., Flavián, C., & Ibáñez-Sánchez, S. (2020). Influencers on Instagram: Antecedents and consequences of opinion leadership. *Journal of Business Research*, 117, 510–519.

Chen, X., Van Der Lans, R., & Phan, T. Q. (2017). Uncovering the importance of relationship characteristics in social networks: Implications for seeding strategies. *Journal of Marketing Research*, 54(2), 187–201.

Cheong, C. (2022). *A timeline of the Ava Majury case, the 15-year-old Florida TikToker whose father shot and killed a man she said was stalking her*. Insider. https://www.insider.com/ava-majury-timeline-tiktok-stalker-case-dismissed-by-court-2022-3

Cooley, D., & Parks-Yancy, R. (2019). The effect of social media on perceived information credibility and decision making. *Journal of Internet Commerce*, 18(3), 249–269.

Cropanzano, R., Anthony, E. L., Daniels, S. R., & Hall, A. V. (2017). Social exchange theory: A critical review with theoretical remedies. *Academy of Management Annals*, 11(1), 479–516.

Dahl, D. W., Fuchs, C., & Schreier, M. (2015). Why and when consumers prefer products of user-driven firms: A social identification account. *Management Science*, 61(8), 1978–1988.

De Freitas Netto, S. V., Sobral, M. F. F., Ribeiro, A. R. B., & Soares, G. R. D. L. (2020). Concepts and forms of greenwashing: A systematic review. *Environmental Sciences Europe*, 32(1), 1–12.

De Jans, S., & Hudders, L. (2020). Disclosure of vlog advertising targeted to children. *Journal of Interactive Marketing*, 52(1), 1–19.

De Jans, S., Van de Sompel, D., De Veirman, M., & Hudders, L. (2020). # Sponsored! How the recognition of sponsoring on Instagram posts affects adolescents' brand evaluations through source evaluations. *Computers in Human Behavior*, 109, 106342.

De Veirman, M., Cauberghe, V., & Hudders, L. (2017). Marketing through Instagram influencers: The impact of number of followers and product divergence on brand attitude. *International Journal of Advertising*, 36(5), 798–828.

De Veirman, M., & Hudders, L. (2020). Disclosing sponsored Instagram posts: The role of material connection with the brand and message-sidedness when disclosing covert advertising. *International Journal of Advertising*, 39(1), 94–130.

Deborah, A., Michela, A., & Anna, C. (2019). How to quantify social media influencers: An empirical application at the Teatro alla Scala. *Heliyon*, 5(5), e01677.

del Fresno García, M., Daly, A. J., & Segado Sanchez-Cabezudo, S. (2016). Identifying the new influences in the internet era: Social media and social network analysis. *Revista Española de Investigaciones Sociológicas*, 153(1), 23–40.

Delbaere, M., Michael, B., & Phillips, B. J. (2021). Social media influencers: A route to brand engagement for their followers. *Psychology & Marketing*, 38(1), 101–112.

Dhaoui, C., & Webster, C. M. (2021). Brand and consumer engagement behaviors on Facebook brand pages: Let's have a (positive) conversation. *International Journal of Research in Marketing*, 38(1), 155–175.

Diener, E., Lucas, R. E., & Scollon, C. N. (2009). Beyond the hedonic treadmill: Revising the adaptation theory of well-being. In E. Diener (Ed.), *The science of well-being: The collected works of Ed Diener* (pp. 103–118). Springer.

Digital Marketing Institute. (2021). *20 surprising influencer marketing statistics*. https://digitalmarketinginstitute.com/blog/20-influencer-marketing-statistics-that-will-surprise-you

Djafarova, E., & Rushworth, C. (2017). Exploring the credibility of online celebrities' Instagram profiles in influencing the purchase decisions of young female users. *Computers in Human Behavior*, 68, 1–7.

Djafarova, E., & Trofimenko, O. (2019). 'Instafamous'–credibility and self-presentation of micro-celebrities on social media. *Information, Communication & Society*, 22(10), 1432–1446.

Eisenhardt, K. M. (1989). Building theories from case study research. *Academy of Management Review*, 14(4), 532–550.

e-Marketer. (2023). *Influencer marketing in 2023*. https://on.emarketer.com/Roundup-20230606-LTK_BusRegpage.html?Source=SOC100

Feng, Y., Chen, H., & Kong, Q. (2021). An expert with whom I can identify: The role of narratives in influencer marketing. *International Journal of Advertising*, 40(7), 972–993.

Fowler, K., & Thomas, V. L. (2023). Influencer marketing: A scoping review and a look ahead. *Journal of Marketing Management*, 39(11–12), 933–964.

French, J. R., Raven, B., & Cartwright, D. (1959). The bases of social power. *Classics of Organization Theory*, 7(311–320), 1.

Friestad, M., & Wright, P. (1994). The persuasion knowledge model: How people cope with persuasion attempts. *Journal of Consumer Research*, 21(1), 1–31.

Garimella, K., Morales, G. D. F., Gionis, A., & Mathioudakis, M. (2018). Quantifying controversy on social media. *ACM Transactions on Social Computing*, 1(1), 1–27.

Gerber, J. P., Wheeler, L., & Suls, J. (2018). A social comparison theory meta-analysis 60+ years on. *Psychological Bulletin*, 144(2), 177.

Gerstner, W. C., König, A., Enders, A., & Hambrick, D. C. (2013). CEO narcissism, audience engagement, and organizational adoption of technological discontinuities. *Administrative Science Quarterly*, 58(2), 257–291.

Giakoumaki, C., & Krepapa, A. (2020). Brand engagement in self-concept and consumer engagement in social media: The role of the source. *Psychology & Marketing*, 37(3), 457–465.

Goanta, C., & Ranchordás, S. (Eds.). (2020). *The regulation of social media influencers*. Edward Elgar Publishing.

Goffman, E. (1959). *The presentation of self in everyday life*. Doubleday & Company.

Goldenberg, J., Han, S., Lehmann, D. R., & Hong, J. W. (2009). The role of hubs in the adoption process. *Journal of Marketing*, 73(2), 1–13.

Goldfarb, A., & Tucker, C. (2019). Digital marketing. In J.-P. Dube & P. E. Rossi (Eds.), *Handbook of the economics of marketing* (Vol. 1, pp. 259–290). North-Holland.

Goldhaber, M. H. (1997). *The attention economy and the net*. First Monday.

Granovetter, M. S. (1973). The strength of weak ties. *American Journal of Sociology*, 78(6), 1360–1380.

Griffith, F. J., & Stein, C. H. (2021). Behind the hashtag: Online disclosure of mental illness and community response on Tumblr. *American Journal of Community Psychology*, 67(3–4), 419–432.

Guardian. (2022). 'They've lost the plot': Leading cosmetic doctor says under-30s are overdoing Botox and fillers. https://www.theguardian.com/lifeandstyle/2022/dec/18/cosmetic-surgeon-botox-fillers-instagram-generation-safety-concerns

Haenlein, M., & Libai, B. (2013). Targeting revenue leaders for a new product. *Journal of Marketing*, 77(3), 65–80.

Hao, A. W., Paul, J., Trott, S., Guo, C., & Wu, H. H. (2021). Two decades of research on nation branding: A review and future research agenda. *International Marketing Review*, 38(1), 46–69.

Hearn, A. (2008). Meat, mask, burden: Probing the contours of the branded self. *Journal of Consumer Culture*, 8(2), 197–217.

Hillis, K., Paasonen, S., & Petit, M. (Eds.). (2015). *Networked affect*. MIT Press.

Hinz, O., Skiera, B., Barrot, C., & Becker, J. U. (2011). Seeding strategies for viral marketing: An empirical comparison. *Journal of Marketing*, 75(6), 55–71.

Horton, D., & Richard Wohl, R. (1956). Mass communication and para-social interaction: Observations on intimacy at a distance. *Psychiatry*, 19(3), 215–229.

Hovland, C. I., & Weiss, W. (1951). The influence of source credibility on communication effectiveness. *Public Opinion Quarterly*, 15(4), 635–650.

Hoyer, W. D., Chandy, R., Dorotic, M., Krafft, M., & Singh, S. S. (2010). Consumer cocreation in new product development. *Journal of Service Research*, 13(3), 283–296.

Hudders, L., & De Jans, S. (2022). Gender effects in influencer marketing: an experimental study on the efficacy of endorsements by same-vs. other-gender social media influencers on Instagram. *International Journal of Advertising*, 41(1), 128–149.

Hudders, L., De Jans, S., & De Veirman, M. (2021). The commercialization of social media stars: A literature review and conceptual framework on the strategic use of social media influencers. *International Journal of Advertising*, 40(3), 327–375.

Hughes, C., Swaminathan, V., & Brooks, G. (2019). Driving brand engagement through online social influencers: An empirical investigation of sponsored blogging campaigns. *Journal of Marketing*, 83(5), 78–96.

Hulland, J., & Houston, M. B. (2020). Why systematic review papers and meta-analyses matter: An introduction to the special issue on generalizations in marketing. *Journal of the Academy of Marketing Science*, 48, 351–359.

Hu, M., Zhao, Y., Liu, Z., Li, Z., & Kong, X. (2021). Just my imagination: The influence of celebrities' romantic relationship announcements on romance fans and friendship fans. *Psychology of Popular Media*, 10(4), 434.

Iyengar, S., Lelkes, Y., Levendusky, M., Malhotra, N., & Westwood, S. J. (2019). The origins and consequences of affective polarization in the United States. *Annual Review of Political Science*, 22, 129–146.

Jenkins, H. (2006). *Fans, bloggers, and gamers: Exploring participatory culture.* NYU Press.

Jiménez-Castillo, D., & Sánchez-Fernández, R. (2019). The role of digital influencers in brand recommendation: Examining their impact on engagement, expected value and purchase intention. *International Journal of Information Management*, 49, 366–376.

Jin, S. V., & Muqaddam, A. (2019). Product placement 2.0: "Do brands need influencers, or do influencers need brands?". *Journal of Brand Management*, 26, 522–537.

Jin, S. V., Muqaddam, A., & Ryu, E. (2019). Instafamous and social media influencer marketing. *Marketing Intelligence & Planning*, 37(5), 567–579.

Johnson, R. W., Voorhees, C., & Khodakarami, F. (2023). Is your brand protected?: Assessing brand safety risks in digital campaigns. *Journal of Advertising Research*, 63(3), 205–220.

Just, S. N. (2019). An assemblage of avatars: Digital organization as affective intensification in the GamerGate controversy. *Organization*, 26(5), 716–738.

Kamins, M. A. (1990). An investigation into the "match-up" hypothesis in celebrity advertising: When beauty may be only skin deep. *Journal of Advertising*, 19(1), 4–13.

Kapitan, S., & Silvera, D. H. (2016). From digital media influencers to celebrity endorsers: Attributions drive endorser effectiveness. *Marketing Letters*, 27, 553–567.

Karagür, Z., Becker, J. M., Klein, K., & Edeling, A. (2022). How, why, and when disclosure type matters for influencer marketing. *International Journal of Research in Marketing*, 39(2), 313–335.

Katz, E., Lazarsfeld, P. F., & Roper, E. (2017). *Personal influence: The part played by people in the flow of mass communications*. Routledge.

Kay, S., Mulcahy, R., & Parkinson, J. (2020). When less is more: The impact of macro and micro social media influencers' disclosure. *Journal of Marketing Management*, 36(3–4), 248–278.

Khamitov, M., Koushyar R., Huang, D.W., & Hong, Y. (2024). Consumer trust: Meta-analysis of 50 years of empirical research. *Journal of Consumer Research*, 51(1) (2024): 7–18.

Kim, Y. (2021). Eating as a transgression: Multisensorial performativity in the carnal videos of mukbang (eating shows). *International Journal of Cultural Studies*, 24(1), 107–122.

Knittel, C. R., & Stango, V. (2014). Celebrity endorsements, firm value, and reputation risk: Evidence from the Tiger Woods scandal. *Management Science*, 60(1), 21–37.

Kostygina, G., Tran, H., Binns, S., Szczypka, G., Emery, S., Vallone, D., & Hair, E. (2020). Boosting health campaign reach and engagement through use of social media influencers and memes. *Social Media+ Society*, 6(2), 2056305120912475.

Kowalczyk, C. M., & Pounders, K. R. (2016). Transforming celebrities through social media: The role of authenticity and emotional attachment. *Journal of Product & Brand Management*, 25(4), 345–356.

Kozinets, R. V., Gretzel, U., & Gambetti, R. (2023). *Influencers and Creators: Business, Culture and Practice*. SAGE.

Layman, G. C., Carsey, T. M., & Horowitz, J. M. (2006). Party polarization in American politics: Characteristics, causes, and consequences. *Annual Review of Political Science*, 9, 83–110.

Leung, F. F., Gu, F. F., & Palmatier, R. W. (2022). Online influencer marketing. *Journal of the Academy of Marketing Science*, 50(2), 226–251

Libai, B., Muller, E., & Peres, R. (2013). Decomposing the value of word-of-mouth seeding programs: Acceleration versus expansion. *Journal of Marketing Research*, 50(2), 161–176.

Lou, C., & Yuan, S. (2019). Influencer marketing: How message value and credibility affect consumer trust of branded content on social media. *Journal of Interactive Advertising*, 19(1), 58–73.

Lu, L. C., Chang, W. P., & Chang, H. H. (2014). Consumer attitudes toward blogger's sponsored recommendations and purchase intention: The effect of sponsorship type, product type, and brand awareness. *Computers in Human Behavior*, 34, 258–266.

Luo, X., Cheah, J. H., Hollebeek, L. D., & Lim, X. J. (2024). Boosting customers' impulsive buying tendency in live-streaming commerce: The role of customer engagement and deal proneness. *Journal of Retailing and Consumer Services*, 77, 103644.

Luoma-aho, V., Pirttimäki, T., Maity, D., Munnukka, J., & Reinikainen, H. (2019). Primed authenticity: How do vlog audiences view the authenticity of influencers and sponsoring brands? *International Journal of Strategic Communication*, 13(4), 352–365.

Maisto, S. A., Carey, K. B., & Bradizza, C. M. (1999). *Social learning theory*. In K. E. Leonard & H. T. Blane (Eds.), *Psychological theories of drinking and alcoholism* (2nd ed., pp. 106–163). The Guilford Press.

Martínez-López, F. J., Anaya-Sánchez, R., Fernández Giordano, M., & Lopez-Lopez, D. (2020). Behind influencer marketing: Key marketing decisions and their effects on followers' responses. *Journal of Marketing Management*, 36(7–8), 579–607.

Maxwell, A. L., Gardiner, E., & Loxton, N. J. (2020). Investigating the relationship between reward sensitivity, impulsivity, and food addiction: A systematic review. *European Eating Disorders Review*, 28(4), 368–384.

Mihalache, M., & Mihalache, O. R. (2016). A decisional framework of offshoring: Integrating insights from 25 years of research to provide direction for future. *Decision Sciences*, 47(6), 1103–1149.

Mishra, R., Singh, R. K., & Koles, B. (2021). Consumer decision-making in Omnichannel retailing: Literature review and future research agenda. *International Journal of Consumer Studies*, 45(2), 147–174.

Moscovici, S. (1963). Attitudes and opinions. *Annual Review of Psychology*, 14(1), 231–260.

Mullainathan, S., & Shleifer, A. (2005). The market for news. *American Economic Review*, 95(4), 1031–1053.

Munnukka, J., Maity, D., Reinikainen, H., & Luoma-aho, V. (2019). "Thanks for watching". The effectiveness of YouTube vlog endorsements. *Computers in Human Behavior*, 93, 226–234.

Naderer, B., Matthes, J., & Schäfer, S. (2021). Effects of disclosing ads on Instagram: The moderating impact of similarity to the influencer. *International Journal of Advertising*, 40(5), 686–707.

Nascimento, T. C. D., Campos, R. D., & Suarez, M. (2020). Experimenting, partnering and bonding: A framework for the digital influencer-brand endorsement relationship. *Journal of Marketing Management*, 36(11–12), 1009–1030.

Niinimäki, K., Peters, G., Dahlbo, H., Perry, P., Rissanen, T., & Gwilt, A. (2020). The environmental price of fast fashion. *Nature Reviews Earth & Environment*, 1(4), 189–200.

Nyangwe, S., & Buhalis, D. (2018). Branding transformation through social media and co-creation: Lessons from Marriott international. In *Information and communication technologies in tourism 2018: Proceedings of the international conference in Jönköping, Sweden*, January 24–26, 2018 (pp. 257–269). Springer.

Ohanian, R. (1991). The impact of celebrity spokespersons' perceived image on consumers' intention to purchase. *Journal of Advertising Research*, 31(1), 46–54.

Oliver, R. L. (1993). Cognitive, affective, and attribute bases of the satisfaction response. *Journal of Consumer Research*, 20(3), 418–430.

Osei-Frimpong, K., & McLean, G. (2018). Examining online social brand engagement: A social presence theory perspective. *Technological Forecasting and Social Change*, 128, 10–21.

Parmigiani, G. (2021). Magic and politics: Conspirituality and COVID-19. *Journal of the American Academy of Religion*, 89(2), 506–529.

Paul, J., & Rosado-Serrano, A. (2019). Gradual internationalization vs born-global/international new venture models: A review and research agenda. *International Marketing Review*, 36(6), 830–858.

Petty, R. E., & Briñol, P. (2011). The elaboration likelihood model. *Handbook of Theories of Social Psychology*, 1, 224–245.

Pfeffer, J., & Salancik, G. (2015). External control of organizations—Resource dependence perspective. In J. B. Miner (Ed.), *Organizational Behavior 2* (pp. 373–388). Routledge.

Pradhan, D., Duraipandian, I., & Sethi, D. (2016). Celebrity endorsement: How celebrity–brand–user personality congruence affects brand attitude and purchase intention. *Journal of Marketing Communications*, 22(5), 456–473.

Pradhan, B., Kishore, K., & Gokhale, N. (2023). Social media influencers and consumer engagement: A review and future research agenda. *International Journal of Consumer Studies*, 47(6), 2106–2130.

Purohit, D., & Srivastava, J. (2001). Effect of manufacturer reputation, retailer reputation, and product warranty on consumer judgments of product quality: A cue diagnosticity framework. *Journal of Consumer Psychology*, 10(3), 123–134.

Raun, T. (2018). Capitalizing intimacy: New subcultural forms of micro-celebrity strategies and affective labour on YouTube. *Convergence*, 24(1), 99–113.

Ravenswood, K. (2011). Eisenhardt's impact on theory in case study research. *Journal of Business Research*, 64(7), 680–686.

Roose, K. (2019). *The making of a YouTube radical*. The New York Times. https://www.nytimes.com/interactive/2019/06/08/technology/youtube-radical.html

Sah, S., Malaviya, P., & Thompson, D. (2018). Conflict of interest disclosure as an expertise cue: Differential effects due to automatic versus deliberative processing. *Organizational Behavior and Human Decision Processes*, 147, 127–146.

Schouten, A. P., Janssen, L., & Verspaget, M. (2021). Celebrity vs. Influencer endorsements in advertising: The role of identification, credibility, and product-endorser fit. In S. Yoon, Y. K. Choi, & C. R. Taylor (Eds.), *Leveraged marketing communications* (pp. 208–231). Routledge.

Shahbaznezhad, H., Dolan, R., & Rashidirad, M. (2021). The role of social media content format and platform in users' engagement behavior. *Journal of Interactive Marketing*, 53(1), 47–65.

Shan, Y., Chen, K. J., & Lin, J. S. (2020). When social media influencers endorse brands: The effects of self-influencer congruence, parasocial identification, and perceived endorser motive. *International Journal of Advertising*, 39(5), 590–610.

Shiau, W. L., Dwivedi, Y. K., & Lai, H. H. (2018). Examining the core knowledge on Facebook. *International Journal of Information Management*, 43, 52–63.

Shore, J., Baek, J., & Dellarocas, C. (2018). Twitter is not the echo chamber we think it is. *MIT Sloan Management Review*, 60(1), 1–5.

Silva, M. J. D. B., Farias, S. A. D., Grigg, M. K., & Barbosa, M. D. L. D. A. (2020). Online engagement and the role of digital influencers in product endorsement on Instagram. *Journal of Relationship Marketing*, 19(2), 133–163.

Sokolova, K., & Kefi, H. (2020). Instagram and YouTube bloggers promote it, why should I buy? How credibility and parasocial interaction influence purchase intentions. *Journal of Retailing and Consumer Services*, 53, 101742.

Smith, C. T., De Houwer, J., & Nosek, B. A. (2013). Consider the source: Persuasion of implicit evaluations is moderated by source credibility. *Personality and Social Psychology Bulletin*, 39(2), 193–205.

Statista. (2021). *Global digital population as of January 2021*. Statista. https://www.statista.com/statistics/617136/digital-population-worldwide/

Stern, B. B. (1994). A revised communication model for advertising: Multiple dimensions of the source, the message, and the recipient. *Journal of Advertising*, 23(2), 5–15.

Stubb, C., & Colliander, J. (2019). "This is not sponsored content"–The effects of impartiality disclosure and e-commerce landing pages on consumer responses to social media influencer posts. *Computers in Human Behavior*, 98, 210–222.

Sundermann, G., & Raabe, T. (2019). Strategic communication through social media influencers: Current state of research and desiderata. *International Journal of Strategic Communication*, 13(4), 278–300.

Swaminathan, V., Gupta, S., Keller, K. L., & Lehmann, D. (2022). Brand actions and financial consequences: A review of key findings and directions for future research. *Journal of the Academy of Marketing Science*, 50(4), 639–664.

Taylor, C. R. (2020). The urgent need for more research on influencer marketing. *International Journal of Advertising*, 39(7), 889–891.

Torres, P., Augusto, M., & Matos, M. (2019). Antecedents and outcomes of digital influencer endorsement: An exploratory study. *Psychology & Marketing*, 36(12), 1267–1276.

Trivedi, J., & Sama, R. (2020). The effect of influencer marketing on consumers' brand admiration and online purchase intentions: An emerging market perspective. *Journal of Internet Commerce*, 19(1), 103–124.

Van Dam, S., & Van Reijmersdal, E. (2019). Insights in adolescents' advertising literacy, perceptions and responses regarding sponsored influencer videos and disclosures. *Cyberpsychology: Journal of Psychosocial Research on Cyberspace*, 13(2), Article 2.

Van Dijck, J., Poell, T., & De Waal, M. (2018). *The platform society: Public values in a connective world*. Oxford University Press.

Veresiu, E., & Parmentier, M. A. (2021). Advanced style influencers: Confronting gendered ageism in fashion and beauty markets. Journal of the Association for Consumer Research, 6(2), 263-273.

Voorveld, H. A. (2019). Brand communication in social media: A research agenda. *Journal of Advertising*, 48(1), 14–26.

Vrontis, D., Makrides, A., Christofi, M., & Thrassou, A. (2021). Social media influencer marketing: A systematic review, integrative framework and future research agenda. *International Journal of Consumer Studies*, 45(4), 617–644.

Wang, C. L., & Chugh, H. (2014). Entrepreneurial learning: Past research and future challenges. *International Journal of Management Reviews*, 16(1), 24–61.

Wang, X., Tang, L. R., & Kim, E. (2019). More than words: Do emotional content and linguistic style matching matter on restaurant review helpfulness? *International Journal of Hospitality Management*, 77, 438–447.

Weiner, B. (1985). An attributional theory of achievement motivation and emotion. *Psychological Review*, 92(4), 548.

Wellman, M. L., Stoldt, R., Tully, M., & Ekdale, B. (2020). Ethics of authenticity: Social media influencers and the production of sponsored content. *Journal of Media Ethics*, 35(2), 68–82.

Woodcock, J., & Johnson, M. R. (2021). Live streamers on Twitch.tv as social media influencers: Chances and challenges for strategic communication. In N. S.

Borchers (Ed.), *Social media influencers in strategic communication* (pp. 88–102). Routledge.

Ye, G., Hudders, L., De Jans, S., & De Veirman, M. (2021). The value of influencer marketing for business: A bibliometric analysis and managerial implications. *Journal of Advertising*, 50(2), 160–178.

Yoganarasimhan, H. (2012). Impact of social network structure on content propagation: A study using YouTube data. *Quantitative Marketing and Economics*, 10, 111–150.

7

THE DARK SIDE OF SOCIAL MEDIA LIVESTREAM INFLUENCER MARKETING FOR BRANDS AND PROFITS

Jingyun Hu and Kevin Flynn

The Dark Side of Social Media Livestream for Brands and Profits

Livestream commerce is a type of e-commerce which enables firms to sell products directly to online audiences through real-time streaming. It allows firms to interact with consumers dynamically and offers consumers a unique shopping experience that incorporates entertainment and social interaction elements. Based on the latest government report on China Internet Network Information Center (CNNIC, 2022), as of June 2022, the population of internet livestream users in China reached 716 million, an increase of 12.9 million compared to December 2021 and constitutes 68.1% of the total number of internet users in the country. The number of livestream commerce users is 469 million, contributing a significant proportion of the total number of livestream users. The Chinese livestreaming market is dominated by three leading platforms: Douyin, Kuaishuo, and Taobao. These platforms have established their dominant positions in the market through their substantial user base, high levels of engagement, and effective monetization strategies.

Very recent scholarship has explored livestreaming commerce – a field that has seen explosive growth as brands have learned to leverage this medium to reach customers and increase sales.

Much of the literature has focused on positive relationships between brands and customers and the advantages of livestreaming to achieve success. Several theoretical papers have posited what should work to provide optimal profits for the two parties – influencers and brands – but to our knowledge these theories have not been tested with livestreaming empirical data. This chapter seeks to look at this area of livestreaming commerce that has not received much attention – contracts between brands and livestreaming

DOI: 10.4324/9781032670546-10

influencers. In particular, our findings will add deeper understanding of the best way to structure contracts with profitability goals in mind.

This chapter is organized as follows. We begin by reviewing relevant literature in this area with a focus on profits. Next, we pose the question, what is the best way to structure contracts for livestreaming influencers in the Chinese market? To analyze practitioner experiences, we utilize a data set from the group of influencers with over 10 million followers on the Chinese livestreaming platform Douyin to see if theory matches practice. We provide summary tables and charts that explore the observations and illustrate supervising gaps between theoretical and actual contract structures in one Chinese livestreaming platform. We conclude by pointing out a surprisingly low percentage of profits among livestreaming parties and provide possible solutions to provide influencers and brands more win-win opportunities.

Literature Review: Livestreaming Influencer Marketing

The use of livestreaming influencers by brands has generated a considerable volume of academic research. Much of the early research focused on relationships among influencers, platforms, and brands with regards to risks and rewards associated with this new channel of e-commerce. Research into the careers of video game streamers on the Twitch platform was explored by Woodcock and Johnson (2019) who found many streamers were self-taught and developed capabilities without formal journal or communications education. These authors found streamers often worked longer hours than traditional jobs, often over 70 hours a week without days off. Johnson and Woodcock found that, in order to succeed in this challenging environment, video game streamers had to be outgoing and passionate about this career. The upsides of streaming mentioned in the author's study included being your own boss. However, the authors pointed out there was a tension between the security of working for a firm and the tenuous short-term employment opportunities of video game streamers.

E-Commerce Shopping

There is a rich history of e-commerce in the literature. Senecal and Nantel (2004) discovered the importance of online recommendations on consumer purchase behavior finding that those who consulted online recommendations were two times more likely to select a product than those who did not look at online recommendations. Ryan et al. (2012) found a trade-off exists for firms that consider using online marketplaces like Amazon. In exchange for access to more customers, the firm must pay fees to the marketplace therefore lowering profits. In addition, there is risk that the firm may directly compete with the marketplace's products. Authors Cui et al. (2012) analyzed new product reviews on Amazon.com and found a positive effect after a product launch – the more reviews the higher the sales and that inventory availability matters. In a study of video games involving 200 titles for PlayStation 2 and Xbox, Zhu, and Zhang (2010) found reviews had bigger impacts on less popular products and online games showing that game characteristics moderated the effect on online reviews on sales.

Livestreaming Development

Livestreaming development is uneven with greater popularity in China than North America (Lu et al., 2018). Several North American platforms have entered into the livestreaming channel including YouTube Live, SnapChat Live Stories, and Facebook Live (Lu et al., 2018). The authors point out fairly limited livestreaming use in North America – essentially for concerts – while in China there are multiple uses including streamer talk shows, individual performances, knowledge sharing, and e-commerce among others (Lu et al., 2018). These authors find that the difference in popularity between the two cultures stems from the concept of guanxi – a system of social networks and relationships that facilitates business. Chinese livestreams are interactive and a social interaction that circulates guanxi and preserves face. Livestreaming is an important subset of internet commerce in China with over 716 million users according to the latest Chinese government statistics from June of 2022 (CNNIC, 2022). The livestreaming users make up over 68% of all internet users in China. Three livestreaming platforms are the leading players in China – Douyin, Kuaishuo, and Taobao. Within the growth of livestreaming, there are studies that point to increased sales for companies willing to adopt this channel, for example, Chen et al. (2019) find that product sales volume increased by 21.8% when firms adopt livestreaming strategies.

Influencers and Brands

Many studies look at the impact of influencers on brands. According to De Veirman et al. (2017), social media influencer marketing is becoming more important to brands because of consumer's rising use of advertising-blocking programs or software. Lou and Yuan (2019) found when influencers post they deliver informative value and credibility that helps consumers build trust with the brand and ultimately lead to higher purchase intent. Authors Martínez-López et al. (2020) found that if brands exert too much control over influencers, then the messages of the influencers lose credibility with online consumers. In another study, Leung et al. (2022) found that online influencer marketing improves targeting, creativity, positioning, and brand trust. De Veirman et al. (2017) reported that the number of followers that an influencer has increases their opinion leadership but if a product is divergent, then having a large number of followers is not a great choice for brands. In another study, Breves et al. (2021) found influencer–brand fit has a positive impact on the influencer's image and on the advertising effectiveness. In another study, De Veirman and Hudders (2020) found that sponsorship disclosure by Instagram influencers negatively impacts brand attitudes causing ad skepticism if the influencer utilizes one-sided messages. Authors Lee and Eastin (2020) found that influencer personality impacts brands when there is a good match between utilitarian brands and those influencers with high levels of sincerity. Next, we will examine the financial incentives between influencers and brands in the livestreaming environment.

Influencers and Livestreaming

The literature on the financial arrangements of livestreaming influencers and brands has grown as this channel has rapidly expanded. Livestreaming e-commerce is a significant phenomenon in China, home to platforms like Kuaishuo, Taobao, and TikTok with sales of products above 100 billion yuan ($13.7 billion US dollars) and growth rates approaching 400% as of 2018 (Liu & Liu, 2021). Research in livestreaming includes understanding what motivates three parties, the livestreaming platforms, consumers, and influencers. Appel et al. (2020) predict that livestreaming by influencers will continue to grow and that virtual influencers may become prominent on streaming platforms.

In another study, researchers conclude that influencers often gauge how much demand there will be for a product more accurately than the product manufacturers according to Qi et al. (2022). Liu and Liu (2021) investigated contracts between influencers and Chinese livestreaming platforms. The authors found setting a high revenue-sharing rate actually hurts profits for both parties. The mechanism of high revenue sharing caused less platform investment required in order to match streamers with customers. Influencers would therefore have smaller audiences to influence, ultimately reducing their profits as well. Liu (2023) analyzed over 1 million consumers who completed over 1.5 million transactions to understand platform profits when using dynamic coupon targeting. The author found dynamic coupon targeting improves platform profits compared to static coupon strategies. Qi et al. (2022) found that in Chinese livestreaming contracts between manufacturers and influencers the most mutually profitable agreements included a mix of profit sharing and commissions. However, there has not been a study that examines which contract details work best between livestreaming influencers and brands. In the next section, we explore this potentially rich area of livestreaming through an empirical study.

Please refer to Table 7.1 for more detail on how scholars have investigated livestreaming and consumer behavior, brands, and influencers.

TABLE 7.1 Studies on E-Commerce, Live streaming and Influencers and Brand Interplay

Authors	*Objective*	*Sample*	*Main Results*
Senecal and Nantel (2004)	To examine how online recommendation sources impact consumer purchase behavior	487 convenience sample of three web user populations	Subjects who consulted online product recommendations chose them twice as often as those who did not look at recommendations. Recommender systems were the most influential source.
Cui, Lui, and Guo (2012)	To examine how eWOM in the form of product reviews in terms of volume influence sales	7,470 product reviews from Amazon.com on 332 new products	The volume of reviews has a significant + effect on the beginning period following the launch of a new product.
Lou and Yuan (2019)	To examine the effects of influencer marketing's message features and influencer credibility components on consumer behavior	538 respondents with either YouTube, Instagram, or Facebook accounts that followed influencers	This study's findings point to influencer posts' informative value and credibility positively affects followers' trust in branded posts, which affects brand awareness & purchase intentions.
Liu and Liu (2021)	Investigated the financial relationship between live streamers and livestreaming platforms to understand what types of contracts benefited both parties	computer generated	The revenue-sharing rate should not be excessively high because both the influencer and platform will lose.
Liu (2023)	To understand platform profits when using dynamic coupon targeting strategies and consumers' trade-offs associated with these strategies	1,020,898 consumers during three months in 2019 who received 25,886,094 coupons and completed 1,539,424 transactions while watching 200,568 distinct live streams, created by 11,926 hosts	Using a model that uses batch deep reinforcement learning the platform's revenues increase by twice that of static targeting and 20% more than other models.

(*Continued*)

TABLE 7.1 (Continued)

Authors	*Objective*	*Sample*	*Main Results*
Qi, Sethi, Wei, and Zhang (2022)	Examined contracts between two types of influencers and manufacturers on livestreaming shopping platforms using game theory	Computer generated	Manufacturers should use contracts that have commission-plus-profit sharing terms when using influencers in live streaming. These terms should help both the manufacture and influencer improve their respective profits.
Ryan, Sun, and Zhao (2012)	Investigated selling goods on Amazon compared to a firm selling directly to consumers	Computer generated	There is a trade-off, selling on a marketplace such as Amazon increased expenses for the firm in the form of fixed participation fees or revenue sharing compared to a direct-to-consumer method, however using a marketplace like Amazon expands reach beyond a company's website audience. Companies may find they are directly competing with the marketplace's own products in exchange for accessing more customers.
Shen, Cheng, He, and Yang (2022)	Develop theory on what type of contracts between platforms and influencers are best to achieve a win-win outcome	Computer generated	Sales-based contracts work best with low quality products, participation-based contracts work best with high quality products. There is no consensus on the correct contract for medium quality products.
Wang, Tao, Liang, and Gou (2019)	Investigates unions representing streamers and how they impact streamer salaries	Computer generated	This paper predicts if a streamer will join a union or work independently based on the streamer's individual ability. Unions must balance the trade-offs of elite talent and huge crowds.

Johnson and Woodcock (2019)	Examined streamers who professionalized on Twitch. tv	39 experienced streamers	This paper focused on the lives of streamers attempting to make a full-time living broadcasting video game and found that these individuals worked longer than traditional hours but experienced unpredictable earnings compared to salaried traditional careers.
Chen, Hu, Lu, and Hong (2019)	Examine if live streaming improves product sales	10.7 million product reviews on Taobao as a proxy for sales	When firms execute livestreaming sales volume improves by 21.8%. Annual platform promotions also contribute to product sales volume gains.
Lu, Xia, Heo, and Wigdor (2018)	Explore the role rewards play into streamers and users	527 Chinese survey respondents	Providing rewards such as virtual gifts are not impulsive in the Chinese context of live streaming. These gifts to streamers are important for circulating guanxi keeping face among Chinese fans of the streamers.
Zhu and Zhang (2010)	To examine how product and consumer characteristics moderate the impact of online reviews on sales	Reviews of 220 game titles sold between 2003 and 2005	The authors found reviews were more important for less popular games and online games sales.
Martínez-López, Anaya-Sánchez, Esteban-Millat, Torrez-Meruvia, D'Alessandro, and Miles (2020)	To understand how influencers and brands should engage with regards to control over online messaging	503 students at the University of Malaga	Brands must not try to control influencers or the message from the influencer will not be credible. Credibility of influencers must be maintained when they endorse brands because consumers will view content with skepticism.
Appel, Grewal, Hadi, and Stephen (2020)	To examine the future of social media research	The authors drew on academic research, discussion with industry leaders.	The authors predict live streaming by influencers will continue to grow. They also believe virtual influencers will become more prominent on social media.

(*Continued*)

TABLE 7.1 (Continued)

Authors	*Objective*	*Sample*	*Main Results*
Leung, Gu, and Palmatier (2022)	To develop a framework for online influencer marketing	58 Master's students from Hong Kong	The authors develop a framework for online influencer marketing, OIM, the improves targeting, positioning, creativity, and trust. Types of products impact how effective content is, certain products work well on live streaming such as cosmetics because these products require demonstrations.
Breves, Amrehn, Heidenreich, Liebers, and Schramm (2021)	To understand how influencers and brand congruence impact advertising	Two online studies	Influencer–brand fit affects the influencer's credibility, which has a positive effect on brand evaluations and behavioral intentions.
De Veirman, Cauberghe, and Hudders (2017)	To understand how to identify the right influencers for a brand	117 Instagram users in the United States	The ratio of social media followers to followers is a good assessment tool of an influencers, if an influencer has too high a number of followers this may negatively impact influencer likeability.
De Veirman and Hudders (2020)	To examine sponsorship disclosure and brand attitudes with Instagram influencers	355 participants recruited from Amazon's Mechanical Turk	Sponsorship disclosure negatively affects brand attitudes causing ad skepticism. Influencer credibility and brand attitude are negatively affected if the influencer utilizes one-sided messages.
Lee and Eastin (2020)	To examine brand type and influencer personality relationships	234 respondents recruited from Amazon's Mechanical Turk	Influencers that had attributes of high sincerity helped utilitarian brand endorsements. A more positive attitude toward the brandfor the utilitarian product was superior when a high-sincerity influencer was used versus a low-sincerity influencer.

Methods: Empirical Study

Douyin, a social media platform owned by privately held Chinese company ByteDance, was introduced to the Chinese market in 2016. Since its introduction, Douyin has gained widespread popularity and has become one of the most widely adopted social media platforms in China and the world. As of 2022, the platform has over 800 million monthly active users, and 88.3% of them watch livestream according to an industry report released from QuestMobile (2022). Douyin differentiates itself from other platforms by emphasizing "interest e-commerce." This approach aims to engage the user through visually appealing content that meets their needs and to further stimulate their consumption by incorporating products into the content. A typical Douyin livestream involves influencers, firms, audiences, and the platform itself.

Many papers have used theoretical models to elucidate the operational dynamics amongst influencers, corporations, and their respective platforms. Ryan et al. (2012) model the relationship between the market firm and retailer as a revenue-sharing relationship with a fixed fee. The selection of commission rate or fixed commission in livestream commerce has a significant influence on the profit of the platform, firms, and influencers. Liu and Liu (2021) theoretically investigate the interaction between influencers and platforms, revealing that both parties might experience a decrease in revenue due to excessively high revenue-sharing commission rates. Some works concentrate on the selection process of firms and influencers on online platforms. Shen et al. (2022) utilize game-theoretical models to deduce that firms and influencers can attain mutually beneficial outcomes by adopting diverse types of contracts, particularly when the quality of the product varies. While the existing literature is predominantly based on theoretical models, our study ventures into the practical aspects of how corporations, influencers, and platforms operate.

While a majority of scholarly articles primarily center their analysis on Douyin, they often overlook a critical distinction. Douyin principally facilitates interaction between influencers and consumers, whereas the business transactions between firms and influencers predominantly occur on a separate segment known as JuLiangXingTu.

Our contribution lies in being one of the first empirical studies conducted in the Douyin livestream market, which sets it apart from the majority of published papers that predominantly focus on theoretical models. These theoretical models often make assumptions that may not accurately reflect real-world operations. In contrast, our research is grounded in the actual market mechanisms, providing valuable insights into the workings of firms and influencers in the livestream market.

To assess the collaboration between firms, influencers, and the platform, the choice of contract plays a crucial role in shaping the outcomes and decisions made by all parties involved. In addition to influencing the collaboration between firms and influencers, the chosen contract can also affect how the platform receives payment. The platform's revenue model may be tied to the contractual terms agreed upon by the parties.

Data Patterns and Stylized Facts

Setting of Livestream Shopping. Our study utilizes two empirical frameworks. First, we explore the intricacies of livestream shopping. Second, we examine the process and impact of firms engaging influencers. Liu (2023) carries out an exhaustive empirical investigation of livestream shopping, with a particular emphasis on Taobao Live, one of China's leading livestream platforms. Unlike online shopping platform Taobao Live, influencers on Douyin must produce brief, compelling videos designed to attract viewers, convert them into followers, and subsequently engage them in e-commerce livestreams. This process implies that Douyin's algorithm, attuned to your preferences, persistently presents you with your favorite influencer's short videos and livestreams. This is a notable distinction when compared to the search page functionality on Taobao Live.

Setting of Influencer Selection. JuLiangXingTu, the top influencer sourcing platform in China, distinguishes itself as the sole platform within the Douyin framework specifically designed to accommodate commercial ventures. It boasts a comprehensive suite of tools, including those for the administration of orders and contracts, the production of project summaries, and the undertaking of data analysis. As recorded in November 2022, the platform has successfully attracted in excess of 2 million creators, along with over 1500 Multi-Channel Network (MCN) agencies, and more than 1,000 service providers. Remarkably, it has fostered collaborations between approximately 1.9 million brands and influencers, a testament to its broad-reaching capabilities and influence.

A comprehensive workflow for a firm intending to collaborate with influencers on this platform can be delineated as seen in Figure 7.1.

How Influencers Work with JuLiangXingTu. JuLiangXingTu permits registration for influencers with over a certain number of followers, and certain fields require influencers to possess relevant certifications to participate. Influencers have the option to browse and select tasks such as promotional content writing, video promotion, and others, and set their desired pricing for each task. Influencers are expected to complete their assigned tasks within JuLiangXingTu and receive feedback from the collaborating firms. Based on this feedback, influencers are expected to make necessary revisions before publishing the content. In the event that influencers are not affiliated with

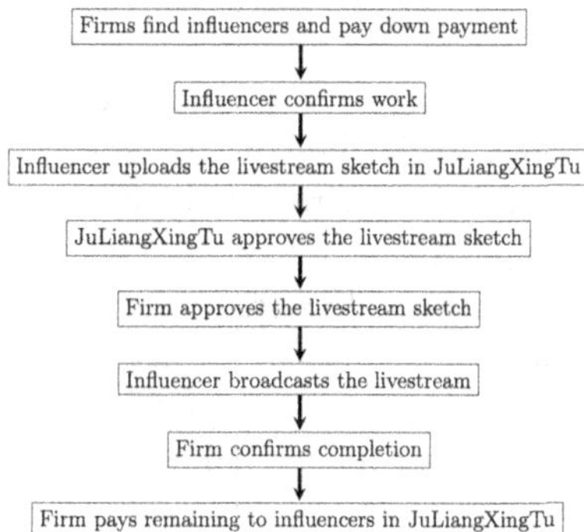

FIGURE 7.1 Flowchart of Working Process between Firms, Influencers and JuLiangXingTu

any MCN, they will receive 95% of the revenue generated by their completed task, while JuLiangXingTu retains 5% of the task.

How firms work with JuLiangXingTu. JuLiangXingTu mandates that firms must upload their official certification prior to commencing any promotional activities. Upon successful registration, firms gain access to the influencer selection pool within JuLiangXingTu for brand promotion. Once a preferred influencer is identified, firms are required to pay the task fee plus a 5% service charge to JuLiangXingTu, with a 10% down payment. JuLiangXingTu offers two modes for influencer promotion: brand promotion and e-commerce promotion. Influencers are selected by firms for promotion through livestreaming on Douyin.

Influencer Price Setting

Influencers who have more than 1,000 followers are eligible to promote products through livestreams and videos, but they are not able to set their own prices; instead, they must promote products at a commission rate. However, influencers who have more than 100,000 followers are empowered to set their own prices for product promotion and are provided with a unique link on their Douyin ID page for businesses to connect with them directly. Influencers have two primary pricing options: setting a price with a commission rate, which allows them to share in the revenue generated from product promotion, or setting a fixed price without any commission rate, which is akin to working on a labor basis for a set salary. In certain industries, such as gaming and online services, revenue sharing is not solely based on sales but can also be based on registrations or other key performance indicators. In addition, influencers can offer promotional packages based on either a daily or hourly rate. For the purpose of daily promotions, this refers to a livestream duration of at least six hours, regardless of the number of livestreams conducted.

Summary Statistics

Data were collected on a sample of 411 influencers, each of whom had cultivated a following of over 10 million by the end of October 2022. In the span of a half-year, from April 25 to October 21, 2022, these influencers collectively hosted an impressive total of 28,736 livestream events. Out of these, 12,929 were e-commerce livestreams incorporating product sales. Furthermore, these influencers engaged in synergistic collaborations with an extensive array of 10,783 unique brands, featuring a diverse collection of 93,671 unique individual products, all within the framework of their e-commerce livestream endeavors.

Our data collection exclusively targets top influencers due to their significant dominance and market share within the livestreaming industry. Qi et al. (2022) find that collaboration with high-profile influencers is identified as a strategy that enhances system efficiency, although it may compromise the manufacturer's profit. It is posited that these top influencers are inclined to invest greater effort in product promotion, leveraging their professionalism, which contributes to their efficiency in this role.

Raw Variables

Our data are at the livestream product level. Table 7.2 defines the variables in each observation.

As previously discussed, companies have two primary strategies when partnering with influencers for livestream promotions. The first strategy involves an exclusive promotion, where the influencer dedicates a substantial period, such as an entire hour or day, to endorse a single brand exclusively. This approach allows for concentrated exposure and depth in showcasing the brand's offerings. Alternatively, the second strategy involves a multi-brand promotion, where the influencer highlights a particular brand alongside others within the same livestream. This scenario provides an opportunity to present a variety of brands simultaneously, broadening the scope of the product exposure during the livestream event.

We eliminate two conditions. The first being that a brand manage its own livestreams, thereby negating the need to collaborate with external influencers. The second condition to be removed is the requirement for influencers to promote their own brands during their livestreams. We focus on the sales of brands promoted during an influencer's livestream. There are 284,846 recorded instances pertaining to individual brands during various livestreams. Table 7.3 presents the number of products, their introduction time, and corresponding brand sales.

The commission rate is often considered as a measure of bargaining power between influencers and firms in theoretical research. The commission rate

TABLE 7.2 Data Overview

Category	*Variable*	*Definition*
Influencer Identity	Influencer Name/ID	The influencer's unique identifier
	Influencer Type	Each influencer is classified into specific categories, such as news or makeup.
	Influencer Fans	# of influencer follower's number
	Influencer Fee Revenue Share Option	Dummy variable whether influencer have revenue share option for brands to choose
	Influencer Fee Fix Price Option	Influencer fee for fix price based on time or product
Livestream Identity	Livestream Name and Start Time	The live stream's unique identifier
	Livestream Duration	The duration of one live stream
	Livestream Total Views	# of people view in live stream
	Livestream Total Products	# of product in live stream
	Livestream Sales Volume	# of sales generated in live stream
	Livestream Sales	Revenue generated from live stream
	Livestream Likes	Number of likes in live stream
Product Identity	Product Order	Product Order in live Stream
	Product Name	The product's unique identifier
	Product Brand	The product's brand
	Product Category	The product's category
	Product Coupon	A discount or special limited offer on the product or service being promoted by the influencer
	Product Price After Coupon	Price that a consumer needs to pay after applying a coupon
	Product Sale Volume	Total number of the product sale in live stream
	Product Sales	Product revenue generated from live stream
	Product Commission Rate	Percentage of the revenue from the sale of a product that is paid to influencer
	Product Introduce Time	The duration of the influencer introducing a product in a live stream
	Product Return	The count of the item that customers have returned to the seller after buying them during a livestream event

represents the percentage of sales or revenue that an influencer receives as compensation for promoting a product or brand. Many theoretical studies overlook an important aspect of real-world revenue-sharing contracts between firms and influencers. In practice, these contracts often involve two

TABLE 7.3 Brand Sales in Live Stream

	Product Numbers	*Product Introduce Time (Hour)*	*Product Sales*
mean	1.37	0.18	55,811.54
std	2.01	1.00	380,071.93
min	1.00	0.00	0.00
25%	1.00	0.03	30.00
50%	1.00	0.06	1,000.00
75%	1.00	0.13	10,000.00
max	100.00	115.26	51,800,000.00

key components: a fixed cost element and revenue sharing based on the commission rate. However, the details of these contracts, particularly the fixed cost component, are not publicly disclosed, as indicated by JuLiangXingTu. We can only observe the product commission rate with livestream records.

In our data set, we have observed that there are 75,256 products with no commission rate. On the other hand, we have data available for 476,854 products that include the commission rate. From Figure 7.2, we can see the distribution of the commission rate in livestream. Based on the density distribution, the majority of product commission rates cluster around 1%. However, it is worth noting that there are several distinct density clusters observed at commission rates of 10%, 20%, and 50% for certain products. Additionally, the average price varies across different levels of product commission rates. We can observe the price comparison for each product category across different levels of product commission rates. These rates have been categorized into three distinct levels for analysis: "Low Commission Rate" for products with a commission rate of less than 1%; "Medium Commission Rate" for those above 10% but less than 20%; and "High Commission Rate" for products with a commission rate exceeding 50%.

From Table 7.4, we can see the majority of product prices in the Low Commission Rate category are higher than those in the High Commission Rate category. There are no products from the Jewelry, Local, and Luxury categories present in the High Commission Rate level. Shen et al. (2022) highlight the decision-making process involved in selecting between revenue-sharing and nonrevenue sharing contracts, a choice which hinges on the product quality.

In livestream marketing, renowned brands seldom rely on high commission rates to incentivize influencers to vigorously promote their products. These well-established brands already possess a strong market reputation, and influencers are often eager to endorse their products due to their superior quality and standing.

Influencer Fee Option. We now review the fee options for influencers as shown on the JuLiangXingTu website. One limitation is that it does not allow

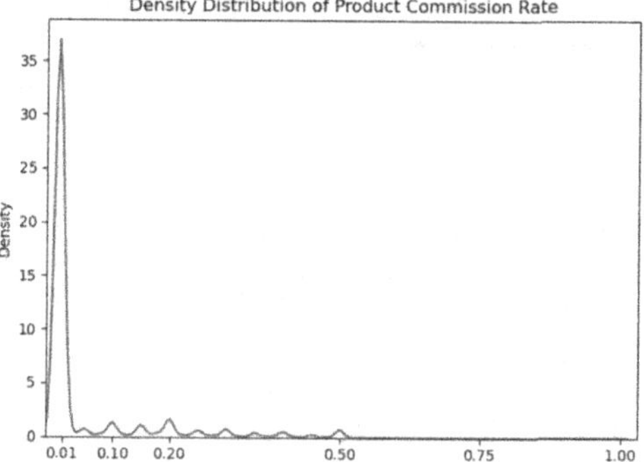

FIGURE 7.2 Product Commission Rate Density Distribution

TABLE 7.4 Average Product Price by Product Category and Commission Rate Level

Product Category	*Low Commission Rate*	*Medium Commission Rate*	*High Commission Rate*
3CDigital	1,413.69	263.79	131.27
Agricultural & Plants	30.94	44.26	10.60
Book & Movie	102.76	56.61	56.81
Clothes	198.34	136.65	24.98
Food & Drink	84.38	43.11	11.47
Gifts	136.38	116.69	10.70
Home	251.42	109.69	20.04
Jewelry	2,894.36	346.35	Na
Local	2,759.60	3,532.33	Na
Luxury	1,657.28	Na	Na
Makeup	158.56	91.52	15.10
Others	61.05	63.15	10.92
Parenting & Pets	101.29	72.26	Na
Personal Care	123.65	55.36	26.08
Plays	244.23	86.12	18.67
Shoes & Bags	387.37	129.96	14.60
Sports & Outing	107.03	81.40	12.62
Virtual Pay	557.21	167.83	1.00
Watch & Accessories	937.35	288.31	19.18
Fresh	87.25	59.20	1.00

us to ascertain the fixed price coupled with the commission. However, the commission rate can be derived from the records of the livestream sessions. Given that our livestream records originate from 2022, while the influencer prices were captured in 2023, there may be some discrepancies. It is feasible that some influencers who were inactive on livestreams in 2022 started participating in these activities in 2023. The records reveal that 164 out of

TABLE 7.5 Nonrevenue-Sharing Fee for Day, Hour, and Multiple Products

	One Day for One Brand	*One Hour for One Brand*	*One Product for Multiple Brands*
mean	403,992.08	143,086.63	45,072.74
std	700,837.81	191,444.83	78,295.15
min	6,000.00	1,000.00	600.00
25%	60,000.00	30,000.00	10,000.00
50%	200,000.00	80,000.00	19,000.00
75%	450,000.00	175,000.00	43,650.00
max	5,000,000.00	1,246,750.00	500,000.00

411 influencers engaged in e-commerce livestreaming. Further scrutiny of the influencer fee options data indicates that 193 influencers out of the total pool of 411 have specified their fee prices. Moreover, 56 influencers among them offer revenue-sharing fee options to firms.

Table 7.5 presents the influencer fee structure, based on whether the influencer's engagement involves one brand and varies depending on the duration, i.e., by the hour or the day. This option tends to be more cost-effective compared to exclusive one-brand selling.

Influencer Fees among different Influencer Types. Table 7.6 provides a detailed comparison of the various nonrevenue-sharing fees charged by influencers across 25 distinct types defined by the platform. Each influencer has the flexibility to collaborate with diverse industries; however, they are restricted to categorizing themselves under a single type. There are two primary reasons that may explain why, for some types of influencers, the hourly fee is higher than the daily fee. Firstly, there are instances where influencers choose to charge the same rate for both hourly and daily services. Secondly, certain influencers may exclusively provide hourly pricing options, opting not to offer a daily rate at all. However, from a business perspective, companies tend to opt for the most cost-effective solution when choosing to collaborate with influencers. They typically select the payment option that provides them with the greatest value at the lowest cost.

Research Question 2: Do Influencers with a Larger Following Charge More?

Influencers with a large number of followers often command higher fees due to their extensive reach and potential audience. However, the effectiveness of reaching and engaging with this audience, and ultimately converting them into loyal customers, is a critical consideration for both firms and influencers. Based on the data presented in Figure 7.3, it can be observed that the majority of influencers in our data set have approximately 20 million followers.

TABLE 7.6 Nonrevenue-Sharing Fee with Different Types of Influencers

Influencer Types	*One Day for One Brand*	*One Hour for One Brand*	*One Product for Multiple Brands*
Agriculture	80,000.00	80,000.00	Na
Art	1,652,575.83	168,482.03	9,384.62
Beauty	179,589.25	99,232.47	20,249.11
Career	Na	Na	Na
Cars	1,762,803.03	435,392.67	135,653.41
Comics	750,000.00	139,676.19	73,200.00
Education	225,000.00	99,871.66	48,810.27
Emotion	Na	Na	Na
Fashion	600,000.00	60,636.84	8,290.67
Film & TV	89,601.27	847,436.22	170,791.02
Foods	380,855.00	124,224.49	29,733.11
Games	14,952.90	8,968.05	7,273.68
Home	320,000.00	175,000.00	30,000.00
Life	178,566.15	140,093.52	65,449.61
Makeup	Na	650,400.00	10,000.00
Music	600,000.00	101,977.94	29,860.00
News	75,083.90	60,208.01	18,675.19
Parenting	10,465.86	23,932.04	6,362.06
Pets	33,736.35	88,880.22	17,772.31
Photography	4,595,193.26	392,504.10	72,065.22
Sports	59,400.00	32,600.00	6,520.00
Story	362,771.32	490,517.90	106,413.39
Technology	1,680,000.00	180,000.00	Na
Testing	200,000.00	70,000.00	20,000.00
Travel	400,000.00	95,327.08	25,347.65

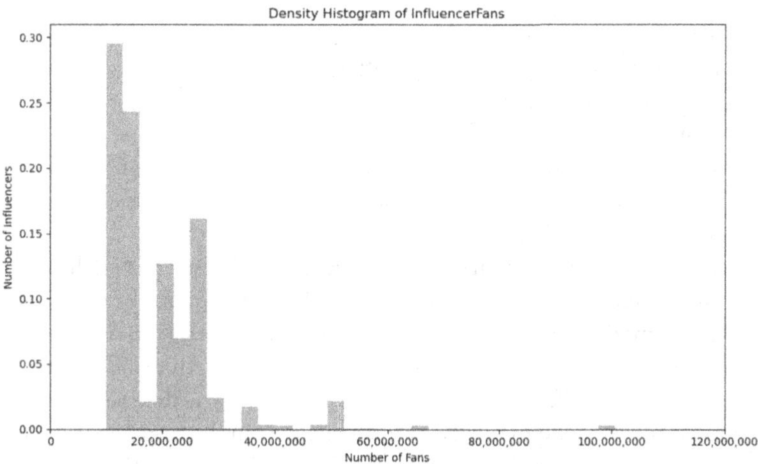

FIGURE 7.3 Product Commission Rate Density Distribution

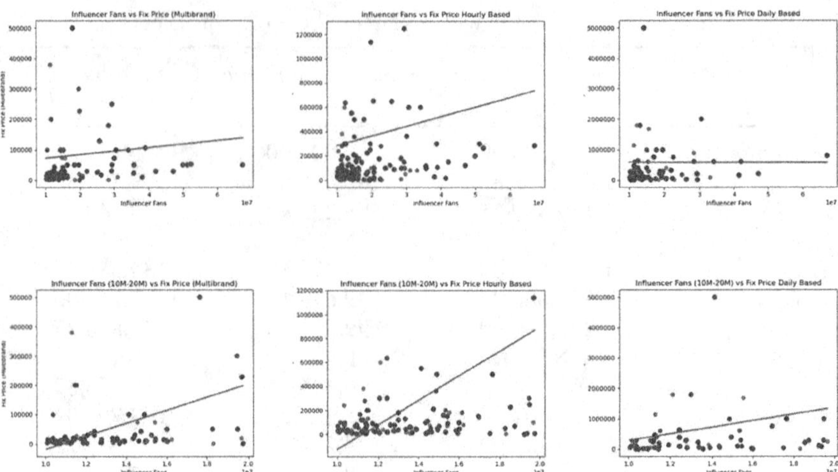

FIGURE 7.4 Product Commission Rate Density Distribution

In Figure 7.4, we found a stronger positive correlation coefficient between influencer followers and price fees in the group of influencers with fewer than 20 million followers. This suggests that influencers in this group tend to charge higher fees as their number of followers increases. In contrast, the relationship between followers and price fees for all influencers (including those with more than 20 million followers) is not as pronounced. Overall, our findings indicate that follower count has a greater impact on price fees for influencers with fewer than 20 million followers.

Contract Problems

One of the limitations of our data is the lack of direct observations on the contract choices between firms and influencers. However, we can infer certain aspects from our livestream records, specifically whether a product has a commission rate or not. Based on this information, we assume that if a product has a commission rate, it indicates that the firm is using a revenue-sharing contract. Conversely, if a product does not have a commission rate, it suggests that the firm is not using a revenue-sharing contract.

From the perspective of firms, there were 868 firms that exclusively utilized nonrevenue-sharing contracts in the livestream market. In contrast, 7,035 firms opted for revenue-sharing contracts, while 2,880 firms employed a combination of both contract types. From the perspective of influencers, out of the total of 411 influencers, 33 of them exclusively utilize revenue-sharing contracts. However, the majority of influencers utilize a combination of both contract types, incorporating revenue-sharing contracts into their agreements.

We conducted a comparative analysis between two payment models in relation to sales. Our findings indicate that under a fixed payment structure, most

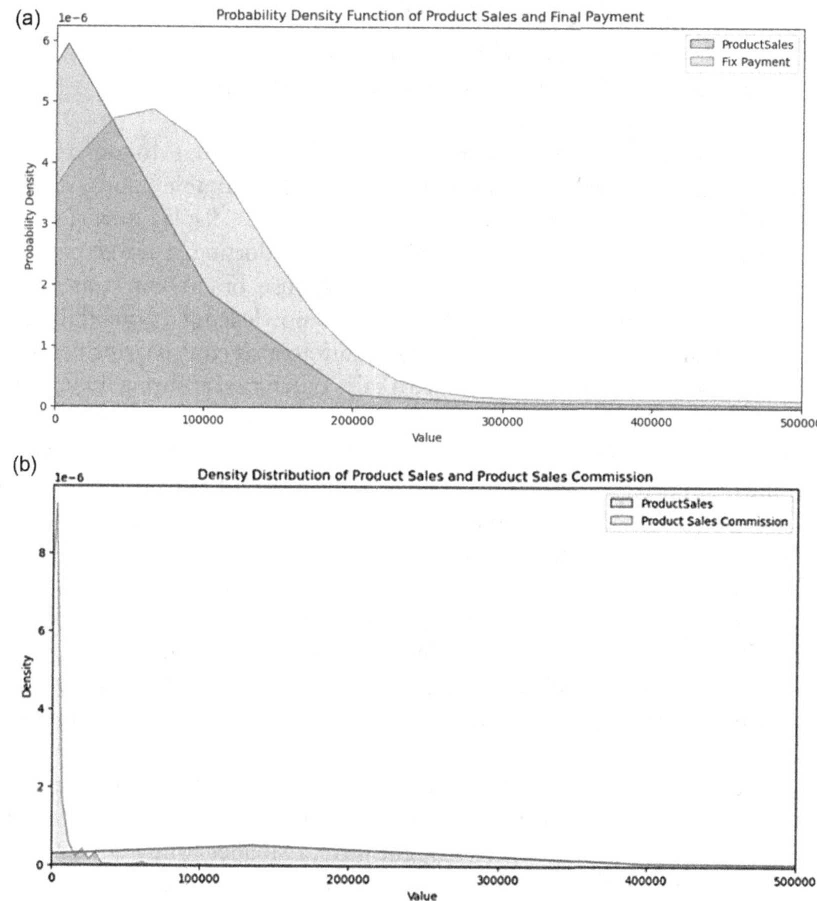

FIGURE 7.5 (a) Probability of Product Sales and Final Payment (Probability Density). (b) Sales and Product Sales Commission (Density Distribution)

brands experience a decline in revenue. Conversely, with a commission-based payment model, certain brands benefit financially. This is attributed to influencers being incentivized to exert greater effort in promoting the brand, as this directly correlates with their potential earnings. Figure 7.5 shows the probability density function of product sales and final payments, or the product sales and commission payment distribution of revenue share firms.

Solutions to the Profit Problems for Livestream Social Media E-Commerce

Influencer contracts are a big problem in the livestream market, for brands, influencers, and platforms. Each party must decide whether to use a revenue-sharing contract or a fixed payment contract. Several factors make this choice difficult: the influencer's experience, the promotion skill of the influencer, consumers' level of brand loyalty, product characteristics, and the target segment characteristics. Potential solutions include the following:

1 When evaluating product characteristics, it's imperative to differentiate between durable and nondurable goods. For non-durable goods, characterized by frequent consumption, consumers often display strong brand loyalty. Given the uncertainties linked with endorsing a novel product, influencers might initially be reluctant. In response, brands can strategically offer a fixed payment to these influencers, acknowledging a potential initial dip in revenues. In later collaborations, a shift to a revenue-sharing compensation model can be more aligned with sales outcomes, ensuring influencers' earnings are directly tied to performance. On the other hand, durable goods typically carry a higher price tag than non-durable goods. Hence, even if brands compensate influencers with a fixed payment for promoting such products, any potential revenue loss is likely to be relatively minimal.
2 When opting for a fixed payment promotional strategy, brands can provide influencers with additional coupons to stimulate consumption. Even though influencers may lack strong motivation to promote products due to the absence of revenue sharing, offering products at a significantly reduced price during their livestreams can enhance their reputation. This approach ensures that the influencers maintain their credibility by offering tangible value to their audience.
3 Should brands aim to amplify their exposure and boost consumer engagement, a combination of macro and micro-influencers can be a strategic choice. While micro-influencers might have a smaller follower base, they often enjoy significant follower loyalty. Brands can offer a fixed payment structure for micro-influencers, capitalizing on their niche audience engagement. Concurrently, adopting a revenue-sharing model for macro influencers can be beneficial, ensuring that their broader reach translates directly into sales.
4 Consider transforming influencers into stakeholders of your brand. Numerous influencers have established their own brands or hold significant market shares in existing brands. When influencers become stakeholders, they often require reduced promotional fees and are intrinsically motivated to promote the product with greater dedication and authenticity.

References

Appel, G., Grewal, L., Hadi, R., & Stephen, A. T. (2020). The future of social media in marketing. *Journal of the Academy of Marketing Science*, 48(1), 79–95.

Breves, P., Amrehn, J., Heidenreich, A., Liebers, N., & Schramm, H. (2021). Blind trust? The importance and interplay of parasocial relationships and advertising disclosures in explaining influencers' persuasive effects on their followers. *International Journal of Advertising*, *40*(7), 1209–1229.

Chen, C., Hu, Y., Lu, Y., & Hong, Y. (2019). Everyone can be a star: Quantifying grassroots online sellers' live streaming effects on product sales. In *Proceedings of the 52nd Hawaii International Conference on System Sciences*.

CNNIC. (2022). *The 50th statistical report on China's internet development*. https://www. cnnic.net.cn/NMediaFile/2022/0926/MAIN1664183425619U2MS433V3V.pdf

Cui, G., Lui, H. K., & Guo, X. (2012). The effect of online consumer reviews on new product sales. *International Journal of Electronic Commerce*, *17*(1), 39–58.

De Veirman, M., Cauberghe, V., & Hudders, L. (2017). Marketing through Instagram influencers: The impact of number of followers and product divergence on brand attitude. *International Journal of Advertising*, *36*(5), 798–828.

De Veirman, M., & Hudders, L. (2020). Disclosing sponsored Instagram posts: The role of material connection with the brand and message-sidedness when disclosing covert advertising. *International Journal of Advertising*, *39*(1), 94–130.

Johnson, M. R., & Woodcock, J. (2019). 'It's like the gold rush': The lives and careers of professional video game streamers on Twitch.tv. *Information, Communication & Society*, *22*(3), 336–351.

Lee, J. A., & Eastin, M. S. (2020). I like what she's# endorsing: The impact of female social media influencers' perceived sincerity, consumer envy, and product type. *Journal of Interactive Advertising*, *20*(1), 76–91.

Leung, F. F., Gu, F. F., & Palmatier, R. W. (2022). Online influencer marketing. *Journal of the Academy of Marketing Science*, *50*(2), 1–26.

Liu, H., & Liu, S. (2021). Optimal decisions and coordination of live streaming selling under revenue-sharing contracts. *Managerial and Decision Economics*, *42*(4), 1022–1036.

Liu, X. (2023). Dynamic coupon targeting using batch deep reinforcement learning: An application to live stream shopping. *Marketing Science*, *42*(4), 637–658.

Lou, C., & Yuan, S. (2019). Influencer marketing: How message value and credibility affect consumer trust of branded content on social media. *Journal of Interactive Advertising*, *19*(1), 58–73.

Lu, Z., Xia, H., Heo, S., & Wigdor, D. (2018, April). You watch, you give, and you engage: A study of live streaming practices in China. In *Proceedings of the 2018 CHI conference on human factors in computing systems* (pp. 1–13).

Martínez-López, F. J., Anaya-Sánchez, R., Esteban-Millat, I., Torrez-Meruvia, H., D'Alessandro, S., & Miles, M. (2020). Influencer marketing: Brand control, commercial orientation and post credibility. *Journal of Marketing Management*, *36*(17–18), 1805–1831.

Qi, A., Sethi, S., Wei, L, & Zhang, J. (2022, September). *Top or regular influencer? Contracting in live-streaming platform selling*. https://papers.ssrn.com/sol3/papers.cfm?abstract_id=3668390

QuestMobile. (2022). *Questmobile 2022 china mobile internet half-year report*. https:// www.questmobile.com.cn/research/report/313.

Ryan, J. K., Sun, D., & Zhao, X. (2012). Competition and coordination in online market-places. *Production and Operations Management*, *21*(6), 997–1014.

Senecal, S., & Nantel, J. (2004). The influence of online product recommendations on consumers' online choices. *Journal of Retailing*, *80*(2), 159–169.

Shen, B., Cheng, M., He, R., & Yang, M. (2022, September). Selling through social media influencers in influencer marketing: Participation-based contract versus sales-based contract. *Electronic Commerce Research*, 1–24.

Wang, X., Tao, Z., Liang, L., & Gou, Q. (2019). An analysis of salary mechanisms in the sharing economy: The interaction between streamers and unions. *International Journal of Production Economics*, *214*, 106–124.

Woodcock, J., & Johnson, M. R. (2019). The affective labor and performance of live streaming on Twitch. tv. *Television & New Media*, 20(8), 813–823.

Zhu, F., & Zhang, X. (2010). Impact of online consumer reviews on sales: The moderating role of product and consumer characteristics. *Journal of Marketing*, 74(2), 133–148.

8

THE DARK SIDE OF MEMES FOR BRANDS AND SOCIETY

Kat Williams and Scott R. Stroud

From "Grumpy Cat" to "Distracted Boyfriend" and all the copypastas in between, memes are everywhere. No longer relegated to the discussion boards of niche online communities, memes have spread throughout the digital sphere to assume roles of significance on mainstream social media platforms. Both within and across sites like Facebook, Instagram, and TikTok, memes are talked about in a variety of contexts for different purposes – from everyday individuals just looking to share a laugh with friends, to government entities communicating official positions (Khurshudyan, 2022; Roach, 2022).

According to the Pew Research Center, "85% of Americans say they go online on a daily basis. That figure includes the 31% who report going online almost constantly" (Perrin & Atske, 2021). While millennials and Gen Z are the most meme-savvy generations (Cole, 2018), because memes exist on nearly every social media platform, whether one is internet-addicted or just a casual peruser, it is likely that anyone who spends even a cursory amount of time online has likely seen a few memes – probably many. Furthermore, because memes have come to influence "irl" (in real life) communication as well, one need not necessarily spend time online to be at least somewhat familiar with them. Indeed, though they began online, memes may be alluded to in casual conversation, be spotted in public art or on protest signs, and even be featured on legacy media outlets (Brown, 2022).

Though memes may appear to just be goofy internet posts, Limor Shifman (2013a) argues that "we live in an era driven by a hypermemetic logic in which almost every major public event sprouts a stream of memes… Ostensibly, they are trivial pieces of pop culture; yet a deeper look reveals that they play an integral part in the defining events of the twenty-first century"

DOI: 10.4324/9781032670546-11

(pp. 5–6). Because of this, more and more people are taking memes seriously. For example, scholars from a variety of disciplines like communication studies and psychology have studied memes as discourses of everyday public engagement (e.g., Milner, 2013) or attachment generators that can promote and sustain collectives (e.g. Milligan, 2019). Similarly, business and advertising experts have examined the potential of "meme marketing" for brands seeking a larger presence online (Sharma, 2018; Tama-Rutigliano, 2018).

Despite all of the fun and good memes can promote, they are not without problems. In this chapter, we contribute to the growing body of literature on memes by taking an ethical perspective. First, we provide an overview of meme theory, the historical rise of memes online, and the functions that make them so popular. Then, by pointing to a variety of cases, we demonstrate just a few of the many ways that memes can promote problematic ideas and behavior, both online and off. Finally, by appealing to Immanuel Kant's moral philosophy, we propose guidelines that may be used to engage with memes in an ethical and respectful manner.

What Are Memes?

While many may assume they "know it when they see it," succinctly and accurately defining memes has been a conceptually difficult task. Especially since the word "meme" is often used variably and interchangeably with related, but distinct, online phenomena (Shifman, 2013a). For this reason, it's important to be clear about the bounds of our subject.

Perhaps surprisingly, the term "meme" originated in the field of evolutionary biology well before the ubiquity of the internet. In his 1976 book *The Selfish Gene*, Richard Dawkins theorized memes as "small units of culture that spread from person to person by copying or imitation" (Shifman, 2013a, p. 2; Dawkins, 1976). Like genes, "memes are defined as replicators that undergo variation, competition, selection, and retention" (Shifman, 2013a, p. 9). Unlike genes, however, "memes are any non-genetically based idea and behaviors" that spread within a culture via human interaction, such as music, fashion, architecture, and abstract belief systems (Sanchez, 2020, p. 2). In other words, "memes are distinct from genes because memes are *learned* and subject to *interpretation*, while genes are biologically-based and transferred through DNA" (Sanchez, 2020, p. 2, emphasis added; Davison, 2012). While *internet* memes arguably adhere to Dawkins' definition in a broad sense – especially since he placed "no discrete limit on the scope of any one meme" (Lee, 2020, p. 92; Dawkins, 1976) – popular understanding of the term has come to refer to much more specific communication behaviors and artifacts. In this sense, the very word "meme" – much like any individual meme online – is "a highjacking of the original idea" (Pryde, 2015; Wiggins & Bowers, 2015).

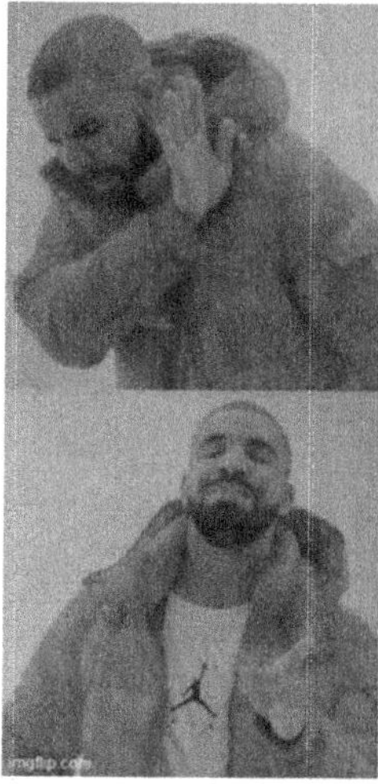

FIGURE 8.1 Know Your Meme. "Drakeposting – That's Marketing." https://knowyourmeme.com/photos/2025504-drakeposting

When thinking of internet memes, one may imagine a humorous post online featuring a photo with text commentary that may or may not directly relate to the image itself, such as the Drake meme depicted in Figure 8.1. While internet memes are most often associated with funny pictures, they can also come in the form of videos, GIFs, text, and –especially with the rise of TikTok– audio (Dickerson & Hodler, 2021; Huntington, 2016; Shifman, 2013a). Importantly, what makes these kinds of posts "memes" rather than just "jokes" is that something about the post is imitated, transformed, and circulated through digital collaboration so frequently that the components become recognizable in the memescape – "the virtual, mental, and physical realms that produce, reproduce, and consume Internet memes" (Wiggins & Bowers, 2015, p. 1893).

Furthermore, Davison (2012) argues that internet memes can be categorized into two basic types: memes "for view" and memes "for use" (p. 126; Sanchez, 2020). On one hand, the former are memes that are shared many times and circulated widely in their original form, while the latter "are created through the replication and modification of original memes" (Sanchez, 2020; Davison, 2012). For instance, the memetic practice of discreetly posting a link to a YouTube video of Rick Astley's hit song "Never Gonna Give You Up" (also known as "Rickrolling") could be considered a meme "for view," since most internet users typically only *share* the music video without necessarily *altering* it in any way. Memes "for view" are also more likely to become "viral posts," which Grossman (2006) describes as those that "spread rapidly via clicking and sharing without significant change" (Johnson, 2013,

FIGURE 8.2 Know Your Meme. "Drakeposting – Bed vs. Cardboard Box." https://knowyourmeme.com/photos/1345946-drakeposting

p. 2). Indeed, the term "virality" also harkens back to meme's etymological roots in evolutionary biology as a metaphor to describe the rapid uptake and spread by thousands of people online, much like how a virus invades the human body and passes from host to host (Shifman, 2013b, p. 364).

While "for view" memes "spread content as is by forwarding, linking, or copying," Shifman notes that, on the other hand, "people do choose to create their own versions of internet memes in starling volumes" (Shifman, 2013b, p. 365; Seaver, 2019, p. 108). Thus, "for use" memes typically function as templates that "lure extensive creative user engagement in the form of parody, pastiche, mash-ups, or other derivative work" (Shifman, 2011, p. 90). In this way, internet memes are also similar to genes because they "undergo a number of mutations," which in turn further the meme because "online users are enticed to continue the cycle of contributing their own memes" with slight modifications that suit their own needs, such as the different versions of the Drake meme in Figures 8.2 and 8.3 (Sanchez, 2020, p. 5; Knobel & Lankshear, 2007; Sharma, 2018).

Though individual memes are often transformed in some way, the creator must simultaneously abide by the meme's (or meme genre's) boundaries of style, type of humor, usage, stylistic features, themes, topics, intended audiences, etc. (Quinones Valdivia, 2019; Yates & Orlikowski, 1992). Doing so not only signifies that the creator knows the culturally recognized "rules" of the meme, but also ensures that the meme resembles the original template enough that it is recognizable as such (Lee, 2020, p. 104). With this in mind, Shifman (2013a) proposes a three-pronged definition of Internet

FIGURE 8.3 Know Your Meme. "Drakeposting – Trumposting." https://knowyourmeme.com/photos/1406753-drakeposting

memes as "(a) a *group* of digital items sharing common characteristics of content, form, and/ or stance, which (b) were created with awareness of each other, and (c) were circulated, imitated, and/or transformed via the Internet by many users" (p. 7, emphasis added).

Importantly, then, unlike Dawkins' original meme theory, human beings are not simply passive "*vectors* of cultural transmission" for "ideas and culture to spread independently of us the way genes do," but *actors* who choose to disseminate and transform internet memes based on intentional decision-making factors like social norms, perceptions, and preferences (Shifman, 2013a, p. 12; Lee, 2020, p. 93; Blackmore, 1999, p. 8; Coker, 2008, p. 907). Indeed, internet memes can *only* thrive in a participatory culture, and "in the digital era where the delineation between consumers and producers often collapses" (Quinones Valdivia, 2019, p. 10; Literat, 2018), ordinary internet users have considerable power in "choosing what to disseminate, what to participate in, and what to propel forward" (Dobson & Knezevic, 2018, p. 383; Johnson, 2013, p. 3).

Of course, humor and play may be the most apparent motivations for spreading memes. When a meme can make us laugh, we often feel compelled to share it with others. In fact, Shifman argues that "humor has become a dominant mode of online communication, and humorous content has significantly increased in scale and speed of diffusion" (Yoon, 2016, p. 96; Shifman, 2014a, 2014b). Although meme humor often boils down to structures consistent with long-standing theories of humor –such as "playfulness (making light of dominant ideals), incongruity (pointing out conflicts in situations), or superiority (emphasizing the opinion stated in the meme as superior to alternative views or interpretations)" (Moody-Ramirez, Tait, & Bland, 2021, p. 377) – at the same time, making memes online often departs from "IRL" (i.e., in real life) jokes in important ways. In particular, "internet humor is no longer predominantly verbalized; rather, it is heavily based on visual formats that can be diffused quickly and easily across the world," which may explain why memes have become so popular in the first place (Yoon, 2016, p. 97; Shifman, 2014a, 2014b).

Indeed, in a highly saturated media environment where information overload limits human attention to any one stimulus, internet users typically only give most posts only a quick glance before they continue scrolling. In this way, Quinones Valdivia (2019) argues that memes function as "fragments" rather than "finished discourses," relying on the audience to "fill-in" their meaning (p. 12). Whether a meme is used to simply poke fun at a common human experience or offer sociopolitical commentary, visual meme humor requires the viewer to make quick connections, often requiring sophisticated media and meme literacy (Shifman, 2013a).

Furthermore, because their humor style is so unique, internet memes "are one of the clearest manifestations of the fact there is such a thing as digital culture" (Gerbaudo quoted in Brown, 2022). Even across the world and in different languages, memes can connect individuals from different political persuasions or cultures. Some studies have even suggested that memes can help connect people who otherwise would not want to engage with one another (Masullo, 2022). For example, "relatable memes" that poke fun at day-to-day life (like being grossed out by dirty dishwater or forgetting to apply deodorant) are not just funny – they unify people through common experiences (Sanchez, 2020, p. 5). And in their popularity, memes build community and show patterns of collectively accepted ideas through the number of views, likes, and shares they gather (Sanchez, 2020, pp. 5, 8). Ultimately, then, as memes (especially viral ones) circulate online spaces, "they come to (intentionally or not) create a shared cultural experience" (Shifman, 2013b, p. 367).

However, even as there may exist a general digital culture, memes do not just build community for the greater internet but create in-group identification for many smaller groups across the web. While some memes can (and do) go viral, non-viral memes are shared within the confines of more specific communities that the bulk of internet users are not necessarily familiar with. With knowledge (or lack thereof) of certain memes, individuals signal their familiarity not only with general internet culture, but also their specific communities. Because most memes (especially those "for use") function as templates, "different memetic variants [of the same meme can] represent diverse voices and perspectives" (Shifman, 2013a, p. 8).

In this way, using certain memes or memes for particular purposes not only signals one's belonging to a group but can also help maintain or spread said group's views through humorous memes. Such unique memes function as "identificatory markers of affiliation articulated across social media platforms" and allow the sharers/creators to "form a bond with those 'in the know'" (Peters & Allan, 2022, p. 219; Shifman, 2013a, p. 28). For example, although most internet users are likely familiar with Grumpy Cat, fewer may be familiar with Loss. Because of this, we follow Yoon's line of reasoning that memes "should be investigated as a site of ideological reproduction," both on a micro and macro scale (Yoon, 2016, p. 93).

The Dark Side of Memes

Despite their ability to invoke laughter and identification, memes also have a dark side. Folklorist Gregory Schrempp (2009) argues that

> Right from the start, th[e] culture-building function of the meme was accompanied by morally negative insinuations – foremost, the 'selfish' theme from the 'selfish gene' root metaphor, but also a series of analogies to entities and processes that humans regard negatively: disease, viruses, and epidemiology. Anthropomorphized in these terms, it seems in the very nature of memes, even good memes, to behave badly. Memes are like politicians: they will not remain what they are unless they win; hence, they are necessarily pushy, exploitive, and self-promotional… As dictated by their very nature, a certain amount of sleaze necessarily runs through the life of all memes and meme theory.
>
> *(p. 93)*

While Schrempp specifically refers to memes in a general Dawkins' sense, his critique certainly applies to internet memes as well (see also Pimple, 1996). Indeed, when anything can be done "for the lulz" with little to no accountability, memes can quickly become problematic. In this section, we outline several stakeholders who are part of the memetic process who can be (and as we will show, *have been*) hurt by the memes created just for fun.

One of the very first memes to go viral online offers a salient example of the frighteningly harmful power of memes. Even during the internet's infancy without the technologically advanced platforms or tools that are taken for granted today, the memetic impulse to share and remix information ad nauseam led to severe consequences for one Canadian high school student. In 2002, 14-year-old Ghyslain Raza filmed himself awkwardly failing around in his school's AV club, making his own action-packed sound effects while wielding a golf ball retriever in imitation of Darth Maul's dual-ended lightsaber from Part I of the *Star Wars* film franchise.

Though he never intended for anyone to see the footage, Raza simply left the tape in the school's basement, where it was discovered by classmates a year later. Without Raza's knowledge or consent, his peers shared the video around school and eventually uploaded it to Andy Baio's waxy.org blog, where Raza was officially dubbed "Star Wars Kid." At this point, the footage was completely out of Raza's hands, and he could only watch in horror as lightsaber effects were grafted onto his golf ball retriever and he was photoshopped into various scenes such as *The Matrix* or canoe races. Even professional entertainment referenced him, including shows like *Arrested Development, Family Guy, The Colbert Report, American Dad,* and *South Park* (Taylor, 2020).

While the entire world giggled at various parodies of the Star Wars Kid, it was "a very dark period" in Raza's life (Raza quoted in Maclean's, 2013). In an interview with French Canadian magazine *L'actualité* (translated to English by *Maclean's*), Raza explains that he faced "immediate and intense" bullying at school: "In the common room, students climbed onto tabletops to insult me" (Maclean's, 2013). Of course, comments from internet users around the world also flooded in, but few were positive. Many took aim at Raza's chubby teenage physique, calling him names like "Darth Haul," or "The little known Jedi, Luke Piestalker," while some went even further referring to him as a "pox on humanity" and saying he should commit suicide (Taylor, 2020).

Even as "every single talk show in America wanted [him] as a guest," Raza wanted to avoid being "turn[ed] into a circus act" as much as possible and ultimately had to finish his high school career in a psychiatric ward (Taylor, 2020). Sadly, Raza is not the only person to face harassment after becoming a meme. Internet personalities like Boxxy and Rebecca Black have also experienced bullying and doxing (Know Your Meme, "Boxxy" & Know Your Meme, "Rebecca Black – Friday"). Thus, those who are featured in popular memes are often on the frontlines of facing potentially dark consequences.

More than just the actual individuals depicted, however, memes can also harm entire groups of people. Despite early hopes that the internet would revolutionize democratic society, the digital sphere has not fully lived up to that potential. Indeed, because "the participatory nature of social media offers the potential for more diverse portrayals of human experience," many early adopters were cautiously optimistic that harmful hegemonies could be disrupted as marginalized voices obtained unprecedented access to public expression unavailable to them through legacy media (Dobson & Knezevic, 2018, p. 393). However, "while more diversity *can* exist on [social media] platforms," new problems developed along with widespread use of the internet (Dobson & Knezevic, 2018, p. 393).

As Merlyna Lim (2013) writes, "social media has dramatically accelerated the production and circulation of information, necessitating simpler and shorter narratives" (Dobson & Knezevic, 2018, p. 393). Moreover, social media not only divides people into filter bubbles and algorithmic enclaves where "groups of like-minded individuals reinforce and legitimize each other's beliefs" (Lim, 2017), "virtual distance" from others and the ability to remain anonymous online "also allow for interactions that are less restrained [because] they seem less consequential" (Lim, 2013, p. 14; Dickerson & Hodler, 2021). Altogether, then, in many ways, social media has served as reductionist or essentialist echo chambers and breeding grounds for oversimplified, discriminatory discourse (Dobson & Knezevic, 2018, p. 393).

For example, Daniels (2013) notes that "race and racism persist online in ways that are both new and unique to the internet, alongside vestiges of centuries-old forms that reverberate both offline and on" (p. 696). Bonilla and Rosa (2015) and Brock (2009) also note the importance of considering race. Especially because memes are often made without attribution or become disarticulated from their creators through their circulation, memes depicting unfiltered and offensive content can be (and are) (re-)posted with impunity, both purposefully and on accident (Dickerson & Hodler, 2021; Yoon, 2016; Hill, 2008). In particular, two salient viral memes of the early 2010s exemplify the blurry lines between willful and unintentional participation in racially problematic content.

On July 29, 2010, Huntsville, Alabama residents Kelley Dodson and her brother Antoine Dodson appeared on a local news broadcast to warn others of a rapist in the Lincoln Country Projects where they lived. Kelley, a young Black woman, explained to news anchor Elizabeth Gentle that around 3am the previous night, a strange man climbed through her window and attempted to rape her as she slept in bed with her child. As she woke up to see the intruder, she let out a scream and Antoine, an openly gay Black man, rushed upstairs to protect his sister. Unfortunately, while Antoine attended to Kelley, the man was able to escape. Though Kelley was the primary victim in this attack, the news team focused primarily on Antoine who, rightfully upset, exclaimed to the camera:

> Well, *obviously* we have a *rapist* in Lincoln Park! He's climbin' in yo' windows, snatchin' yo people up so y'all need to hide ya kids, hide ya wives, and hide ya husbands 'cause they rapin' er'body out here! We got yo' t-shirt, you done left fingerprints and all, you are so dumb, you are really dumb, for real. You don't have to come and confess that you did it, we lookin' for you, we gon' find you. I'm lettin' you know na. So you can run 'n' tell that Homeboy.
>
> *(Peoples, 2020, p. 174; @iKING on YouTube, 2010)*

Shortly after airing, the newscast was posted to YouTube and quickly went viral with "millions of views in a matter of days" (Carvin, 2010). On July 31st, The Gregory Brothers –a musical quartet known for "songifying" viral news videos with auto-tune – released the "Bed Intruder Song" on their

YouTube channel @schmoyoho. Perhaps unsurprisingly, the songifyed version of the video went viral again and even sold more than 60,000 copies on iTunes within the first two-and-a-half weeks of release (Johnson, 2013, p. 2). Moreover, internet users across the web joined in the remixing fun to create many more versions of the meme through songs, art, op-eds, and more (Johnson, 2013, p. 2). In response to his virality, Antoine Dodson "embraced his [unexpected] online celebrity" by launching his own official social media accounts and holding meet-and-greets with his fans (Carvin, 2010). He also went on to perform the Bed Intruder Song at the 2010 BET Hip-Hop Awards, appear in commercials (in particular, for the iPhone Sex Offender Tracker App), and be featured in numerous televised interviews (Johnson, 2013, pp. 2–3). With these appearances, Dodson soon "made enough money to purchase a home for his family away from the projects and start a foundation for juvenile diabetes, a disease that affected his sister and mother" (Johnson, 2013, p. 3).

Similarly, on April 8, 2012, Kimberly "Sweet Brown" Wilkins, a middle-aged Black woman, appeared on a news broadcast for Oklahoma City NBC affiliate, KFOR-TV. In the now infamous segment, Wilkins explains how she discovered and reacted to a fire in her apartment building:

> Well I woke up to go get me a cold pop. And then I thought somebody was barbequin'. I said oh lord Jesus it's a fire! Then I ran out, I didn't grab no shoes or nothin' Jesus! I *ran* fo' my life! And then the smoke got me- I got bronchitis! Ain't nobody got time fo' that!
>
> *(@KFOROklahoma'sNews4 on YouTube, 2012)*

After a Reddit user uploaded the clip to YouTube later that day, Wilkins quickly went viral with almost 3 million views within only 48 hours (Dobson & Knezevic, 2018, p. 387). Of course, parody videos and still image memes began spreading throughout the digital sphere, and all of this attention suddenly thrust Wilkins into the spotlight. Like Antoine Dodson, Wilkins would go on to appear on numerous television shows –including *Jimmy Kimmel Live!, Dr. Oz,* and *The View* – be featured in dozens of national and local commercials, and even start her own t-shirt and barbeque sauce lines (Dobson & Knezevic, 2018, pp. 387–388).

In these cases, unlike Star Wars Kid and others "who have been victimized by out-of-control memes," Dodson and Wilkins gained fame and fortune through taking control of their memes (Thurston quoted in Carvin, 2010). Nonetheless, though Dodson and Wilkins *as individuals* were able to benefit from their internet exposure as memes, many have argued that their memes have done harm to greater communities – specifically poor, Black, and queer communities – by perpetuating stereotypes. That is, despite both Dodson and Wilkins having the media literacy and business savvy to make the most of their unexpected internet fame, "based on the participatory culture that is meme sharing and virality, [internet] users... chose to focus on the stereotyped aspects of their performances," thereby allowing audiences "a pass" to mimic, ridicule, and ultimately make bigoted assumptions about all poor, Black, and/or queer folks (Johnson, 2013, p. 11; Ball, 2012; Dobson & Knezevic, 2018). About Sweet Brown in particular, Dobson and Knezevic (2018) write that:

> Over and over... she is framed as a joke. Her images invite viewers to laugh with and at her. The humor obscures the class conditions that created the situation that launched her to fame in the first place. Her complicity in this framing gives the audiences the permission to laugh not just at her, but also at everyone else the audiences might want to believe are like her—African Americans, low-income Americans, people with gold teeth, do-rags, or whatever else the character has been associated with.
>
> *(p. 392)*

While the reception of Dodson and Wilkins as individuals was overwhelmingly positive, the fact that "digital media [has the capacity] to generate new narrative forms that move beyond the individual story" points to troubling consequences of their vial memes (Johnson, 2013, p. 4; Murray, 1998). Indeed, it is questionable at best whether non-Black internet users wearing do-rags and mimicking Dodson's or Wilkins' style of speech is appropriate. Even without any ill-intent, "humor is heavily dependent on context; depending on the joker, audience, time, and place" (Yoon, 2016, p. 98). "Some have used the term 'digital blackface' to describe how racial stereotypes are often mimicked and appropriated online through memes, gifs, and 'humorous' online personas meant to resemble and evoke offensive 'thug' or 'ghetto' tropes" (Dobson & Knezevic, 2018, p. 383).

For others, "watching the wider Web jump on this meme... seemed like a form of 'class tourism' [where] folks with no exposure to the projects could dip their toes into YouTube and get a taste" (Thurston quoted in Carvin, 2010). Moreover, even as most of the memes about Dodson and Wilkins poked fun at general human experiences, some memes were created with a clear intent to be racially insulting, operating on stereotypes that associate Black Americans with "bad English" or particular diets (Dobson & Knezevic, 2018, p. 390). Ultimately, whether intentional or not, "racial discourse surrounding these memes reflects negative stereotypes and colorblindness... Even if the intention of these memes is satirical, they function to create a space where people can mock and ridicule people of color" (Yoon, 2016, p. 109). Thus, while Dodson and Wilkins were able to turn lemons into lemonade as individual microcelebrities, they were also targets for exploitation as "visual synonyms for poverty" and Blackness, "ultimately framing them as people that everyone is allowed to ridicule" (Dobson & Knezevic, 2018, pp. 390–391). In this sense, "memes can maim and even become toxic, discrediting an entire people" (Moosa quoted in Guidos, 2019).

Going further, it could also be argued that the Dodson and Wilkins memes not only perpetuated racist stereotypes but also made light of and completely glazed over devastating situations. Weaver (2011) notes the racism embedded in many jokes spread on the internet. Indeed, within hours of going viral, "social commentary ceased asking about the rapist [and fire], and regarded the incident[s] with nonchalance," as audiences of both social media and legacy news media homed in on Dodson and Wilkins as individuals (Johnson, 2013, p. 3; Dobson & Knezevic, 2018). While it is common and often helpful for human beings to use humor for coping with difficult situations, ethical questions arise when serious situations are trivialized through humor. For example, "in late 2020, a [memetic] trend under the hashtag #HolocaustChallenge went viral on TikTok, which consisted of users pretending to be deceased Holocaust victims" (Matamoros-Fernández, 2023, p. 2). Jackson (2016) notes what is called hashtag activism. Even more, hashtags can be sabotaged or taken over akin to hijacking a car (Jackson & Foucalt Welles, 2015).

Similar examples, unfortunately, abound – from police brutality, domestic violence, and mass shooting memes, to "Trayvoning," "arrest the cops who killed Breonna Taylor," and 9/11 memes. These memes encapsulate what Matamoros-Fernández (2023) refers to as "'legal but harmful,' where internet users unreflexively use their privileged position as non-victims of [some tragedy] to subordinate victims as mere caricatures 'for the clout'" (p. 2). Sanchez (2020) likewise argues that this usage of memes contributes to desensitization of the public. Noting that because "past research has linked violent media to physiological desensitization," it is plausible that humorously framing violent or sensitive events can also correlate to desensitization (p. 8). Because memes work by creating copy upon copy, each imitation not only distances the meme from its original context but individuals may become less and less sensitive to the content. In this way, when tragic events become memeified, they subsume more important public conversations and potentially minimize the seriousness of certain events or normalize conditions that ought to be actively resisted (Carvin, 2010).

In addition to the individuals depicted in a meme or the greater groups that inadvertently become associated with a meme, memes can also harm those who see and participate in the meme's circulation. In one sense, there are those who laugh and spread the memes around, thinking they are just having fun without really knowing or caring about the folks in the memes. In another sense, however, memes can entice viewers to participate in dangerous trends and behaviors.

For example, one meme that took the US by storm in 2018 also took 134 people to the hospital after "intentional exposure to laundry packets" (Sleight-Price et al., 2018, p. 90; Selyukh, 2018). The Tide Pod Challenge pokes fun at the incongruity of design and function of Tide Pods – laundry detergent packs that happen to resemble gummy candies with their bright colors and squishy texture. Though they appear delicious, of course, they are highly toxic and inedible. Because of this, Tide Pods soon became a staple of the "forbidden snacks" meme genre, which eventually inspired the memetic challenge of eating (or, more often, licking and biting) a Tide Pod on camera and "post[ing] the inevitable #fail" to social media for others to laugh at (Sleight-Price et al., 2018, p. 86; Del Monico, 2015). While Sleight-Price et al. fairly note that children of all generations engage in dangerous "deep play" (such as chicken and chandeliers among others) and that 134 is a relatively small number of cases given the challenge's association with the entire generation of zoomers (individuals born from 1997 to 2012), it is nonetheless inarguable that "an internet meme encouraged human beings to put deadly chemicals in and near their bodies" (Sleight-Price et al., 2018, p. 94).

Moreover, impressionable children and teens are not the only people who fall prey to the dangerous slippery slope of internet memes. For example, the "wine mom" meme genre associates adult mothers (in particular, middle-aged, middle-class white Americans) with high alcohol-consumption habits in order to bear the stress of modern motherhood. While it is true that many mothers consume wine to wind down at the end of a busy day and there's nothing wrong with mothers bonding over humor, Seaver (2019) argues that the overabundance of "mommy juice" memes online "trivialize overconsumption and might influence or even exacerbate an individual's susceptibility to experiencing an Alcohol Use Disorder" by normalizing, expecting, and even actively encouraging mothers to drink (pp. 104, 107). It is important to note that humor is subjective and can have a dark side (Morrell, 2005). There are limits to humor (Pickering & Lockyer, 2005) and this is especially apparent in the meme culture.

In particular, "to speak of an alcoholic beverage so flippantly is to downplay its power as a habit-forming intoxicant that can lead to addiction and the many concomitant problems associated with it" (p. 104). While it is difficult to empirically prove whether exposure to these memes result in more mothers forming unsafe drinking habits, there is some statistical evidence to support this conclusion (Seaver, 2019, pp. 105–106). Furthermore, based on individual experiences, some mothers believe that the excessive "mommy juice" memes readily posted on social media and parenting websites, as well as the material culture spurred offline (e.g., "things like the wide assortment of customized beverage containers, home décor, and apparel available to the target demographic"), contributed to an increase in their drinking (Seaver,

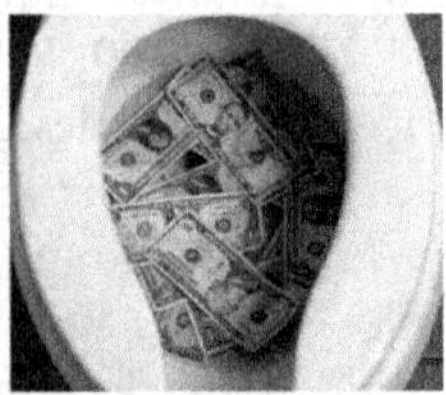

FIGURE 8.4 Know Your Meme. "Android Users Vs. iPhone Users – Phones." https://knowyourmeme.com/photos/1461409-android-users-vs-iphone-users

2019, pp. 115, 117). It is possible to "digitize cultures", and such can be harmful (Nakamura, 2008).

The Tide Pod Challenge and wine mom memes also implicate another category of stakeholder that can cause harm and be harmed by memes: brands. Like funny pictures or news stories, businesses or their products and services can become memeified, just as Tide Pods were. Unfortunately, companies have little to no control over how internet users invoke their brand in a meme. Of course, P&G – the parent company that produces Tide – would never advise customers to consume laundry detergent. Yet, the brand was nonetheless forced to respond to and grapple with the ramifications of a meme it had no hand in creating. Indeed, it was pertinent for P&G representatives to respond to the meme swiftly and unambiguously tell consumers that their product should not be ingested.

Besides memes that pose a danger to a brand's customers, companies may also be faced with memes that pose a danger to their reputation or sales. For example, "Android vs. iPhone" is a common genre of memes that poke fun at the different smartphone platforms by disparaging one in favor of the other (Know Your Meme, "Android Users Vs. iPhone Users"). Depending on the preference of the individual creator, these memes may focus on the (perceived) superiority of one brand's camera quality or the (perceived) excessive pricing for another brand's products, such as in Figures 8.4 and 8.5. While brands like Android and Apple are consistently in competition with each other, because these memes are made by anonymous internet users, the brands have little recourse for responding to every single one or may incidentally become associated with "attack ads," despite having no control over the memes.

While some brands have faced potential PR disasters due to memes created by internet users, other brands purposefully participate in meme culture. Because modern consumers – especially younger demographics – engage with

FIGURE 8.5 Know Your Meme. "Android Users Vs. iPhone Users - Android users be like, SELFIE!" https://knowyourmeme.com/photos/1461333-android-users-vs-iphone-users

social media online more than institutionalized legacy media, many brands have turned to "mining popular memes as a cultural strategy model to branding" (Sharma, 2019, p. 305; Holt & Cameron, 2010). Despite being an effective way to connect with online audiences and demonstrate digital culture literacy, intentional "meme marketing" still suffers from a lack of control in the memescape. The memescape has a clear directionality (Wiggins, 2016). Even if businesses create a new meme or contribute to an already existing meme, "the brand might struggle to maintain control of the message" (Sharma, 2019, p. 305).

Most importantly, it is crucial for brands to tread carefully when engaging with already existing memes. For example, Seaver (2019) notes that "predominately white women of child-bearing age, especially those who live in middle- and upper-middle-class suburban areas, are the same demographic that is frequently targeted by advertisers marketing wine products," as a proliferation of wine names like Girls' Night Out, MommyJuice, and Mommy's Time Out have become available for purchase (p. 106). In this sense, some brands within the larger alcohol industry may attempt to demonstrate cultural literacy by playing into wine mom memes which developed organically online, but in doing so, may only contribute to the larger sociocultural problem of normalizing alcohol overconsumption.

Ethical Meme Engagement through Kantian Moral Philosophy

As we have seen, despite initial appearances, memes are not just fun and games, but significant cultural artifacts that carry deep ethical implications.

Memes affect people and the personal or professional brands they associate themselves with through mediated means such as social media. Whether intentionally or not, individuals and brands can become deeply entangled in memetic instances of internet snark and fun. How can we tell when memes cross ethical lines? If we are in a position to enable or curtail the reach of certain memes, what should be done – and under what conditions should we do it? To begin answering deeper questions about the ethics of memes, we need some sort of normative structure that can be used in evaluating memes and how they treat individuals.

Because of the previous section's unearthing of the tensions among humor and honesty, helping and entertaining, creativity, and destructive juxtapositions, we turn to a thinker who has provided clear ideas of what respecting persons means: Immanuel Kant. This Prussian philosopher has been a central figure in Western ethics since the 1700s – and for good reason. His moral philosophy is elaborate and unique as it is convincing (to some). Kant represents one of the few thinkers that divides the right thing to do from that which secures happiness. On a straightforward reading of his complex thought, Kant's ethics can be reduced to seeing moral action as that which is motivated by respect for the moral law. A vital entailment of this moral law is the respect it gives to humans and rational beings that have a grasp on the moral imperative. In this final section, we briefly review Kant's moral philosophy to articulate and suggest some guiding principles for ethical meme engagement relative to personal and corporate brands.

Kant's moral philosophy gets one of its most memorable presentations in his short but complex 1785 work, *Groundwork for the Metaphysics of Morals* (translated in Kant, 1996a). It is in this important text that Kant outlines the parameters of his moral thought. Humans have the ability to resist the causal forces in the world of nature and instead choose to act from incentives and motivations within their faculty of practical reason. In other words, Kant reminds us that humans have the ability to think beyond normal, self-focused ways of acting. Humans could think about what their – or anyone's – duty might be in a given situation and act accordingly, even if that way of acting promises them only unhappiness or suffering.

Kant explores what it means to act – or "will to act" – out of respect for the moral law within our powers of reason. His first formulation of this "law" is what he calls the Formula of Universal Law (FUL): "act only in accordance with that maxim through which you can at the same time will that it become a universal law" (Kant, 1996a, 4:421). Here, Kant is getting at an important feature of our volition abilities: our capacity to make choices that prioritize us and our interests, or in ways that anyone might act. While the FUL test is notoriously difficult, we can see the useful aspect of it for the inquiry into memes as this: when we choose to create, share, or otherwise engage memes in a certain way, on what sort of principles is this based? Are these principles – or "maxims," as Kant would label them – universal and applicable to all? Or are they oriented toward interests largely applicable to only ourselves?

Focus on a person acting on certain guidelines gets additional meaning when we see Kant's next iteration of the moral law in his *Groundwork* text. Exploring the values of entities and things in the world, Kant stakes out the position that humans are *intrinsically* valuable (valuable in and of themselves), whereas objects are only *instrumentally* valuable (valuable only to the extent that they are useful). This is because humans (or rational beings in general) serve as the source of valuation in the world of causal interactions. Values have something to do with our capacities for *choice*. Ethics has long been associated with situations of choice and value, so Kant's account is particularly useful insofar as it strongly emphasizes the importance of choice in scheming out moral principles. Put simply, moral duty demands we respect the power of choice in humans (and other rational beings) to set their own ends and to select means to achieve these goals. In his later thought, Kant would denote this power of choice with the freedom of spontaneity, or the ability of humans to break free from the causal determinations of this world.

What this implies for ethics is what Kant calls the Formula of Humanity as an End in Itself (FHE): "So act that you use humanity, whether in your own person or in the person of any other, always at the same time as an end, never merely as a means" (Kant, 1996a, 4:428–29). This is a powerful version of the same moral law that FUL represents. In many ways, it's Kant's strongest contribution to ethics – a point that he seemingly concurs with, given that the vast majority of the duties he derives in his later work, the 1797 *Metaphysics of Morals*, come from FHE instead of FUL (Kant, 1996b).

The usefulness of Kant's notion of duty circulates around the special value of humanity. FHE is a version of the moral law, and as such, it can serve to test our specific maxims or guide us in formulating new ways to act. The morally advisable ways to act, and those that will "pass" FHE, will be courses of action that respect human agency. Note that the emphasis on humanity is really an underlining of *agency* – the ability of humans to plot their course in the world. Of course, the concerns of morality do not end there because one's freedom should not be allowed to trump or preempt the freedom of other agents. Kant's agents demand a systematicity of action and motivation among a set of agents living among each other. Thus, FHE spells out the respect we ought to give to the agency of others, and even to ourselves.

The challenge is figuring out what sort of actions align with the respect we owe FHE and humanity. Kant sees this respect as preserving and promoting the human agency of ourselves and others (Guyer, 2000). What his ethics points to is the ideal of how we can be fully rational agents – ones that respect the agency of others as well. Some of this comes in how we conceive of and judge our own action and self-conception (Korsgaard, 1996, 2009).

Do we see ourselves as transcending our self-focused desires and achieving the state of willing out of respect for rational agency in self and others? For Kant's ethics, our maxims are vital. Human actions are guided by principles (or "maxims"), even if we are not consciously aware of this guidance in any given action.

However, we have the capacity to reflect on these maxims and change them if necessary. Thus, the question becomes – if some action is to be moral, how do we know it respects rational agency in self and other? Even though Kant's ethics are renowned as deontological (duty-based) and opposed to consequentialist approaches, he is not ignorant of cause and effect in human action. Actions affect others. The question for Kant is complex: what sort of foreseeable effects on others and self ought to be worked into our reflection on our guiding maxims? In other words, what principle is suggested by how a certain maxim leads us to treat self and others?

Thus, Kant would encourage us to engage the topic of memes and ethics from two vantage points. First, we should enunciate what sort of maxims or general principles we are operating on when we create, share, or view internet memes. Some of these principles or maxims might pass the test of FHE, and thereby respect human agency. Other principles might be noteworthy because they *fail* to uphold the standards of FHE and the respect it demands. Based on our previous review, most internet users seem to create and share memes based on a general principle of increasing happiness and enjoying creativity – through humor and/or creating a sense of identification with others who are "in on" the joke.

While individuals are likely not fully conscious of this guiding principle all the time, and while propagating memes to spread joy appears harmless at first glance, like Kant, we argue that happiness and good consequences are not the best principles to base moral judgments on. That is, humor and happiness are too subjective – what is humorous to one person can be hurtful to another. Moreover, even if happiness was universal, seeking it by any means necessary still creates ethical problems. In other words, we cannot prioritize happiness over all other duties and, in some cases, we should *not* seek happiness if it comes at the expense of something else. Indeed, sometimes the most virtuous act is that which will not increase happiness.

Fortunately, human beings are endowed with the agency and rationality to reflect on and change our maxims if necessary. We have the capacity to think beyond our habituated ways of acting. Clicking a button to share a meme is extremely easy and may even seem like an automated or compulsive reaction for some. However, rather than immediately sharing a meme we find humorous, Kant would urge us to slow down, pause, and consider whether this *normal* behavior is how we *ought* to behave, or whether we have any particular moral duty in the face of certain memes. Even if it means missing out in participating in the latest trendy joke, as we have shown, sometimes it is more important to avoid propagating memes that can (intentionally or not) cause harm to various stakeholders.

Second, Kant's ethics instruct us to consider when and how individuals are treated with disrespect. In the *Groundwork*, Kant describes this as using others as "mere means." But humans often engage others in strategic or purposive ways. For example, when a patron orders food at a restaurant, they "use" the waiter as a means to receive food. What is the difference between this everyday "use" of others and the sort that FHE screens out? While Kant's account of FHE is as rich as it is ambiguous, we can add some more clarity here. Kant suggests two criteria, at least when FHE concerns the treatment of other agents. First, agents are used as mere means when we interact with them and fail to give them necessary *information* in the interaction crucial to preserving and promoting the exercise of their free choice. In other words, Kant argues that agents ought to be fully informed as to the use they are being put, or as to what sort of situation and goals they are entering into.

Relatedly, is how much *choice* we allow them in the situation. Information can be limited or maximized, with obvious impacts on choice. However, choice itself can also be inclined one way or another through overt or covert uses of force. Thus, ethical agents should be concerned about whether the choice of others is forced to some extent, or even ignored altogether. A central tenor to Kant's ethics is that our capacity for freely directing our lives, in cooperation with others, ought not be unreasonably abridged by the uses of freedom by another agent. Do we respect others to give them a free choice in some mediated use of them or their image?

Thus, in addition to identifying (and possibly changing) the maxims that guide meme engagement online, we should also consider when and how the agency of others is disrespected in the memetic process. In terms of full information and free choice, before propagating any particular meme, we should ask if and to what extent the subject of the meme was able to make an informed choice. That is, was the agent given full information about how their likeness would be used for memetic purposes? Was the agent given a choice in whether or how their likeness would be mediated for use online?

To compare cases like Star Wars Kid (see Trudel, 2013) to Dodson and Wilkins, while only the former faced immediate and individualized harm, none of these agents were given an informed choice in becoming a meme. In fact, it appears doubtful at best that full information is even *possible* to provide when creating a new meme. Because an internet meme only actually becomes a "meme" when it has received significant engagement in the form of circulation, imitation, and/or transformation, no agent can necessarily predict how much or what kind of attention different internet users will bring to the meme. Thus, if full information is inherently limited in the memetic process, then free choice and informed consent may also be difficult to obtain.

Furthermore, the operationalization of FHE also concerns the "use" of one's *self*. That is, Kant does not just want us to respect the humanity in others, but also in ourselves. For example, becoming hopelessly addicted to drugs, even if no harm is foreseen to others, would still be problematic on the grounds of Kant's ethics because it short circuits skills and capacities needed for choice in predictable future situations. In other words, this is an instance of *self-directed* behavior that seems to treat *our agency* as not worth protecting. Other actions –such as participating in meme culture online– might not be as severe as a hard drug addiction, but the same criterion applies. When we participate in the memescape, are we treating our ability to direct our life and to respect ourselves, now and in the future, with the maximum respect? Do we hurt or put at risk our own capacity for autonomy?

The Tide Pod Challenge and wine mom memes may be two of the more obvious ways individuals can disrespect or harm themselves when participation in a meme goes too far. However, even engagement with memes that do not appear to cross the (blurred) boundary from the digital world into the physical world can harm us in less obvious ways. Transcending self-focused desires not only respects the humanity of others who are directly involved in any particular meme, but also respects ourselves in becoming the kind of person who exercises a healthy sense of humor. For example, even if a non-Black internet user shares a meme of Dodson or Wilkins to a non-Black audience with no racist intent, doing so nonetheless contributes to a larger pattern of propagating anti-Black stereotypes. In this sense, the meme sharer not only disrespects the agency of a larger community but also disrespects their own capacity for understanding and empathy. Again, rather than mindlessly spreading memes that appear humorous at first glance –while likely done in an attempt to make others laugh and experience joy– caring for ourselves seems to also entail a re-evaluation of the maxims which guide current patterns of meme engagement online. As such, we end by exploring some potential principles that individuals and brands can adopt in an effort to uphold Kant's FHE.

As we have seen, memes are more ethically complicated than we may initially assume. However, we do not suggest that anyone should stop participating in meme culture altogether. On the one hand, simply being online in any capacity nearly ensures that one will always be confronted by various memes. Even if one decides to never create or share memes again, simply by virtue of seeing them (like all pieces of media we encounter), it is important to critically interpret the media we consume. On the other hand, because memes are such important cultural artifacts that are continuously spreading across the digital and physical worlds, meme literacy is becoming a part of media literacy overall. In such a case, it is crucial for individuals and businesses to, at least minimally, keep up with popular memes. For these reasons, rather than give up on memes altogether, we should reflect on how we can continue to engage with memes but in a more ethical way that respects the agency of self and others.

One problem with a variety of online memes concerns the lack of informed consent. That is, the agents who are pictured, named, or implied by memes are not always provided full information about how their likeness will be used, nor are they given a free choice to opt in or out of being depicted in a meme. As mentioned previously, because the very definition of memes requires a variety of engagement, but the digital sphere is often marked by chaos and anonymity, even if a meme creator attempted to obtain consent to use someone's likeness in a meme, that creator could not provide full information because it is impossible to predict if and how the internet will engage with any meme. If this is the case, then informed consent is elusive at best. For example, as we saw with Star Wars kid (Tunison, 2017), even if Raza was given a chance to approve uploading his video to the internet, no one could have predicted that the video would become a meme, spread as far as it did, or lead to online and offline bullying. One potential way around this problem is to avoid engaging with memes that depict or implicate a living person or group. Instead, memes that utilize images of animals or fictional characters are less likely to cross ethical lines because there is no living entity that can be harmed.

Of course, there are some cases where the individual depicted in a meme may encourage the spread of their meme, as we saw with Dodson and Wilkins. However, because their memes implicate larger groups of people, it is still important for individual meme sharers to consider whether it is appropriate for them to participate in the meme. In these cases, one should pause and consider who the meme was created by, who the meme was created for, and who benefits or is disadvantaged by the spread of the meme. For example, engaging with memes that depict stereotypes of an entire culture or community is probably inappropriate for those who are not a member of the group implicated by the meme.

However, we also want to avoid overgeneralizations or speak in absolutist terms, so we do not want to suggest that all memes depicting individuals or implicating groups are always, already unethical. Instead, we want to encourage active reflection over habituated participation. In other words, before engaging with these types of memes, at minimum, one should research the meme before using or sharing it to determine whether it is distasteful or could offend the community if used outside of the in-group. Indeed, memes often function as markers of in-group identification, so it is unlikely that memes poking fun at an entire (sub-)culture will ever disappear completely. Because we are almost guaranteed to encounter such memes at some point, and while we may laugh when we see them, we have a moral obligation to consider whether or not the memes are universally appropriate for everyone to engage with.

Finally, regardless of whether a meme depicts a living person or not, we recommend avoiding engagement with any memes that encourage dangerous behavior. Indeed, even if one shares a Tide Pod meme thinking it is too silly for anyone to actually attempt, these memes are often better left unshared. While perhaps counterintuitive, even sharing these memes only for the purpose of *criticizing* them contributes to their spread, provides an impetus for impressionable audiences to rebel, and/or intensifies the "forbidden fruit" effect (Seaver, 2019).

Brands especially should exercise caution when participating in meme marketing. Even if a company only intends to playfully join in on memes like the wine mom genre, commercializing the meme by creating Mommy Juice branded wines and other merchandise only furthers the normalization of alcohol consumption. In these cases, we argue that it is best to just slow and stop the spread of these memes altogether, in the hope that they never reach audiences who might take the meme too far.

Ultimately, while no meme is guaranteed to result in dark consequences, all memes have power. Because they function as modern-day folklore that can make people laugh or feel included in a community, they hold a certain allure that should not be understated. Even as they appear to be nothing more than harmless or silly jokes online, a meme is never just a meme – they can create targets for vulnerable individuals, reproduce disrespectful cultural assumptions, and even desensitize audiences. Given both the ubiquity of memes and the variety of ethical dilemmas they present, it is crucial for internet users to consider the moral duties we owe with respect to humanity when we engage with memes online and off. Here, we have appealed to Kant's FHE to suggest maxims of (1) avoiding memes that depict real, living entities in favor of non-human/fictional subjects; (2) avoiding, or at least thoroughly researching, memes that implicate entire groups; and (3) stopping the spread of memes that encourage high-risk behavior, including criticizing them. In abiding by these guiding principles, we not only exercise respect for the agency of others, but also for ourselves in becoming moral people who do not perpetuate or derive joy from bullying individuals and communities, making light of serious public tragedies, or weaponizing brands.

Of course, acting in accordance with these guidelines may initially prove difficult or even seem burdensome, given that most people are deeply entrenched in the habit of unreflexively participating in meme culture. However, doing the right thing is not always the easy thing. As Kant reminds us, human beings have the capacity to make ethical choices, shake ourselves out of established patterns of behavior, and chart new ways of living. To do so, we must slow down in the face of the ever-changing memescape to more thoughtfully and purposefully engage with memes that respect the humanity of self and others, and disconnect from memes that do not.

References

Ball, C. (2012). The sweet brown viral video: Embarrassed why you shouldn't be. *MadameNoire*. http://madamenoire.com/161568/the-sweet-brown-viral-video-embarrassed-why-you-shouldnt-be/2/

Blackmore, S. (1999). *The meme machine*. Oxford University Press.

Bonilla, Y., & Rosa, J. (2015). # Ferguson: Digital protest, hashtag ethnography, and the racial politics of social media in the United States. *American Ethnologist*, 42(1), 4–17.

Brock, A. (2009). "Who do you think you are?" Race, representation, and cultural rhetorics in online spaces. *Project on Rhetoric of Inquiry*, 6(1), 15–35.

Brown, H. (2022, September 28). The surprising power of internet memes. *BBC*. https://www.bbc.com/future/article/20220928-the-surprising-power-of-internet-memes

Carvin, A. (2010, August 5). 'Bed intruder' meme: A perfect storm of race, music, comedy and celebrity. *NPR*. https://www.npr.org/sections/alltechconsidered/2010/08/05/129005122/youtube-bed-intruder-meme

Coker, C. (2008). War, memes and memeplexes. *International Affairs*, 84(5), 903–914. https://doi.org/10.1111/j.1468-2346.2008.00745.x

Cole, A. (2018, July 19). More than a trend: Meme marketing is here to stay. *Forbes*. https://www.forbes.com/sites/forbesagencycouncil/2018/07/19/more-than-a-trend-meme-marketing-is-here-to-stay/?sh=c275b812487a

Daniels, J. (2013). Race and racism in Internet studies: A review and critique. *New Media & Society*, 15(5), 695–719.

Davison, P. (2012). The language of internet memes. In M. Mandiberg (Ed.), *The social media reader* (pp. 120–134). NYU Press.

Dawkins, R. (1976). *The selfish gene*. Oxford University Press.

Del Monico, D. (2015, December 8). So help me god, I'm going to eat one of those multicolored detergent pods. *The Onion*. https://www.theonion.com/so-help-me-god-i-m-going-to-eat-one-of-those-multicolo-1819585017

Dickerson, N., & Hodler, M. (2021). "Real men stand for our nation:" Constructions of an American Nation and anti-Kaepernick memes. *Journal of Sport and Social Issues*, 45(4), 329–357.

Dobson, K., & Knezevic, I. (2018). "Ain't Nobody Got Time for That!" Framing and stereotyping in legacy and social media. *Canadian Journal of Communication*, 43(3), 381–397.

Grossman, L. (2006). How to become famous in 30 seconds. *TIME*. https://time.com/archive/6676899/how-to-get-famous-in-30-seconds/.

Guidos, R. (2019, October 26). The dark side of memes: Spreading untruths about religion. *CRUX*. https://keough.nd.edu/the-dark-side-of-memes-spreading-untruths-about-religion/

Guyer, P. (2000). *Kant on freedom, law, and happiness*. Cambridge University Press.

Hill, J. H. (2008). *The everyday language of white racism*. Wiley-Blackwell.

Holt, D., & Cameron, D. (2010). *Cultural strategy: Using innovative ideologies to build breakthrough brands*. OUP Oxford.

Huntington, H. E. (2016). Pepper spray cop and the American dream: Using synecdoche and metaphor to unlock Internet memes' visual political rhetoric. *Communication Studies*, 67(1), 77–93.

Jackson, S. J. (2016). (Re)imagining intersectional democracy from Black feminism to hashtag activism. *Women's Studies in Communication*, 39(4), 375–379.

Jackson, S. J., & Foucault Welles, B. (2015). Hijacking #myNYPD: Social media dissent and networked counterpublics. *Journal of Communication*, 65(6), 932–952.

Johnson, A. (2013). Antoine Dodson and the (mis) appropriation of the Homo Coon: An intersectional approach to the performative possibilities of social media. *Critical Studies in Media Communication*, 30(2), 152–170.

Kant, I. (1996a). Groundwork for the metaphysics of morals. In M. J. Gregor (trans.), *Practical philosophy* (pp. 37–108). Cambridge University Press.

Kant, I. (1996b). The metaphysics of morals. In M. J. Gregor (trans.), *Practical philosophy* (pp. 353–604). Cambridge University Press.

Khurshudyan, I. (2022, January 26). Ukraine's showdown with Russia plays out one meme at a time. *The Washington Post*. https://www.washingtonpost.com/world/2022/01/26/ukraine-russia-memes-social/

Knobel, M., & Lankshear, C. (2007). Online memes, affinities and cultural production. In C. Bingum & M. Peters (Eds.), *A new literacy sampler* (pp. 199–227). Peter Lang Publishing.

Know Your Meme. (n.d.). *Android Users Vs. iPhone Users*. https://knowyourmeme.com/memes/android-users-vs-iphone-users

Know Your Meme. (n.d.). *Boxxy*. https://knowyourmeme.com/memes/boxxy

Know Your Meme. (n.d.). *Rebecca Black - Friday*. https://knowyourmeme.com/memes/rebecca-black-friday

Korsgaard, C. M. (1996). *Creating the kingdom of ends*. Cambridge University Press.

Korsgaard, C. M. (2009). *Self-constitution: Agency, identity, and integrity*. Oxford University Press.

Lee, B. (2020). 'Neo-Nazis Have Stolen Our Memes': Making Sense of Extreme Memes. Digital extremisms: Readings in violence, radicalisation and extremism in the online space, 91–108.

Lim, M. (2013). Many clicks but little sticks: Social media activism in Indonesia. *Journal of Contemporary Asia*, 43(4), 636–657.

Lim, M. (2017). Freedom to hate: Social media, algorithmic enclaves, and the rise of tribal nationalism in Indonesia. *Critical Asian Studies*, 49(3), 411–427.

Literat, I. (2018). Make, share, review, remix: Unpacking the impact of the Internet on contemporary creativity. *Convergence: The International Journal of Research into New Media Technologies*, 25(1), 135485651775139.

Maclean's. (2013, May 9). 10 years later, 'Star Wars Kid' speaks out. https://macleans.ca/news/canada/10-years-later-the-star-wars-kid-speaks-out/

Masullo, G. (2022, April 28). Bridging political divides with Facebook memes. *Center for Media Engagement, University of Texas at Austin*. https://mediaengagement.org/research/bridging-political-divides-with-facebook-memes/

Matamoros-Fernández, A. (2023). Taking humor seriously on TikTok. *Social Media and Society*, 9(1), 20563051231157609.

Milligan, S. (2019). *A rhetoric of zaniness: The case of Pepe the frog*. Dissertation. Wayne State University.

Milner, R. M. (2013). Pop polyvocality: Internet memes, public participation, and the Occupy Wall Street movement. *International Journal of Communication*, 7, 2357–2390.

Moody-Ramirez, M., Tait, G., & Bland, D. (2021). An analysis of George Floyd-themed memes: A critical race theory approach to analyzing memes surrounding the 2020 George Floyd protests. *The Journal of Social Media in Society*, 10(2), 373–401.

Murray, J. (1998). *Hamlet on the Holodeck: The future of narrative in cyberspace*. MIT Press.

Nakamura, L. (2008). *Digitizing race: Visual cultures of the internet*. University of Minnesota Press.

Peoples, G. A. (2020). The forgotten Kelly Dodson: Viral performance and the interplay of excess and erasure. *Women & Performance: A Journal of Feminist Theory*, 30(2),170–194. https://doi.org/10.1080/0740770X.2020.1869412

Perrin, A., & Atske, S. (2021, March 26). About three-in-ten U.S. adults say they are 'almost constantly' online. *Pew Research Center*. https://www.pewresearch.org/short-reads/2021/03/26/about-three-in-ten-u-s-adults-say-they-are-almost-constantly-online/

Peters, C., & Allan, S. (2022). Weaponizing memes: The journalistic mediation of visual politicization. *Digital Journalism*, 10(2), 217–229.

Pickering, M., & Lockyer, S. (2005). Introduction: The ethics and aesthetics of humour and comedy. In S. Lockyer & M. Pickering (Eds.), *Beyond a joke: The limits of humour* (pp. 1–24). Palgrave Macmillan.

Pimple, K. (1996). The Meme-Ing of Folklore. *Journal of Folklore Research: An International Journal of Folklore and Ethnomusicology*, 33(3), 236–240.

Pryde, E. (2015). This is what happens when you become a meme. *VICE*. https://www.vice.com/en/article/yvwk5j/what-happens-to-people-when-they-become-a-meme-078

Quinones Valdivia, F. I. (2019). *From meme to memegraph: The curious case of Pepe the Frog and white nationalism*. Dissertation.

Roach, S. (2022, February 28). Ukraine's meme war is a 'desperate' cry for help. *Protocol*. https://www.protocol.com/policy/ukraine-twitter-memes

Sanchez, B. C. (2020). Internet memes and desensitization. *Pathways: A Journal of Humanistic and Social Inquiry*, 1(2), 5.

Schrempp, G. (2009). Taking the Dawkins challenge, or, The Dark Side of the meme. *Journal of Folklore Research*, 46(1), 91–100.

Seaver, J. B. (2019). Mommy juice: Internet memes and the dark humor of wine consumption among American mothers. *New Directions in Folklore*, 17(1), 102–126.

Selyukh, A. (2018, January 30). Teenagers are still eating tide pods, but don't expect a product redesign. *NPR*. https://www.npr.org/2018/01/30/581925549/teenagers-are-still-eating-tide-pods-but-dont-expect-a-product-redesign

Sharma, H. (2018). Memes in digital culture and their role in marketing and communication: A study in India. *Interactions: Studies in Communication & Culture*, 9(3), 303–318.

Shifman, L. (2011). An anatomy of a YouTube meme. *New Media and Society*, 14(2), 187–203. doi:10.1177/1461444811412160

Shifman, L. (2013a). *Memes in digital culture*. MIT Press.

Shifman, L. (2013b). Memes in a digital world: Reconciling with a conceptual troublemaker. *Journal of Computer-Mediated Communication*, 18(3), 362–377.

Shifman, L. (2014a). Internet humor. In S. Attardo (Ed.), *Encyclopedia of humor studies* (pp. 390–393). Sage.

Shifman, L. (2014b). *Memes in digital cultures*. The MIT Press.

Sleight-Price, C., Ahlstone, D., & Jones, M. W. (2018). Forbidden foodways: Tide pods, ostensive practice, and intergenerational conflict. *Contemporary Legend*, 8, 86–114.

Tama-Rutigliano, K. (2018, August 10). Memes: A digital marketing tool for every industry. *Forbes*. https://www.forbes.com/sites/forbescommunicationscouncil/2018/08/10/memes-a-digital-marketing-tool-for-every-industry/?sh=4a9832b92664

Taylor, C. (2020, October 28). Reconsidering 'Star Wars kid,' the early internet's meanest moment. *Mashable*. https://mashable.com/article/star-wars-kid-cyberbullying

Trudel, J. (2013, May 8). Star Wars Kid brise le silence. *L'actualité*. https://lactualite.com/societe/le-retour-du-star-wars-kid/

Tunison, M. (2017, August 6). The incredibly sad saga of Star Wars Kid. *Daily Dot*. https://www.dailydot.com/unclick/star-wars-kid-meme/

Weaver, S. (2011). Jokes, rhetoric and embodied racism: A rhetorical discourse analysis of the logics of racist jokes on the Internet. *Ethnicities*, 11(4), 413–435.

Wiggins, B. E. (2016.) Crimea river: Directionality in memes from the Russia-Ukraine conflict. *International Journal of Communication*, 10, 451–485.

Wiggins, B. E., & Bowers, G. B. (2015). Memes as genre: A structurational analysis of the memescape. *New Media and Society*, 17(11), 1886–1906.

Yates, J., & Orlikowski, W. J. (1992). Genres of organizational communication: A structurational approach to studying communication and media. *Academy of Management Review*, 17, 299–326.

Yoon, I. (2016). Why is it not just a joke? Analysis of Internet memes associated with racism and hidden ideology of colorblindness. *Journal of Cultural Research in Art Education*, 33(1), 92–123.

@iKING. (2010, July 29). Woman wakes up to find intruder in her bed. *YouTube Video*. https://www.youtube.com/watch?v=uzKtPezPsqE

@schmoyoho. (2010, July 31). Bed intruder song!!! *YouTube Video*. https://www.youtube.com/watch?v=hMtZfW2z9dw

@KFOROklahoma'sNews4. (2012, April 11). Sweet brown on apartment fire: "Ain't nobody got time for that!" *YouTube Video*. https://www.youtube.com/watch?v=ydmPh4MXT3g

INDEX

Note: **Bold** page numbers refer to tables; *italic* page numbers refer to figures and page numbers followed by "n" denote endnotes.

Printed in the United States
by Baker & Taylor Publisher Services